ROUTLEDGE LIBRARY EDITIONS: COLONIALISM AND IMPERIALISM

Volume 35

JAMES SMITH

JAMES SMITH

The Making of a Colonial Culture

LURLINE STUART

Routledge
Taylor & Francis Group
LONDON AND NEW YORK

First published in 1989 by Allen & Unwin

This edition first published in 2023
by Routledge
4 Park Square, Milton Park, Abingdon, Oxon OX14 4RN

and by Routledge
605 Third Avenue, New York, NY 10158

Routledge is an imprint of the Taylor & Francis Group, an informa business

© 1989 Lurline Stuart

All rights reserved. No part of this book may be reprinted or reproduced or utilised in any form or by any electronic, mechanical, or other means, now known or hereafter invented, including photocopying and recording, or in any information storage or retrieval system, without permission in writing from the publishers.

Trademark notice: Product or corporate names may be trademarks or registered trademarks, and are used only for identification and explanation without intent to infringe.

British Library Cataloguing in Publication Data
A catalogue record for this book is available from the British Library

ISBN: 978-1-032-41054-8 (Set)
ISBN: 978-1-032-42473-6 (Volume 35) (hbk)
ISBN: 978-1-032-42475-0 (Volume 35) (pbk)
ISBN: 978-1-003-36293-7 (Volume 35) (ebk)

DOI: 10.4324/9781003362937

Publisher's Note
The publisher has gone to great lengths to ensure the quality of this reprint but points out that some imperfections in the original copies may be apparent.

Disclaimer
The publisher has made every effort to trace copyright holders and would welcome correspondence from those they have been unable to trace.

JAMES SMITH

The Making of a Colonial Culture

LURLINE STUART

Allen & Unwin
Sydney London Boston Wellington

To Peter and John

© Lurline Stuart 1989

This book is copyrighted under the Berne Covention. No reproduction without permission. All rights reserved.

First published in 1989
Allen & Unwin Australia Pty Ltd
An Unwin Hyman company
8 Napier Street, North Sydney, NSW 2060
Australia

Allen & Unwin New Zealand Limited
75 Ghuznee Street, Wellington
New Zealand

Unwin Hyman Limited
15–17 Broadwick Street, London WIV 1FP
England

Allen & Unwin Inc.
8 Winchester Place, Winchester, Mass 01890
USA

National Library of Australia
Cataloguing-in-publication
Stuart, Lurline.
  James Smith, the making of a colonial culture
  Bibliography.
  Includes index.
  ISBN 0 04 355033 9.
    1. Smith, James, 1820–1910. 2. Litterateurs—Victoria—Melbourne—Biography. 3. Melbourne (Vic.)—Intellectual life. 4. Melbourne (Vic.)—Social life and customs—1834–1900. I. Title.
994.5'102'0924

Library of Congress Catalog Card Number: 88-83853

Typeset in 10 pt Aster by Best-set Typesetter, Hong Kong
Printed by Kim Hup Lee Printing, Singapore

CONTENTS

Illustrations vii

Acknowledgments ix

Introduction x

1
Melbourne in 1855   1

2
England: 1820–1854   10

3
The immigrant   28

4
Institutions   44

5
Public heroes   64

6
Periodicals   83

7
The drama, the opera and the fine arts   101

8
Literary controversies   119

James Smith

9
Spiritualism   135

10
The return visit   152

11
A new generation   164

12
Declining years   180

Notes   191
Select bibliography   211
Index   217

ILLUSTRATIONS

Loose village (Loose Amenities Association)

On the river, Ware (The Ware Society)

View at Amwell (Hertford County Record Office)

High Street, Salisbury
(*Ancient and Historic Monuments in the City of Salisbury* 1,204)

James Smith as a young man (*Victoria and its Metropolis* 1,502)

James Smith in old age (*Harbinger of Light* 35,1904,8449)

James Smith's *carte de visite*
(La Trobe Collection, State Library of Victoria)

James Smith's memorial ode for Gustavus Vaughan Brooke
(Mitchell Library, State Library of New South Wales)

The bust of actor Gustavus Vaughan Brooke
(La Trobe Collection, State Library of Victoria)

Collins Street, Melbourne, *c.* 1860
(La Trobe Collection, State Library of Victoria)

Collins Street, Melbourne, *c.* 1890
(La Trobe Collection, State Library of Victoria)

The office of the *Argus* and the *Australasian*
(La Trobe Collection, State Library of Victoria)

Nicholas Chevalier's design for the Garibaldi sword
(La Trobe Collection, State Library of Victoria)

Shakespeare statue on subscription card
(La Trobe Collection, State Library of Victoria)

James Smith

The memorial to the explorers Burke and Wills
(La Trobe Collection, State Library of Victoria)

The interior of the Parliamentary Library of Victoria
(La Trobe Collection, State Library of Victoria)

Henry Gyles Turner (La Trobe Collection, State Library of Victoria)

Annie Bright (*Leader*, 7 December 1907, p30)

'A run on the books' (artist unknown)
(La Trobe Collection, State Library of Victoria)

DECIMAL AND METRIC CONVERSIONS

Currency: £.s.d. or pounds, shillings and pence. There were 12 pence to the shilling and 20 shillings to the pound. 21 shillings made 1 guinea. When Australia converted to decimal currency in 1966, $2 was the equivalent of £1.

Measurement: length. 1 inch = 25.4 millimetres; 1 foot = 30.5 centimetres: 1 mile = 1.61 kilometres.

ACKNOWLEDGMENTS

I am grateful for the assistance given by librarians at Australian and overseas libraries, in particular, the State Library of Victoria, the Parliamentary Library of Victoria, the State Library of New South Wales, the National Library of Australia, the British Library and the National Library of New Zealand.

More people gave me willing assistance and encouragement than I am able to name here. Special thanks go to John Arnold, Jim Davidson, Harold Love and Richard White, each of whom read sections of the manuscript and made valuable suggestions for alteration and improvement. John Holroyd was another whose knowledge was most helpful: he seemed always able to answer my questions about literature and the Melbourne book trade. In England, David Perman showed me around Ware, told me its history and made me a member of the Ware Society. Peggy Sims performed a similar service in Loose, pointing out historic details while walking with me through the village and across the fields to Maidstone.

The members of my family have shown whole-hearted support. Peter Arnold found the rare books and pamphlets I needed and Josie Arnold made a number of pertinent comments on the work in progress. Besides reading and re-reading the manuscript, John Arnold helped me with research enquiries, while his children Jessica and Benjamin provided interruptions that were often welcome in a long day's work. My husband Ronald Stuart has been of great help in many different ways.

INTRODUCTION

James Smith came out from England to Australia in 1854, settling in Melbourne, Victoria, where he was to remain until his death in 1910, at almost 90 years of age. He was active culturally from the beginning, forming and joining clubs and societies, serving on councils and committees, supporting cultural movements and foundations and, generally, encouraging the appreciation of art and letters. In the course of his activities, both cultural and professional, he came to know most of the men and women in the colony who joined in the formation of an elite network. The story of his own life as an important colonial figure is interesting enough, but when that life is set in the context of his times as one of a number of like-minded immigrants, it becomes the catalyst for a better understanding of the phenomenon of colonial culture in Victoria.

Smith was one of a remarkable group of middle-class colonists that dominated cultural activity in Melbourne from the time of their arrival during and immediately after the gold rushes of the 1850s until late in the nineteenth century. While most of them hoped to make their fortunes, they were also attracted to Victoria by the prospect of social and occupational advancement made possible through the wealth that had resulted from the discovery of gold deposits. At the same time, involvement in the colonial situation was often a threat to personal security. In order to build a supportive framework of custom and convention within which they might operate successfully, the newcomers were quick to transplant familiar cultures as the basis for a new, yet recognisable, society. European influences were to have some effect, but almost all the members of this group who became permanent residents were British, and the values and institutions that formed the basis for colonial culture were largely derived from their homeland.

Most of those immigrants who carried their culture with them eventually found occupations that suited their diverse talents as well as their common interests. Some were professional and business men who found time in recreation for activity in cultural affairs; others were more directly part of the cultural scene, working as writers, actors or artists. Smith was a journalist, employed by a daily newspaper. His position as a leader writer and critic enabled him to promote cultural activities. Like many of his contemporaries with similar interests, he can aptly be described as a 'cultural activist', that is, one who de-

Introduction

liberately and consistently takes action to promote and disseminate culture. He and his friends and associates adopted this role because of a genuine belief in the intrinsic value of culture. Involvement in cultural affairs was also likely to bring personal benefit when the activist became known as a civic-minded colonist.

The growth and development of Victoria runs parallel to the reign of the British queen for whom the colony was named. Because Queen Victoria also gave her name to the era in which she was on the throne, there has been a common double usage of the term 'Victorian', meaning both a period and a place. This allows 'Victorian' culture, in the sense of the culture that flourished in Victorian England, to appear to be the same as that which spread out from the mother country to become the similar, but distinctive, culture of the colony of Victoria. As a means of avoiding such confusion, 'Victorian' has been used throughout the text to signify nineteenth century imperial culture, and 'colonial' to describe immigrant culture in Victoria.

Victorian culture was far wider ranging than its eighteenth century equivalent. With the rise in the middle classes that was part of the restructuring of English society during the Industrial Revolution, a new group of people evolved with the leisure to pursue cultural and educational interests. Critical appreciation was no longer restricted to a select few and the opportunity of influencing public taste became a goal that might be achieved without the benefit of patronage. Literary periodicals were a useful vehicle for the dissemination of cultural ideas. At first designed for scholarly audiences, these periodicals were modified in order to attract an increasingly literate readership. Criticism in these circumstances became more deliberately didactic, while explanations of various aspects of informed appreciation were governed by an awareness of the function of art and letters as a moral and elevating force. This was a strongly-held concept in the mid-Victorian era, given its greatest credence by John Ruskin and passed on to others, like James Smith, who were influenced by Ruskin's perception of artistic taste.

The term 'man of letters' has virtually passed into disuse. Originally applied to scholars, its meaning extended to cover authors generally. As used in the nineteenth century, it was an appropriate description for a person who, while not necessarily distinguished as an author, made the study and promotion of literature a major interest. Most of the new men of letters were journalists, editing the latest periodicals as well as writing much of the contents. Smith would have considered himself primarily a man of letters. So, also, would many of his contemporaries have thought of their own pursuit of literary activity, whether or not it was their main occupation. The previous generation of literary men had been more likely to have the advantage of private means. Now, in the Victorian era, when men of letters were more common, the journalist was one of the few able to adapt literary interests to a viable career. The others, often equally talented, practised their craft in the leisure time left from different occupations.

Since more books were being published during the nineteenth century and more people were reading for instruction and relaxation than ever before, the man of letters played an important cultural role. While writing was usually his major activity, he might also be a lecturer on a variety of topics. Public lectures were a popular form of entertainment and a good lecturer who knew his subject could attract large audiences. The man of letters, or literary journalist, as he eventually became known, needed to attend theatres, exhibitions, concerts and other activities in order to keep up with cultural trends and activities. In large cities, where he was one of many with similar interests, he might remain undistinguished. In a smaller community, such as a provincial or a colonial town, he could be seen as a leading cultural figure, known by his presence at functions as well as by the reports he wrote for a wider audience. Such a man was James Smith. His biography, therefore, is not only the story of his life and times; it expands, through his involvement in all the important cultural movements of the period, into an account of the development of colonial culture.

Smith came to Melbourne from Salisbury, Wiltshire, where he had been the editor of a provincial weekly paper and a founder and active member of the local literary and scientific institute. In immigrant society, opportunities for cultural activity were necessarily restricted and those with literary and artistic interests were deprived of the cultural institutions that had sustained them in England. A healthy colonial culture could not develop spontaneously. It depended for its vitality upon the active support of those immigrants who most strongly desired its consolation as a defence against the loneliness of absence from a distant homeland. One by one, familiar clubs and societies took on new form and the promoters of colonial periodicals tried to reconstruct a basis for literary endeavour. These men—for with very few exceptions it was men rather than women who were in a position to build up colonial culture—dominated literature and the arts in Victoria until late in the nineteenth century. Those then left alive were to be challenged by a new generation of largely native-born writers and artists with less respect for the traditional points of view that had been transplanted from the old country.

In the Australian colonies, this questioning of the standards set by the original promoters of colonial culture was linked with the growing movement towards nationalism that resulted in Federation and a new sense of identity. Colonial culture was seen to be derivative and outmoded, rather than providing the basis for the development of an Australian culture with its own distinctive features. Rejection of Victorianism as a whole was worldwide. By the time of Queen Victoria's Diamond Jubilee in 1897, many of the attitudes held by the Victorians had lost their validity. There was a strong reaction against the ma-

Introduction

terialism of the industrialists and the seeming hypocrisy of formal religious observance. As part of the general reassessment of values and ideas that was taking place, the strict morality that had informed art and letters in previous years was discarded in favour of a more liberal approach. Those who clung to Victorian standards were considered unprogressive and, therefore, no longer able to act as arbiters of public taste.

Over the last twenty or thirty years, there has been a reassessment of Victorian ideas and attitudes. Just as the heavy furniture and the ornate decoration of the Victorian era have returned to favour as an important aspect of the refurbishing of the solidly-built Victorian houses that are their proper setting, so the standards of aesthetic taste that guided the arbiters of the Victorian era and, in turn, affected the direction of colonial culture, are being reassessed and found valuable in their proper context. In Australia, where research into the colonial period continues to increase and diversify, the Victorian values that were the mainstay of immigrant culture are becoming more widely appreciated as an important basis of colonial society.

James Smith's life is central to the further understanding of those Victorian values, but, like many other minor literary figures of the time, he and his work have almost been forgotten. Apart from theatre and art historians who have found his reviews useful, there are few who now know enough about him to appreciate that he was a leading cultural figure in nineteenth century Melbourne. When he is remembered, it is usually because of his outspoken dismissal of the work of the Australian impressionist painters in 1889. This particular piece of criticism, with its overtones of reaction and outraged authority, has been accepted as typical of the man and his ideas, obscuring the extent of his contribution to the development of art and letters in Australia. When taken out of context and without a detailed knowledge of Smith's life and career, it also diminishes his importance as a cultural activist in an immigrant society. Like Victorianism itself, he needs to be reassessed as a pointer towards appreciating the cultural values that have shaped those that are at present in vogue.

Smith was very much a public figure and that is the way in which he took care to present himself. He left few private papers. There is a diary, kept for one year only, and a collection of letters received from various people which he evidently believed worthy of preservation. There is also a notebook, one of many now lost, where he made notes from his reading and pasted in relevant cuttings. He was inclined to reminisce as he grew older, but the articles that he wrote in this vein are factual, rather than personally revealing. Rarely, in the Smith papers that have survived, is there anything of substance to portray the private man. Because of this, his biography, based largely upon his books, his articles and newspaper reports about his activities, has its major focus on the public life through which he achieved importance.

1
MELBOURNE IN 1855

A series of letters from Melbourne appeared in the *Salisbury and Winchester Journal* at irregular intervals from May to October 1855. Written by James Smith, a former editor of the *Journal*, these letters were intended to provide a first-hand account of colonial life for the benefit of English readers. They also served the more personal purpose of allowing the writer to impose order upon his first impressions and consider his reaction to the experience of being one of many recent immigrants to the gold-rush city. Smith had arrived in Melbourne in December 1854. During the first few weeks of the new year, he went about the necessary business of finding lodgings, securing employment and familiarising himself with the place in which he expected to spend several years, if not the rest of his life. Apart from the need for time to do these things as well as to recover from the hardship and confinement of the long voyage out, he was evidently anxious to avoid hasty conclusions, preferring not to write home until he felt able to express himself 'deliberately and without prejudice'.[1]

In the first letter, sent off almost a month after his arrival, Smith wrote about the topics that he found most commonly discussed among the new immigrants. First impressions were not always favourable:

> Most of the new arrivals expend a deal of invective upon the colony when they first land. Their notions of expenditure are adjusted according to a European standard, and the colonial charges terrify them; they miss the thousand and one little comforts of an English home, without immediately recognising the fact that a climate like that of Australia renders you independent of those comforts, which have been invented at home in special antagonism to the discomforts of the English climate. Then again they cannot dig up gold so easily or so plentifully as they have been accustomed to do potatoes in their own "back gardings;" nor are they waited upon at their hotels or lodging houses by a deputation of employers humbly soliciting the new arrivals to come to work and name their own terms,—for something equivalent to this many have expected,—so they either sit down and write a desponding letter to John or Tom at

home, or else go back (as very many really *have* done of late) in the same ship which brought them out.[2]

For Smith, by then employed at the *Age* office, and confident of a higher place in colonial society than the unsuccessful immigrants he describes, the strangeness of his new life was modified by the prospect of personal advancement. But for most of those who had expected an instant and easy fortune, Melbourne might indeed have been a disappointment. Altogether, 83 410 immigrants arrived in Victoria in 1854, bringing the total population of the colony up to an estimated 312 307.[3] They came for different reasons: some were misfits at home; others were fired with a spirit for adventure, while still others saw opportunities for personal and professional advantage in the freedom of the new world. Whatever their motivation, all were attracted to some extent by the prospect of sharing in the richness of the gold discoveries. A few were successful; many more, caught up in the crowd, found that they were not much better off materially than if they had stayed at home.

For the first years after gold deposits were found in Victoria in 1851, tales of good fortune overshadowed the reality of failure for most of the diggers. Those who wanted to stay in the colony, despite their lack of success on the goldfields, had to seek other means of prosperity. As Smith wrote home:

> The truth is that at Melbourne, as elsewhere, fortune favours the patient, the persevering and the self-reliant, with this advantage in favour of the colony—that fortune is within the reach of many, and competence of all,—that seven or eight millions of gold are annually filtered through the fingers of about a quarter of million of colonists, —that the agricultural and mineral resources of a territory, larger than Great Britain by 10,000 square miles, have yet to be developed, —that industry, sooner or later, is sure to meet with an adequate reward, and that whenever (or rather as soon as—for the time *must* shortly arrive when—) the lands will be "thrown open;" the growth and rapidity of the colony of Victoria will surpass, in rapidity of execution and splendour of results anything of a like nature in the history of the world.[4]

Much of this glowing report was based on future prospects, none of which were to be quickly realised, even by those colonists who were as strongly convinced of the value of the Protestant work ethic as Smith. While pastoral activity remained a favoured source of wealth, the availability of urban labour and the ready market created by a constantly increasing population, encouraged the growth of the manufacturing industry that would become the mainstay of the Victorian economy. But the opening up of the Crown Lands, upon which depended the development of agriculture and the exploitation of a variety of minerals, was long delayed and often mismanaged.[5] However, Smith's confident assertion of a prosperous future for Victoria was shared by most of his fellow colonists.

Melbourne in 1855

His second letter to Salisbury was written after six weeks in the colony. He was gradually becoming accustomed to living and working in the bustling, overcrowded city that was taking shape around him. But there was still much that would have seemed strange; in fact, for Smith, like most of the 1850s immigrants, Melbourne was a phenomenon that almost defied perspective. Yet it had to be described realistically. In this letter, in order that the place might better be understood, he related it to former and more familiar surroundings:

> Take two or three square miles of the most undulating part of Salisbury Plain; scalp it of its turf, denude it of everything like a tree; leave just as much surface soil on the rocky sub-stratum as will make a good solid mud-pudding in winter, and a thick layer of volatile dust in summer; stake out this area into five streets of great breadth, and as many of a narrower width, all running in a direct line from East to West, commencing on an eminence, dipping into a valley, and terminating on another eminence; intersect these streets by half-a-dozen others running North and South; imagine a belt of "Government Reserves" (open spaces, *with* timber, but *without* turf, and eligible as the site of future parks, or public edifices), surrounding this area on the North, East and West, and the river Yarra winding along its Southern boundary, and you have the rudimentary site of Melbourne. Erect upon this site the most heterogenous collection of buildings that were ever grouped together—linen-drapery establishments (at a rental of £4000 and £5000 per annum) worthy of Ludgate-hill,—taverns with palatial facades,—substantial warehouses of brick, stone, and iron,—wooden houses containing a basement story only,—tenements of corrugated zinc, weather-boarding, canvass, calico, sheet-tin and old packing cases,—sprinkle it with churches, chapels, theatres, barracks, a post-office, a prison, and other "evidences of civilization;" and you have a rough outline of the capital of Victoria.[6]

As Smith described it, the rectangular grid that formed the streets was the most orderly aspect of the colonial settlement which, in 1855, was still only twenty years old.[7] During that time it had grown, slowly at first, from a collection of huts and tents along the Yarra banks into a crowded frontier town. At the time that Smith was writing, there was little that was distinguished in the way of architecture. But, despite the confusion of rapid development, substantial buildings were rising in between the makeshifts, altering the streetscapes until they began to assume the look of solid permanence that was to be typical of Melbourne later in the nineteenth century.

Smith went on to remark upon the cosmopolitan nature of the town and its inhabitants, whether English, French, German, Italian, American or Chinese. In all the variety of people and race that he noticed while walking the dusty streets, the diggers were the ones who seemed most to catch his eye:

> Taking them as a body, the diggers—easily distinguishable from the urban population—are as handsome a set of fellows as one could

> desire to see,—a trifle wild and unkempt perhaps in costume and demeanour, but with bronzed faces that glow, and bright eyes that glisten, and lithe and sinewy limbs that are eloquent, of health and vigour, and of a life like that of the foresters of Arden—
> "More sweet
> Than that of painted pomp."
> They come down in great force to Melbourne about Christmas time, and you may generally alight upon a group of them in any auction-room where a land sale is going on; also crowding round the post-office a few days after the English mail is in.[8]

This romanticised picture was drawn more for Smith's English readers than himself. In reality, as anyone on the spot would have been able to see, they were as mixed a group as any other part of the population. But, on a less literary and eulogistic level, he must have recognised that there was an essential difference between the diggers and those colonists who were leading more settled lives. He says nothing here about the recent rebellion at the Eureka Stockade on the Ballarat goldfields, when disgruntled miners in revolt against restrictive administration had taken arms against government troops.[9] Nor does he comment on the advisability of the political and administrative reforms that were to follow. Obviously, he wished to confine himself to first-hand impressions in these letters. It is also likely that, as a man of conservative political views, he may have regarded news of what might be described as a minor democratic uprising unworthy of comment.

In his third letter home, Smith discussed the commercial activities of the colony, with particular reference to the wholesale trade. He noted the excessive importation of soft goods, much of which had to be reshipped unsold. On a local note, he referred to the necessity for importing food, especially dairy produce, into the colony, assuring his readers of the popularity of Wiltshire bacon and North Wiltshire cheeses, provided they were packed well enough to be edible on arrival. Most of this letter is taken up with matters such as these until, in the last paragraph, Smith reminds the friends and acquaintances he had left behind that colonists of British stock are separated only by distance:

> Knowing the demand which the war will make upon your space, I will here conclude, merely observing, in reference to the topic just mentioned, that the news of the gallant actions in the Crimea was received here with the utmost enthusiasm, mingled with a feeling of profound regret for the awful loss of life which has occurred,—regret which will express itself in the tangible form of the contribution by the Australian colonies of (probably) £100,000 to the Patriotic Fund.[10]

The Charge of the Light Brigade had taken place the previous September. News of such events was long delayed, being dependent upon the monthly P & O mail service until the telegraphic system between

Melbourne in 1855

Britain and Australia was opened in 1872. As Smith indicates, the mail and the news it contained was eagerly looked for by the colonists and received with mixed feelings of interest and nostalgia. When the news included an appeal for support, the response was stimulated as much by the satisfaction of sharing in what had happened in some tangible way as by obvious need.

In the fourth letter Smith wrote about religion—or what he saw as the lack of it—in the colony. He found little religious feeling as such, even though the churches of various denominations were well attended. There seemed to him to be two reasons for the noticeable weakness of religious sentiment: the climate, with its stimulus to exertion rather than reflection, and the widespread preoccupation with business affairs. The question of religious observance and belief was one of fairly general interest so far as Smith himself was concerned. While nominally an Anglican, and having at one time contemplated entering the ministry,[11] he no longer appears to have had any strong church affiliation. What did concern him personally was that concentration upon business had the effect of reinforcing his feelings of isolation from home and the best of British and European culture. As he had found it in Melbourne, there was

> no picture gallery, no opera house, no agreeable lounge or gossip at a West-end Club, no dropping down by rail for a day's shooting at a friend's "little box in the country," none of the *délassements*, in short, which are always within easy reach of the prosperous man in the old world.[12]

Whether or not Smith had enjoyed all the pleasures of English society that he now professed to miss, he was undoubtedly sincere in feeling deprived of attendance at established art galleries and theatres because of his removal to a less cultured environment. But, although the predominance of business affairs was an essential aspect of early immigrant life, the colony was already more culturally active than he suggests. The foundation stones of the University and Public Library had been laid on the same day of July in the previous year. There were also two newly-formed learned societies—the Victorian Institute for the Advancement of Science and the Philosophical Society of Victoria—while the Mechanics' Institute, founded as early as 1839, continued to hold regular meetings.

In the last letter, written after Smith had been six months in Melbourne, he referred to the original inhabitants of the site:

> The aborigines of Australia are a very low type of humanity. They are mostly short in stature and repulsive in face; with thin shrunken legs and arms and prominent abdomens. Many of the women have a moustache upon the upper lip and both sexes smoke short pipes. They are impudent mendicants, and will cheat, lie, and drink as freely as Christians.[13]

In a pattern that was common to all the Australian colonies, the local Aborigines had been reduced to this unfortunate state within a few years of white settlement. Like most of his fellow immigrants, Smith probably believed that the dispossessed native race would eventually die out. There was good reason to think so: from a minimum estimated population for Victoria of 15 000 when the Europeans arrived in Australia, there were only 2384 in 1861.[14] Many of them had suffered through contact with unfamiliar diseases; others had been killed in the struggle over possession of the land. At the time when Smith was writing, the survivors had been placed under Government protection, but numbers continued to decline until after the turn of the century, when the trend was gradually reversed.

Apart from his remarks about the Aborigines, the last letter is a cheerful one, and mostly about the climate as Smith had experienced it from midsummer to midwinter. That life in Melbourne suited him is obvious. He writes: 'I have enjoyed such robust health and buoyant spirits ever since I have been in the Colony'.[15] Although he may not have expected to do so at the time, he was to spend the rest of his life there. During the period between his arrival in 1854 and his death in 1910, he would see his new home develop into a thriving metropolis that, despite obvious shortcomings, might validly be called 'Marvellous Melbourne' because of the grand scale of its rapid expansion. Commerical and industrial development ensured the wealth of the city during the years of growth and consolidation and cultural activities provided intellectual stimulus and recreation from matters of business. Smith was to be evangelical as a journalist, writing frequent articles for newspapers and periodicals in which he promoted cultural affairs. At the same time, he formed and joined social and cultural clubs and societies and served on their committees, extending his circle of friends and associates and immersing himself in the literary and artistic life of nineteenth century Melbourne.

With other immigrants of like interest, Smith made a deliberate effort to uphold what he believed to be the best of British and European cultural traditions. For people of similar background, this could, perhaps, be as important as the acquisition of material wealth and its accompanying status. In time, colonial interests would gain in importance when the inability to participate in the activities of familiar institutions was relieved by membership of a local organisation. The development of a colonial culture, however derivative, was also a form of consolation for enforced absence from established cultural centres. As such, it helped to encourage acceptance of permanent residence in the colony.

Among those colonists who arrived in Melbourne during the 1850s, whom Smith came to know as friends and associates, were professional and business men, politicians, journalists, authors, actors, artists and many others of diverse occupations who shared a common interest in cutural affairs. As Smith recalled, 35 years after his arrival:

> Few of us regarded it as our permanent abode. Everybody was going
> to "make his pile," and to do so in a very few years, after which he
> would return "home," and fulfil a good many of the visions of his
> youth. But, with most of us, this expectation of returning "home"
> with a fortune was the most visionary dream of all. Better so in all
> probability, than otherwise. For each of us has been able to contribute
> by the labors of his head or hand, in however small a degree, to the
> building up of a prosperous commonwealth—to the transplantation
> of English ideas, principles, and modes of action—and to the
> foundation of one of innumerable homes, in which the conditions of
> life are easier, and its enjoyments more accessible than they possibly
> can be to the great bulk of the people in a country so densely
> populated as the United Kingdom.[16]

But, although Smith links them together, these immigrants were not so much a cohesive group as members of smaller circles whose interests tended to overlap. They visited each other's homes or met at hotels and clubs. They joined the same societies and served together on councils and committees. They produced and edited periodicals and supported cultural movements and foundations, moving from one circle to another according to the particular interest of the time. Overall, Smith was more involved than most, partly because of his emphatic views on the place of cultural activism as a major factor in colonial progress, but also because his occupation as a journalist gave him the means of promoting current activities as well as opportunities for mixing with those concerned.

Facilities for meeting were necessarily limited during the early years of immigrant life. Reminiscing many years later, Smith described an evening at Butler Cole Aspinall's first home:

> I remember dining with a distinguished barrister, who was
> afterwards Attorney-General, in a little three-roomed cottage in
> Flinders-lane, at which a drayman would now turn up his nose. My
> host's wife was the daughter of a Dublin physician in good practice,
> and did the honours of the house with the grace of a Parisienne. We
> were terribly cramped for room, and the experiments in cooking of a
> raw Irish girl, who had been imported from Connemara, were of the
> most rashly adventurous character; but they were provocative of
> endless amusement. My entertainer's wit crackled and flashed like a
> continuous discharge of musketry, and it was one of the merriest
> evenings I ever remember to have spent in Melbourne.[17]

At other times, groups of men met at one or other of the many Melbourne hotels. The Argus hotel in Collins Street was most often frequented by Smith and his companions. There, at a reserved round table, 'actors, artists, barristers, musicians, doctors and pressmen' used to meet 'at luncheon time and after the theatres had closed'.[18] Aspinall was a notable member of this group. So also were the journalists Charles Bright and Edward Whitty, the actor G. V. Brooke and the dramatist W. M. Akhurst. In the course of his occupation, Smith came to know writers and journalists such as R. H. Horne, Charles Whitehead and Frederick Sinnett, with whom he was associated in the production of colonial periodicals. The banker and literary enthusiast Henry Gyles Turner was to become a close friend. Turner recalled Smith at this time as 'a cheerful blythe companion, most engaging in his manner, and playfully humorous in his talk'.[19] They had first met at the home of the artist Nicholas Chevalier, as part of a circle of colonists interested in literature and the fine arts. When groups of this kind were formalised into clubs and societies, other men with like interests were drawn into purposeful companionship.

While most of the colonists who became friends and associates in this way were of British origin, the cosmopolitan nature of Melbourne's immigrant population brought people of different racial backgrounds together in search of cultural contact. Smith, who had a good knowledge of foreign languages, appears to have mixed with members of the French and Italian communities in particular. Many years later, he recalled visiting the home of the French writer and photographer Antoine Fauchery, who had a studio in Melbourne during the 1850s.[20] The Italian Raffaello Carboni was another foreign immigrant with whom Smith was on good terms. Carboni had taken a leading part in the insurrection at the Eureka Stockade and written a stirring narrative of the event.[21] As Smith described him, he was 'a poet in feeling and temperament, impulsive, courageous, rash, hot-tempered and impatient'.[22]

Not all of those who were active in early cultural circles remained in Victoria. Some, who had come out to the colony in poor health, died young. Others were long-term visitors, rather than serious immigrants. But, whatever the length of their stay, the colonists who arrived with Smith during the 1850s formed the fabric that was to become the basis of colonial culture. They were fortunate in living in Melbourne at a time of rapid development that gave them greater scope for effective action than would have been likely at home. The circumstances of colonial life provoked a lively response. Decisions had to be made quickly and, if cultural growth was to be a vital part of colonial progress, action had to be immediate. Much of what they did was necessarily derivative. British and European culture formed the pattern and these immigrants were transmitters rather than originators of colonial culture. However, they may also be regarded as having acted as instigators, because they provided the next generation of largely native-born colonists with the basis from which an indigenous culture could develop.

These men and others like them were motivated by high standards that influenced the organisation of their clubs and societies and the quality of the periodicals they produced. For most of them, cultural activity was linked with an appreciation of the benefits that might be derived from a wider knowledge and a better understanding of the various aspects of culture. As Smith declared in later years, they had been in a position of acknowledged privilege:

If, in the goodness of Providence, and by favour of natural capacity or of special circumstances, some of us have been placed in a position in which we can say that life is sweet and pleasant to us, and that we find it abound in intellectual enjoyments and innocuous pleasures—we wish, in all these respects, to bring the toiling masses up to our own level, and to make them participators in the *agrémens* familiar to ourselves.[23]

The colonists of whom he was speaking were comparatively few in number and, in the records of their activities, the same names appear in different contexts as presidents and secretaries, editors and contributors. Some were more committed than others, but, as new immigrants, most of them shared in the enthusiasm that inspired James Smith's pursuit of cultural activity.

2
ENGLAND: 1820–1854

Although he eventually adapted himself to colonial life, James Smith never lost his affection for the place that had been his homeland. The prospect of return, unless for a working holiday, became ever less likely when professional and personal obligations tied him to Melbourne. But, like many of his fellow immigrants, he retained fond thoughts of earlier days, drawing upon his memories of home and childhood in order to alleviate the common hardships of separation and distance. As he grew older, he became increasingly fond of reminiscence, writing about his life in England both in private and for publication. Some of these recollections are included in the diary he kept in 1863; others appeared as articles in newspapers and periodicals, while still others formed the basis for autobiography. Smith nostalgically recalled the places he had lived in, writing feature articles in which he described them in fine detail as they were when he was a young child or a schoolboy. He often added vignettes of local inhabitants, but, apart from brief accounts of some of the events of his childhood, he wrote little regarding himself and his family in articles of this kind. Only in fiction or an occasional diary entry did he allow himself the indulgence of close personal recollection. Much of his fiction is based on verifiable fact; the rest is embellished with imaginary characterisation and development of plot, making it less than reliable as an exact source of family information.

According to the local parish register, James Smith was born on 28 April 1820 in the village of Loose, near Maidstone, the county town of Kent, situated thirty-six miles by road south-east of London. Evidently a fragile baby who might not have been expected to live, he was baptised twice, the first time eight days after his birth, and the second seven weeks later, on 30 July.[1] His father, also James Smith, is described in the parish records as an excise officer. Mary Smith, young James's mother, was the daughter of James Wood, the parish clerk, a saintly man to whom James looked up with 'fond reverence, simple homage, admiration, gratitude and love'.[2] The family was an old-established one in the village. As Smith recalled in his diary, there were four generations living

England: 1820–1854

in the house where he was born: his great-grandparents, his grandparents, his parents and himself. His sister Mary was born in 1822.[3] He may have had other sisters and brothers; although not listed in the baptismal section of the register, the infant Lucy Smith was buried in the parish cemetery in 1825.[4] As evident from the dedication to Smith's *Rural Records*, there was also a brother, born in 1828, who died of drowning.[5]

James appears to have been very attached to his mother, using her as a model in the autobiographical novel *Ralph Penfold*, where he described her as an idealised Madonna-like figure:

> Her dress is of black silk, close fitting, with a plain linen collar round the throat, and no ornaments whatever. Bands of light brown hair partially cover a forehead which is as pale as the rest of her face,—a pure oval, regular in features, and remarkable for a certain expression of patient melancholy, which heightened by contrast, the sweetness of her smile.[6]

Ellen Penfold's air of sadness is induced here by the harshness shown her by her husband, a man whom Smith recalled in the novel as being 'austere, almost to moroseness; sombre in countenance, saturnine in manner, sensitive and suspicious'.[7] This assessment of the father's character could be based on the reality of childhood experience; it might also be coloured by literary licence. However, the impression of a sternly authoritarian father is augmented by the short story 'On Christmas Eve', also partly-autobiographical, where relations between the hero and his father are equally strained.[8] Whatever the truth of the strength and the quality of the relationship, father and son were to be separated permanently when James Smith emigrated to Australia. The older man died before James could make a return visit to England; the last form of contact between them was his inheritance of his father's estate in 1879.[9]

The pretty and peaceful village of Loose, where the Smith family lived for the first six years of James's life, seems little changed from the way in which he saw it as a child, despite the urbanisation that surrounds it. Though now almost a suburb of Maidstone, it has been made a Conservation Area, allowing strict controls over further development because of its architectural and historic interest as a rural manufacturing centre.[10] Smith was to revisit Loose only once and then not until 1882, fifty-six years after he had left the village to move on to another part of England. In Australia, he wrote about Loose in times of homesickness, drawing upon childhood impressions. As he remembered it:

> The village nestled in a green and fruitful hollow, through which flowed a bright trout stream, which set in motion the machinery of half-a-dozen paper mills before it reached the place, and did the same good office for as many after it left it and [went] on its way to

> join the Medway, besides turning the overshot wheel of an old flour mill, the lower side of which, as well as the wheel itself, was streaked with patches of rich colour, and decked with pendants of green velvet-looking slime... Except where the stream wound into and wound out of the valley, the village was completely shut in by gently undulating hills, covered with hop-gardens, interspersed with sunken lanes, bordered by thick hedgerows, famous for their nuts and blackberries, while here and there an apple or a cherry orchard, or a farmhouse, or a filbert copse, diversified the fruitful landscape.[11]

This extract is taken from an article written for the *Argus* in 1879, but Smith had described the village in almost identical terms in his 1863 diary, drawing upon his recollections of childhood in order to create a picture of the birthplace that for him seems to have been the epitome of the rural beauty of England. Like other nostalgic immigrants, he kept this picture in his mind as a talisman of the familiar world that had been left behind. When he wrote about Loose after seeing it again in 1882, he was gratified by the faithfulness of his impressions: his village was one of the few that was comparatively little changed.

Smith's lifelong interest in the theatre appears to have begun at Loose, where, aged five, he attended a performance held in the club-room attached to the Chequers, the one public-house in the village. As he recalled it after many years as a drama critic:

> The play was Morton's comedy of Speed the Plough, and the company consisted of marionettes, the dialogue being spoken by the manager and his wife, who seemed to be gifted with flexible voices. I have seen quite as wooden actors since then who were not mechanical puppets. The movements of the latter were deliciously humorous, owing to the looseness of their limbs and other grotesque conditions.[12]

The visit of this itinerant company was an exciting event in village life. So also were the regular festivals that provided memorable occasions for the observant and impressionable children. All were important in recollection as remnants of pre-industrial life in England, especially in distant Australia, where differences in lifestyle and position were increasingly marked as the years since emigration continued. Christmas was one of the most important of the old festivals: groups of villagers went around to each other's houses, acting out the play *St George and the Dragon*, in which the cast consisted of St George, the Dragon, Father Christmas, the King of Egypt, a Turkish Knight, the Great Turpin and a Doctor.[13] At the conclusion of this traditional performance, as Smith remembered it, the actors were rewarded with mulled elder wine and sent on their way to entertain another household.

The young James seems to have been a precocious reader. Taught by his mother, he was reading serious works that included Charles Lamb's *Essays of Elia* at the age of six.[14] From then on, he claimed to have been 'always found wandering, deeply engrossed' in whatever of the whole body of English literature was available to him.[15] At the age of six also, he was sent to a school in Chatham, near Rochester, which was conducted by William Giles, an Oxford graduate and the son of the minister of the Zion Baptist Chapel. This school had been attended earlier by Charles Dickens,[16] a writer with whom Smith was proud to have been associated in this way and whom he was to attempt to emulate in his descriptive writing. Another former pupil was the actor George Rogers, whom Smith was to meet eventually in Melbourne. While living in Chatham, where he was to stay for two years, the boy enjoyed exploring the city of Rochester and finding that the castle and the cathedral were 'never-failing sources of wonder and delight'.[17] He appears to have been interested in almost everything that could be seen about him, contrasting the cathedral city with the quiet village that he had left behind and learning to appreciate its antiquity.

Then came another move, this time to East Dereham, west of Norwich in Norfolk. It is not known whether Smith moved there alone or with his family. His father's duties as an excise officer involved postings to various parts of south-eastern England, but East Dereham was outside this area. The boy may have gone to stay with relatives. If the autobiographical stories are to be relied upon, his mother died when he was a young child, although there is no evidence in the parish register that this happened at Loose. While in East Dereham, it is probable that he attended the National School established in 1812.[18] However, departing from his habit of recalling childhood surroundings and activities, he wrote nothing about the town. The only recollection of this period of his early life is an account of the dismay he claimed to have felt, even as a child, at observing the miserable conditions under which the agricultural labouring population lived and worked. British agriculture was protected against foreign competition at that time by the imposition of tariffs. But Smith recalled that the Norfolk farm labourer was

> working from twelve to fourteen hours a day, in all weathers, for a miserable pittance of seven or eight shillings a week, that meat was never seen upon his table except at Easter, Christmas and Whitsuntide, and that his position was immensely inferior to that of the pigs, horses and cattle on his employer's farm.[19]

A return visit in adulthood confirmed these early impressions of rural poverty in the district. Attributing the suffering of the agricultural labourers to the protective tariffs that were not lifted until the repeal of the Corn Laws in 1846, he became convinced of the benefits to be gained from free trade. Later, in Victoria, where successive democratic governments adopted and maintained protectionism, Smith contributed to the actively opposed free trade movement by writing and lecturing on the subject, using the plight of the Norfolk labourers as illustration.

From East Dereham, Smith moved to Ware, near Hertford, either with his parents or, again, perhaps with relatives. There he lived at Amwell-end, a suburb of the town, going in to school at Ware by coach, joining in local activities, exploring the district and apparently settling happily into a more permanent home than he had had for the past few years. Although he was to retain his sentimental attachment to Loose, he became very fond of Ware and the surrounding countryside. He was particularly impressed with Great Amwell, where, below the church at the centre of the village, an island covered with willows divides the Pool formed out of the New River.[20] When he bought the house at Hawthorn that was to be his home for much of his life in Melbourne, he named it 'Amwell' after this remembered scene of youth. Of all the places that he wrote about from personal experience, Ware was the one most often chosen as the subject for articles or the setting for fiction in which he incorporated his activities as a schoolboy.

On the Old Cambridge Road, about twenty miles north of London, it is an old town with historic associations that reach back to medieval times.[21] When James Smith was a boy, malting was the major industry. Then, as he remembered it:

> The town itself consisted principally of one long winding street, entered at that time from the south by a crazy bridge, spanning the River Lea, a bridge which was the favourite lounging place of the bargemen. A sudden bend of the leading thoroughfare gave it an easterly direction... One side of this street was flanked with antient houses, furnished with huge gateways, nearly every edifice having been formerly an inn. In course of time they were converted to private dwellings, and the range of stabling in the rear had been metamorphosed into malt houses. Behind these, narrow strips of garden ground ran down to the river side, and the sluggish waters of the Lea were overhung with summer houses,—kiosks, if one may so term them—from the windows of which, you might angle for the dace and roach which gleamed below. From the centre of the town arose a fine old cruciform church; opposite to which, a narrow lane conducted to a Priory, embowered in foliage. Another monastic ruin, transformed into a malt house, stood at the northern extremity of the town, with fruit trees overspreading its aged walls and a flower garden creeping up to their very feet.[22]

Here, he went to the parish school for boys, learning Latin and reading the prescribed English classics, as well as occasional schoolboy stories under the desk. For sport, the boys bowled hoops or played cricket, while, when the weather was warm enough, they were released from school an hour early and taken to a sheltered spot on the river to swim. Then, as so often the case in happy scenes of childhood, the sun seemed to him to be always shining. For the immigrant readers for whom he wrote these recollections, now far removed from home by age as well as distance, scenes of this kind had an especially nostalgic appeal.

On 13 October 1830, when the summer holidays were over, James was admitted to the Ware Free Grammar School.[23] His parents, as

England: 1820–1854

recorded in the Minutes of the Ware Charity Meetings, were James and Margaret Smith, a change of name that may simply be a clerical error; it may also indicate a second marriage by the father. But, although in *Ralph Penfold* Smith refers to 'the kind old lady who stood in the relation of a second mother to me',[24] there is no mention of an actual stepmother in this or any other of his stories. He was now ten years old and ready to begin more formal schooling. The Grammar School, founded and endowed during the seventeenth century, had ten free scholars and about twenty more who were paying students. As Smith described it in *Ralph Penfold*:

> The school-room occupied the south-west angle of the church-yard, and was approached by a steep flight of stairs, which seemed to be symbolical of our ascent to a good many branches of learning. A row of dormer windows, while they admitted the light, prevented our attention to our studies being distracted by the sight of external objects, and the massive beams which crossed the room were deeply indented with the names or initials of bygone scholars.[25]

The Reverend John Brittan, the master referred to as 'Burly' in the novel, was the curate of an absentee vicar. 'A scholar, a gentleman, a man of the world, travelled and well read, an agreeable companion, a good whist player, and a bon vivant,'[26] he was much admired by the boys, partly because of these patently good qualities, but also, perhaps, because he was inclined to let them work at their own pace while he spent most of his afternoons in the reading-room at the Town Hall.

Although the successive chapters of *Ralph Penfold* were published anonymously in the first *Victorian Review*,[27] there would have been few of Smith's readers who were not aware of his authorship: he was the editor and major contributor to the literary section of that periodical and his English background was probably generally known. Because of his aspirations as a culturally active figure, it was important to him that the place and the manner of his schooling should be described as favourably as possible. Many of his fellow immigrants had attended small grammar schools similar to his own. Others, though, had had the benefit of higher education and their numbers were to grow as the University of Melbourne became established and attracted men with good degrees for its staff. In future years, the distinction between university and non-university men would become a divisive factor in cultural circles. It is possible that this trend may already have been obvious to James Smith, writing his recollections of schoolboys for Melbourne readers in 1861.

As Smith was also to recall in later years, he had been a shy boy whose air of reserve was sometimes misunderstood:

> Shy, self-distrustful, and studious; precociously thoughtful, but slow of speech and outwardly stupid withal, I see myself as I was then ...with a heart craving for affection, an imagination that had

> undergone no discipline, and a certain reserve of speech and manner, which discouraged others from inviting my confidence, and prevented them from penetrating below the surface of my character.[28]

The inclusion of this description of youthful shyness and reserve in what is otherwise a cheerful account of schooldays suggests that he had not altogether outgrown the self-distrust that sometimes inhibited companionship as a boy. The extract reads like a plea for understanding, or, perhaps, an apology that might be as relevant to current relationships as to those of the past. Certainly, Smith's habit of reserve was to be retained for the whole of his life, despite his liking for agreeable company. In some respects, this reserve acted as a protective device, allowing him to write about his life without intimate detail. With his fondness for recollection and his ability to recreate almost any place or recall any episode that he wished, he might have written the full autobiography that could have proved a valuable record of his life. Instead, preferring to remain a public rather than a private figure, he chose to be selective, highlighting the incidents that he felt able to write about and resorting to fantasy in order to disguise those that might be too revealing.

At Ware, as became his habit wherever he was to live, Smith joined in local activities, enjoying participation in the events that stirred small town life and observing them as possible topics on which to write. One of these exciting events was the contested election held at Hertford, two miles from Ware, prior to the passing of the 1832 Reform Bill. He wrote twice about this election, once in *Ralph Penfold* and, again, as a feature article for the *Argus*. The 'delightful excitement' that he felt as a boy went on for a fortnight, while the Tories established themselves in one hotel and the Whigs at another, and the town divided itself into supporting groups that wore coloured rosettes identifying them with their chosen candidate. As Smith remarked:

> A borough election was not an every day occurrence, and all those who benefited by it virtuously resolved to make hay while the sun shone. On this particular occasion the crop must have been very heavy indeed, and stacked under the most favourable circumstances. The town gave itself up to idleness, excitement, and revelry. Business was partially suspended, and the hourly returns of the poll were looked for with as eager an interest as telegrams from the seat of war in our own days.[29]

The boy James was excited by the whole thing, storing up in his memory all the glitter, the clamour and the ruthless competition of an election which, because of the bribery and corruption that surrounded it, was later to be declared null and void.[30] Although at that time he had supported the unsuccessful Whig candidate, he rejected the liberal movement for Toryism as he grew older, a change in support that is indicated by his acceptance of the editorship of a Tory newspaper in 1840.

England: 1820–1854

While at Ware, Smith looked forward to the annual visit of a group of itinerant players, who beguiled their audience with a mixed programme of tragedy, melodrama and farce. In *Ralph Penfold*, he wrote about his pleasure at the visit of the players and his enjoyment of their productions:

> Never was day so long, or night so short, as the day preceding the wished for evening, and the enchanted night of that memorable entertainment. The awful apprehension lest the long-room should be so full as to compel Mrs. Bullen to refuse us entrance; the rapture of the discovery that the apprehension had been groundless; the exquisite sense of comfort experienced on taking our seats in the warm cheerfully-lighted room; and the sentiment of commiseration felt for the people perched upon the lofty seats at the remote end of the room, appropriated as a gallery; only a schoolboy could imagine; only a schoolboy could describe.[31]

Then he accepted it all uncritically, feeling 'tears, rapture, breathless wonder, plaudits and absolute belief in the reality of the transactions enacted on the stage'. Even so, he was intrigued by the personalities of the actors, going with a group of schoolfellows to interview the female lead and being 'charmed by her affable condescension'. He was also interested enough in the mechanics of stagecraft to take particular notice of the settings and backdrops. This growing interest in the theatre was part of a family tradition of playgoing. Smith's father had a large collection of books and pamphlets on the subject, and, through the older man's recollections, he became familiar at an early age with the style and manner of actors such as the Kembles and Edmund Kean, venerated as exponents of the art. In 1861, at the time of writing about that memorable evening at Ware, Smith was a colonial critic in regular attendance at the theatre. Yet, as is evident from the tone of much of his criticism, he was to retain some of the excitement and the feeling of joyful anticipation that accompanied his youthful experience of involvement in the drama.

It seems likely that he may have had further tutoring immediately after leaving the Grammar School. In *Ralph Penfold*, he tells the story of the hero's years at St Helier on Jersey in the Channel Islands, learning foreign languages as a major part of the extension of his formal education.[32] But, in the story, 'On Christmas Eve', he refers to the private tutor who read with him at Amwell for a given number of hours each day.[33] Whether he studied then at home or abroad, it appears that it was during those years he became fluent in French and Italian, with a reading ability in other foreign languages. At about this time also, he began the literary career that was to be his main occupation. First of all, some letters that he wrote to one of the country papers were used as editorials. Then, inspired by the success of writers such as Charles Lamb and William Hazlitt, whose essays had become an important part of the early Victorian, literary tradition, he began writing topical articles in the hope that they might be suitable for inclusion in one of of the popular periodicals of the time. In 1837, one of these articles was accepted by Douglas Jerrold for publication in *Heads of the People*. At seventeen, Smith was elated at this proof of his ability. In later life, however, he seems to have thought little of his early attempts at writing for publication:

> What so fascinating to the youthful mind as the pleasure of seeing yourself in print? What delightful illusions you indulge in, both with regard to the quality of your present effusions and the brilliancy of your future successes! And how heartily, in course of time, one comes to regret the indolent good nature or benevolent caprice of those who gave publicity to the early, crude productions of your pen. So far as I can remember my own, it would have been a mercy to have consigned them to the flames. Lenient judges thought otherwise, and so determined the bias of my life.[34]

But Douglas Jerrold, well aware of the market for work of the kind, encouraged Smith to continue writing, nurturing him until he produced the successful series of country sketches that appeared in the *Illuminated Magazine* from 1843 to 1845.[35] There were sixteen altogether, in which the author described rural scenes and holidays, retold old tales and recalled old customs. Some of the sketches, including 'Pole's Lane', 'Emma's Well' and 'Woodside Wake' are set in and around Ware. Other locations are less readily identifiable, forming what in effect is a composite village.

The concept was not new; other writers, including William Cobbett and the poet George Crabbe, had captured various aspects of the rural life that was disappearing because of changes in methods of agriculture and the industrialisation of country areas. Smith's immediate model was Mary Russell Mitford, whose sketches of village life, written originally for periodicals, were republished as *Our Village* in five volumes between 1824 and 1832. Unlike both Cobbett and Crabbe, who were more intent on realism, Mitford chose to present a pleasant, sentimentalised view of village life in which there was little to disturb her gentle readers. Anxious to emulate Mitford's success as a writer of 'drawing-room literature', Smith adopted a similar approach with his own rural tales,[36] introducing each sketch with a picture of the general scene before moving inwards to concentrate on the homes of the main characters and, in turn, on the story of their lives, as set in the context of the surrounding village. In following Mitford's approach, rather than attempting an individualistic treatment of his material, Smith was relying on the surer prospect of success promised by the adoption of an established mode of writing. This was a tendency that was to become habitual during his working life. Fifteen of his tales from the *Illuminated Magazine*, together with four more, were collected for publication as *Rural Records* in 1845. As he indicated in the Preface, the sketches had been collected and published 'with no higher object than of amusing the leisure moments of the reader...' The book appears to have been successful in meeting this objective, selling well enough to create a demand for a second edition, published in 1848.

Writing the country sketches and revising them for publication began as a leisure-time occupation. But, in 1840, at the age of twenty, Smith found employment at Hertford as editor of the *County Press*, a weekly paper covering several neighbouring regions.[37] It consisted of four pages in which regional news, divided into local sections, took precedence. Events of national importance were given space also, while national politics were frequent subjects for editorials written from a Tory point of view. There is no reference to the editor by name, nor is there any clear indication that these editorials were Smith's work, even though as editor he must have been responsible for a good many of them. That he succeeded at times in provoking the editor of the rival *Hertfordshire Mercury* is obvious from the reference in that paper to the 'self-satisfied juvenile who occasionally enriches the pages of our truth-loving contemporary'.[38] He remained at the *County Press* for at least two years, developing his skills as a journalist while trying also to establish himself as an author.

Apart from occasional references to events in his adult life, Smith's personal recollections are confined to his youth. Little is known about his activities during the early 1840s. At some time during that period he left Hertford to live in London. On 20 March 1844, he married Annie Feldwick Notcutt, the daughter of a schoolmaster, at the Trinity District Church in the Parish of St Mary Newington.[39] They were to have two children, James Bartlett, born in 1845, and a younger brother, Charles Henry.[40] It seems likely that Smith would have continued working as a writer, but his exact occupation during these years is unknown. He mentions in his recollections that, on 10 April 1848, while still living in London, he enrolled as a special constable in anticipation of a Chartist riot.[41] As it happened, the demonstration at Kennington Common, where Chartist supporters were addressed by their leaders, was remarkably peaceful and the services of Smith and his fellow volunteers were not required. There were six points in the People's Charter: manhood suffrage, annual parliaments, vote by secret ballot, abolition of the property qualification for parliamentary candidates, payment of members of parliament, and the creation of equal electoral districts.[42] While these demands were reasonable as well as being progressive, it was a year of revolution in Europe and those who were more conservative in their approach to reform than the Chartists had some cause to fear that the demonstration could develop into a riot. Along with the other special constables who gathered at Kennington Common, Smith was not in favour of democratic methods of politics. He distrusted the ability of the average man to cast a sensible vote and he deplored the possibility of majority rule by an uneducated mob.[43]

Sometime in late 1848 or early 1849, Smith accepted the position of editor of the *Salisbury and Winchester Journal*. When he arrived at the cathedral city that was to be his home for the next six years, he found that it promised to be an agreeable place in which to live and work. It was then 'a staid and quiet city, serenely respectable and quietly prosperous',[44] with surroundings that seemed as peaceful and picturesque as they had been for centuries past. The *Salisbury and Winchester Journal*, established in 1720 for circulation throughout Wiltshire, Hampshire, Dorset and Somerset, and owned by the Brodie family from shortly after its inception, was the leading weekly newspaper. In 1848, James Bennett bought the paper from William Bird Brodie, the former parliamentary member for the district and a recent bankrupt.[45] Previously inclined to Whig support, the *Journal* became more neutral politically under its new owner, although regular editorials on social and political topics soon began to appear. The recording of general news, particularly that of local interest, was a major feature. Agricultural matters were also given wide coverage. When Smith took over, he retained these familar features while taking steps to diversify and rearrange the content in an effort to add to the interest of the paper as a whole. He was especially anxious to introduce literary items and, on 14 July 1849, he published the first of a series of 'Original Papers', written by himself. Although they were novel features, items such as these, together with notices and reviews of cultural activities in Salisbury and nearby districts, were soon to become an accepted part of the *Journal's* pages.

All seems to have been going well; Smith obviously enjoyed the work of enlivening the *Journal* and he and his family appear to have settled down happily in Salisbury. But in 1849 the epidemic of cholera that had affected other parts of England swept through the city. Annie Smith was one of its victims, dying at her home in the High Street on 19 July.[46] Altogether, 123 people died in Salisbury from cholera and related causes between July and September 1849.[47] The lack of adequate drainage and proper sanitation was largely to blame for the rapid spread of the disease, and, through articles and editorials, Smith gave publicity to the deficiencies in local health services and pressed for an inquiry into the sanitary condition of the city, which was held in 1851. The Board of Health set up in the following year arranged for the provision of water works and supply, together with closed drainage for the whole city.[48] For Smith, personally, it was too late. The work was completed in 1854, the year in which he was to emigrate to Melbourne.

In the meantime, there was much to be done and, probably glad of the demands of his occupation, he was able to turn to it as a palliative for grief and loneliness. He continued his efforts to improve the *Journal* and increase its circulation, determined that in all respects it would be a leading provincial newspaper. The variety and expansion of content that followed was evidently appreciated by local readers. On 10 May 1852, he was able to announce an increase in the size of the pages to allow for the inclusion of more material, based on the confident claim that the circulation of the *Journal* equalled the total of all other Wiltshire papers. These years immediately after the loss of his young wife mark the beginning of his role as a public figure. He had gained local distinction while editing the *County Press* in Hertford. Now, as the older, experienced editor of a more important weekly newspaper, he was in a position to acquire further professional status. The division between public and private life was a noticeable feature of the effects of capitalism during the nineteenth century. When men who had previously been unknown succeeded in establishing themselves as heads of business and industrial enterprises, they tended to acquire a public image that was separate from the roles they assumed in private. So it was with Smith, whose life in Salisbury was essentially that of a public man.

His adoption of a distinctly public role was undoubtedly compounded by the fact that he was now a widower, whose private life had effectively been fragmented Nothing is known of the fate of his children at this time. It is uncertain that Charles Henry was still alive; according to the certificate, he was dead at the time of his father's second marriage in Melbourne in 1857.[49] Since Smith had no relatives in Salisbury so far as is known, arrangements must have been made for the care of James Bartlett and, perhaps, his brother, either at home or away. In 1854, when Smith emigrated to Australia, one or both of the boys may have accompanied him, although there is no record that they did so.[50] Possibly, James Bartlett remained for the time being in England, where he might be better looked after than in the new colony of Victoria. However, he did eventually go out to Australia, perhaps for his health. He died of consumption while teaching in Queensland in 1867.[51]

At Salisbury, aware that as the editor of the local newspaper he was in a position to inform and to influence public opinion, Smith encouraged the foundation of the Salisbury Literary and Scientific Institute. The movement began in 1849 with a letter to the *Journal* signed 'Deo Regi Vincino'. This correspondent deplored the current lack of 'any institution or society for the purpose of collecting together kindred spirits to discuss interesting subjects of a literary or scientific character for mutual improvement'.[52] While there were other 'kindred spirits' who may well have written the letter, it seems likely that Smith himself was the pseudonymous correspondent. He needed something besides his work that would occupy and divert him; the concept of an institute was one that, allowing for his interest in literature and his aspirations as a writer, would undoubtedly appeal; its activities would also provide newsworthy items for his paper, allowing him to assume the role of publicist. The formation of the institute could have been suggested directly in a *Journal* editorial. But, if Smith had used that method of broaching the idea, he would have had less opportunity for effective response than might follow a seemingly unsolicited letter from a public-minded citizen. Whatever the truth of the matter, the suggestion met with enthusiastic support.

Institutes such as that proposed for Salisbury in 1849 were products of the Victorian belief in the moral value of self-improvement. It was obvious to the new middle classes that increased business and professional skills were the key to the achievement of a higher status. A greater degree of appreciation of literature, art and science might also be acquired through reading and discussion. The result would be an extension of knowledge, together with an elevation of taste. Men with sufficient education to promote and participate in intellectual discussion for its own sake joined literary and philosophical societies formed for that purpose. Then, aware of the privilege of being members of a cultural elite of this kind and confident that moral elevation must follow further education, they began to found institutes through which the working classes, particularly skilled tradesmen, might also benefit from the diffusion of knowledge. A Mechanics' Institute, opened in Salisbury in 1833 to provide popular lectures, had gradually declined in importance until its closure in the early 1840s. In 1836, while it was still in full operation, discussions had been held as to the feasibility of incorporation into a literary and philosophical society, but without further action.[53] Now the *Journal's* correspondent urged the foundation of an appropriate body. As editor, Smith welcomed the idea of a local society in which members could listen to knowledgeable speakers and discuss with one another the important literary and scientific questions of the day. On 10 November 1849 he included a paragraph amongst the general news to the effect that it was editorial policy to publicise any initiative in the manner of establishing a Literary and Scientific Society or reorganising the former Mechanics' Institute. At a preliminary meeting of friends and supporters, chaired by the Mayor on 7 December, initial steps were taken for the foundation of the Salisbury Literary and Scientific Institute.[54] By mid-January, there were 60 honorary and 210 ordinary members for whom fortnightly lectures were arranged,[55] together with the use of a library containing 400 volumes.[56] Smith supported the Institute in whatever way he was able, both as publicist and member, until more active involvement came with his election to the committee in 1852. From then on, he acted either as secretary or programme organiser, arranging lectures on a variety of topics, together with readings from the work of prominent authors.[57] In later years he was proud to claim that, at Salisbury, he had given the first public reading in England of Charles Dickens's *A Christmas Carol*.[58] This was true, although Smith was not far ahead of the author. Dickens's first public readings from his books were given in 1853, in aid of the newly-founded Birmingham and Midland Institute. He read *A Christmas Carol* on 27 December.[59] Smith read a compressed version of the novel five days earlier, on 22 December.[60] Readings such as these were to become very popular, both in England, where Dickens prepared special

England: 1820–1854

reading versions of his novels, and in Australia, where Smith was prominent amongst several other exponents.

The year 1852 was an important one for the Salisbury Institute because of its sponsorship of a county exhibition of art and manufactures. This exhibition was the first to be held in a provincial centre following the Great Exhibition of 1851, when exhibitors from all nations displayed the latest achievements in technology and the finest artworks in the Crystal Palace, a spectacularly modern building designed for the purpose and erected in Hyde Park in London. The Salisbury exhibition, though necessarily organised on a much smaller scale, was an ambitious venture that could be expected to draw favourable attention to the Institute and, specifically, to James Smith and W. F. Tiffin, who had been appointed as organisers. Almost 100 applications were received for space to display exhibits that included paintings, embroidery, items of natural history, carpets, woodwork and other local manufactures. Smith, anxious both for the success of the exhibition and his reputation as an efficient organiser, explained through the *Journal* that the task of organisation had been extremely demanding because of

> the brevity of the period during which the preparations have been made, the comparative novelty of the undertaking; the absence of any building sufficiently large to comprehend all the articles sent in, in one group, the season of the year, and the multifarious claims imposed upon the time and attention of the Committee by their professional or other avocations....[61]

Fortunately, Smith, Tiffin and their helpers managed to have everything ready in time for the opening day on 12 October. To their gratification, the exhibition was most successful; interested viewers filled the exhibition halls each day. When it was over and the receipts were counted, the organisers were able to declare a surplus of £100 towards the Institute's funds.[62] Smith and Tiffin were each presented with a purse of sovereigns and a piece of silver plate in popular appreciation of their efforts.[63] It must have been an interesting and a valuable experience, despite the initial difficulties in organisation. For Smith in particular, there were other satisfying rewards. Through his involvement in the preparation and smooth running of the exhibition he had developed his skills as an organiser; he had extended his circle of acquaintance in Salisbury and the surrounding district and, through the successful conclusion of the exhibition, he had added a certain prestige to his growing reputation.

As anticipated when taking up his appointment as editor of the *Salisbury and Winchester Journal*, Smith had been able to find time to continue with other writing besides the editorials and feature articles that he prepared as part of his work as a journalist. He had three books published during his time in Salisbury. The first, *Oracles from the British Poets*, appeared in 1849. Its success, as indicated by a second edition in 1851 and a third in 1862, was largely dependent upon its popularity as an adjunct to a parlour game.[64] Described by the sub-title as 'a drawing-room table book and pleasant companion for a round party', it consisted of a series of questions to be answered by selections from the 'oracles' or verses. Smith acknowledged his reliance on an American prototype in the preface: this was *Oracles from the Poets*, compiled by Caroline Gilman and published in 1844.[65] There is little difference in the methods used by the two compilers. Their questions are identical apart from some slight alterations in the wording, but, while Gilman's 'oracles' were drawn both from British and American poets, Smith confined his selection to 'a fresh and perfectly distinct body of quotations' from the British poets only.[66] Except for its usefulness for the purposes of the game for which it was designed, the *Oracles* is little more than a collection of quotable verses. To some extent, the compilation was a means of recreation for Smith, who, while building upon the work of another author, declared in his Preface that he had found the task of reading and re-reading for his selection 'a labour of love'.[67]

Wilton and its Associations, Smith's history of Wilton House, the home of the Herbert family, was published in 1851 with illustrations by W. F Tiffin.[68] Although Smith did not set out to write a scholarly history, this book was a more serious undertaking than the last, based upon personal observation as well as literary and historical sources. In the course of the work, which covers the period from 800 AD until the time of writing, Smith traces the history of the Earls of Pembroke and introduces stories of the lives of the Herbert family and other noted people connected with the house, including Sir Philip Sidney, George Herbert and Philip Massinger. The final chapter consists of an enumeration of the sculptures and paintings collected and added to by successive Earls of Pembroke, together with descriptions of selected pieces. Although the work is highly derivative, it is not without imaginative passages, such as Smith's sketch of a theatrical performance at Wilton House in honour of James I, where he describes the play, the audience and the scene as they might have appeared to those present in 1603. He retained his interest in the great house and its inhabitants after leaving the district, annotating his own copy of the book with items of particular interest to himself.[69] He also resurrected some of the more self-contained sections in Melbourne many years later, when, acting as editor of the *Victorian Review*, he used them as articles, with the occasional inclusion of additional material.[70]

Lights and Shadows of Artist Life and Character was Smith's fourth book and the last of the three that he either wrote or compiled in Salisbury. Advertised as 'a Christmas gift book', it was published in 1853 in time for the seasonal trade.[71] As explained in the Preface, the book was 'the skeleton of a work of more ambitious character' which had since been abandoned. Smith had collected anecdotes of various kinds in preparation for the original project and he now used them grouped under appropriate headings, such as 'Early intimations of genius', 'Friendships subsisting between artists' or 'Regal patronage of art and artists'. The information that follows is based on the sources given incidentally in the text. As a whole, the work gives the impression of having been an edited version of the art sections in the books of notes and cuttings that Smith had begun to keep. It is, in effect, a digest culled from wide reading for the purpose of providing interest and amusement.

All of these books, however presented as 'labours of love', were money-making projects. Although Smith would have acquired some local status as an author through the production of three books during the time of his editorship of the *Journal*, compilations and digests such as the *Oracles* and *Lights and Shadows* were quickly prepared and only the history of Wilton House, and that marginally, could have assisted the promotion of his ambitions to be a serious writer. It was not easy for him to establish a literary career while in full employment as a journalist. Previous generations of writers had had the benefit of more leisure in which to establish a reputation. Some were fortunate in having inherited the wealth required for the adoption of a literary lifestyle; others benefitted from patronage. It is possible that members of the Herbert family acted as patrons for *Wilton and its Associations*; the work is dedicated to 'The Honourable Mrs. Herbert' and the Countess of Pembroke heads the list of subscribers. However, patronage of this kind was becoming outmoded with the rise of men of self-made wealth and the fact that subscriptions were called for confirms the publisher's need for assurance that the book would be successful. The early records of the *Salisbury and Winchester Journal* are no longer in existence,[72] and Smith's salary as editor is unknown. Since the proceeds of his books, from the first in 1845 to the latest in 1853, would have been inadequate for living expenses, it must have been essential that he should remain in full employment. Any additional income such as that received from book royalties was a bonus.

Lights and Shadows sold well and, with the proceeds, Smith was able to take a long-planned European tour with his friend Walter Tiffin. A trip of this kind was an important part of the attainment of cultural knowledge. It was an opportunity for Smith to develop his fluency in foreign languages as well as to extend his appreciation of the fine arts. Smith and Tiffin travelled through France, Switzerland and northern Italy, making, as he later recalled, 'natural scenery, picture galleries and architecture' their 'objective points of observation'.[73] Though necessarily a shorter and less elaborate trip than the traditional 'grand tour' undertaken by members of the leisured classes, it was an experience that was to have a lasting effect, attracting Smith to the pleasures of travel while informing his artistic sensibilities. In future years, he was to become increasingly appreciative of John Ruskin's views on art and architecture. It is possible that *The Stones of Venice*, recently published as a result of Ruskin's observations on Venetian architecture, may have influenced Smith's decision to travel in Europe in company with an artist, in search of aesthetic experience. On his return, he found that the trip had been advantageous, not only for its own sake, but also in providing material for lectures and articles. On 10 October 1853, he gave a lecture on Venice, illustrated with sketches by Tiffin, at the Assembly Rooms in Salisbury.[74] This lecture was to be repeated on 19 January 1855 at the Mechanics' Institute in Melbourne, soon after his arrival in Victoria.[75] Other recollections of travel in 1853 formed the subject for articles written for colonial newspapers and magazines.[76]

In 1854, the year in which he was to emigrate, Smith had achieved some success as a literary figure: he was successful in his profession as a journalist and he had had four books published. However, he was not in a position to become a full-time author and, even if there had been no concern about making a good livelihood, the success of the books he had already completed provided no assurance that he would eventually produce a great novel or some other memorable work. Certainly, he had proven ability as an editor and compiler. He may, perhaps, have realised by now that his major skills lay in the detailed and accurate description that was most suited to routine journalism or, at best, to leading articles, criticism or other newspaper and magazine features. If he had then decided that skills such as these might provide an opening for further advancement in another place, a new country with seemingly unlimited prospects for success could have had a strong attraction. There were other more personal reasons that probably influenced his departure from the familiar scene. Although a place in which he had made professional progress, Salisbury had unhappy associations because of the loss of his wife. Always inclined to introspection, he had begun to suffer from occasional bouts of melancholy that were aggravated by his intense dislike of the cold dampness of the English winters.[77]

The subject of emigration was a topical one during Smith's stay in Salisbury. After the discovery of gold in 1851, Australia had become increasingly attractive as a land of wealth and opportunity. In Wiltshire, as in many English counties at the time, an emigration association was formed to provide information and encouragement for prospective emigrants, whether independent or assisted by colonial governments.[78] Lectures were given in town centres and articles published in provincial newspapers, containing the latest news on conditions in the Australian colonies, with Melbourne the focus as the centre of the goldfields. The possibility of financial fortune was as attractive to Smith as to any other emigrant. But, even more, he may have looked towards a brighter future as a journalist in a place where, without the competition he faced at home as one among many of equal talent, he might well become a leading figure. Advertisements for passages to Australia appeared frequently in the *Journal*, with the fastest of the ships promising arrival in Port Phillip Bay within ten weeks. It is

England: 1820–1854

possible that Smith travelled as an assisted migrant, although it seems more likely that, given his desire for status as a professional figure, he would have preferred to pay his own passage. The name of the ship that he took and the exact date of his departure are unknown; shipping records for the period are incomplete and his name does not appear on the available lists of passengers arriving in Melbourne in the last weeks of 1854.[79] Sometime, late in September or early October, he left Salisbury to begin his outward journey, perhaps exhilarated at the prospect of a new start, but probably equally apprehensive about the suitability of the employment he hoped to find on arrival. Whatever his feelings on leaving England, there must have been undoubted reassurance in the knowledge that emigration need not be permanent; the length of his stay in Australia would depend upon his reaction to colonial experience.

3
THE IMMIGRANT

Within a few days of his arrival in Melbourne Smith was working on the *Age* as a leader writer and dramatic critic. This newspaper, founded by the mercantile firm Francis Cooke and Company on 17 October 1854, was designed to be 'liberal', 'unsectarian' and 'high in literary character'.[1] The proprietors were not to remain in control for long. According to a report published on 2 January 1855, its assets had been sold on 31 December to a 'new proprietary' with the means to maintain it 'for at least six months', and the services of 'several competent writers' had been secured. Smith was one of those 'competent writers'. Although he probably had been on his way to Australia when the *Age* began publication, it seems likely that he would have made enquiries about opportunities for employment before deciding to emigrate. If so, he may have had prior knowledge that a new paper was about to be founded, and could, perhaps, have been recruited especially. On the other hand, his immediate employment may have been the result of fortuitous circumstance, in that his availability as an experienced journalist met the urgent needs of the 'new proprietary'.

The *Age* was run by a cooperative that included, as editorial staff, former *Argus* journalists Ebenezer Syme, David Blair and Thomas Bright. When this cooperative failed in June 1856, Ebenezer Syme became sole editor and proprietor. In the following September, David Syme joined Ebenezer as co-proprietor. After Ebenezer's death in 1860, David Syme remained in partnership with his brother's heirs until 1891, when he became the sole proprietor. Smith stayed at the *Age* until early in 1856, contributing leading and other articles and acting as a dramatic critic. He was also involved with the foundation of the *Melbourne Leader* (later the *Leader*), a country weekly first published by the *Age* in January 1856. Designed as a family paper, it contained agricultural, sporting and literary sections, as well as a summary of the week's news. Smith was the first editor, but he can have done little more than preside over the first few issues before his resignation from the *Age* in order to join the *Argus*. That newspaper, with which he was to be associated for the next 40 years, had been founded in 1846 by William

The immigrant

Kerr. It was purchased in 1848 by Edward Wilson, but Wilson and his partner J. S. Johnston found it difficult to maintain the venture. It was not until Lauchlan Mackinnon entered partnership with Wilson in 1852, bringing additional capital with him, that the paper began to achieve stability. So it was, in 1856, that Wilson was able to make Smith a 'liberal offer' of employment as leader writer, dramatic, literary and fine arts critic.[2]

Wilson's offer was attractive financially: a salary of £500 per annum assured material comfort.[3] It is likely that Smith was also influenced by *Argus* policy. Wilson had originally adopted a radical approach to colonial politics. Under his editorship, the *Argus* had been antagonistic towards the government during the administration of the Lieutenant-Governor, Charles La Trobe. But, by the time of the diggers' revolt at the Eureka Stockade in December 1854, Wilson had moved to the right, in support of La Trobe's successor, Governor Hotham. This change in policy was the reason for David Blair and other dissatisfied *Argus* employees forming a cooperative to run the *Age* on the more radical principles that had previously motivated the *Argus* proprietors. It is probable that Smith, aligned more closely with Wilson in the new mode than he was likely to have been with Blair, welcomed the opportunity to move to what was now the more conservative of the Melbourne papers. He and Blair may also have found that it was becoming increasingly difficult for them to work together. Blair appears to have had a quarrelsome personality. Influenced, perhaps, by professional jealousy, together with resentment at Smith's readiness to leave the *Age* for the rival *Argus*, he was to make several public attacks on his former employee.

Smith was to stay with the *Argus* for most of his career as a journalist, working either as a salaried employee or, at shorter periods, as the contributor of frequent articles and reviews. In 1858, he was given an opportunity to return to the *Age*, when Ebenezer Syme, then co-proprietor and editor, invited him to become a contributor, on piecework rates or, if preferred, a regular salary. The terms offered for piecework were 30 shillings each for three articles per week, or, for a larger number, £1 each.[4] To match his *Argus* salary, Smith would have had to supply the *Age* with an average of ten articles each week. It is not known whether or not he accepted Ebenezer Syme's offer. Since, as part of his varied journalistic activities at the time, he was editing *Melbourne Punch*, it seems unlikely that he would have been able to accept additional regular employment; nor is there any reference in the biographical material to a break with the *Argus* at this time, even though he seems to have been writing less for that newspaper than when first appointed. He was certainly engaged in profitable freelance work during the late 1850s, writing for several colonial newspapers, including the *Ballarat Star*, the *Geelong Daily News*, the *Mount Alexander Mail*, the *Maryborough Advertiser* and the *Daylesford Mercury*. If he had accepted Syme's offer, it would probably have had to be on that kind of freelance basis. Whether or not the engagement of one of their writers by a rival newspaper would have suited the proprietors of the *Argus* is another matter that would have required serious consideration in the light of Smith's friendship with Edward Wilson. Whatever the arrangement with Syme, which, in any case, might have been altered when David Syme took control of the business after Ebenezer's retirement in 1859 and subsequent death, Smith was again writing regularly for the *Argus* by late 1859 or early 1860. He was not then to return to work as a contributor to the *Age* until the early 1900s.

With his position as a leading journalist seemingly assured, Smith took an important step towards further securing his future in Melbourne when he and Eliza Julia Kelly were married. The ceremony took place at St Mark's Church of England, Collingwood, on 11 April 1857.[5] For this marriage certificate, Smith gave his occupation as that of 'journalist', while his father is described as a 'government officer'. At the time of his first marriage in London in 1844, both were listed as 'gentlemen'. The change in attribution is an interesting indication of the way in which class distinctions might become blurred in the colonies. Since they both worked for a living, neither Smith nor his father were strictly entitled to be called English gentlemen in what was the then accepted meaning of the word. But, in Melbourne, where professional ability could lead to gentlemanly associations, there was less need to claim a position that might not be theirs by right of birth. Eliza's father, William Lancelot Kelly, is described on the certificate as a 'hotel-keeper': he was the proprietor of the Argus hotel in Collins Street where Smith and his friends used to gather. His occupation in England, before emigration, was that of a 'newsagent'.[6]

Eliza Kelly was 17 at the time of her marriage to James Smith. She was born at Tewkesbury in Gloucestershire, where, as she was proud to recall, she had been christened in the Abbey. She was well educated, being a fluent linguist with a particular interest in literature and art; she was also an accomplished needlewoman. In later life she was to become a Vice-President of the Alliance Francaise, acting in that position for 25 years. After her husband's death in 1910, Eliza—or Lizzie, as she was commonly called—moved to Ballarat to live with her son Charles, then editor of the *Ballarat Star*. There, as had been her custom in Melbourne, she involved herself in cultural affairs, becoming President both of the local branch of the Victoria League and the Ladies' Committee of the Ballarat Horticultural Society. She was also a judge of the literary section at the South Street competitions. When she died on 24 May 1927, the writer of the obituary notice in the *Ballarat Courier* described her as 'a brilliant conversationist', whose 'bright personality endeared her to all whom she knew'.[7]

Despite the twenty years' difference in their ages, the marriage seems to have been a happy one, lasting for over 50 years. The couple had six children: two boys and four girls. The boys had literary names: Tennyson Lancelot and Charles Lamb. Tennyson, born in 1858, was the author, with Percy Hulburd, of *Jim the Penman*, published in Melbourne in 1890. Charles, born the following year, adopted his father's profession, training with the *Argus*, and eventually moving to Ballarat to become editor of the *Star*. Edith Mary was born in 1862 and Emily Beatrice in 1864. The last two daughters were Kate Brooke, born in 1866 and named in memory of the Smiths' recently-drowned actor friend,[8] and Maria Theresa, born in 1872 and named after the Austrian Empress. This last child was described by a contemporary in later life as 'a woman of great literary capacity and immense artistic appreciation'.[9]

Others among Smith's fellow immigrants were married at around the same time. He was a witness at Doctor J. E. Neild's wedding in March 1857 and, most likely, a guest, when fellow journalist Frederick Sinnett was married in the following October. Marriage in these circumstances meant more than the establishment of a home. It was a movement towards permanent residence, that, with the birth of children, became more certain. While ties of family and affection still bound the immigrants to their home countries, those who married and founded their own family dynasties were less likely to uproot themselves once more. Marriage had another effect on most of the male immigrants, in that their social habits altered to include more female company, as they visited and, in turn, entertained their married friends and colleagues. Professional activity was still largely centred on male contacts, but the close associations that had characterised the early years of colonial life gradually weakened. Some of the immigrants remained good friends. Others moved apart when acquaintance and interest diversified.

As the immigrants settled down and familiar patterns of social behaviour replaced the less conventional lifestyle that they had adopted as new arrivals, their public life became more tightly structured. Those who, like James Smith, were especially interested in establishing a colonial culture, followed the Victorian model of formalised public culture. Lectures that provided entertainment combined with instruction were an important feature of that culture, often attracting large audiences when topical subjects were treated in a lively and interesting manner. This was a form of public cultural involvement in which Smith achieved considerable success. His friend Henry Gyles Turner recalled that 'his elocutionary powers were exceptional, and he had a clear penetrating voice which he knew how to use to advantage in either pathos or humour, and for a long time he was the best lecturer in Melbourne'.[10] But Smith was not a good impromptu speaker. As Turner continued, 'he had one defect, he could not get away from his manuscript' and, in fact, admitted that he was unable to think 'without a pen in his hand'. Because of this close link between writing and speaking, Smith's articles and lectures were often interchangeable, with one providing the material for the other. Along with other lecturers, such as David Blair, barrister Archibald Michie (later Sir) and journalist

Richard Birnie, who were also becoming prominent in the field, he spoke in town halls, mechanics' institutes, churches, schoolrooms, courthouses, theatres, or wherever suitable premises might be found.

During Smith's early years in Melbourne, most of his topics were literary or historical, but, as he became more actively involved in colonial affairs, he spoke more often on subjects of social and political interest. One such lecture had a particular appeal for a largely immigrant audience. This was 'Mother and Daughter; or Old England and Young Australia Contrasted', first given by Smith at the St Kilda Town Hall on 8 October 1860 and repeated under different, though similar, titles at other suburban locations during following weeks.[11] He introduced his subject with a reference to Janus, the two-headed Roman god who was able to look both ways at once. He then developed his theme of assessment of the differences between the two countries in respect of climate, historical background and social condition. The whole tone of the lecture is one of encouragement to the immigrant, who, while necessarily forward looking, might retain the benefits to be derived from the old society through the transplantation of its best aspects. Smith suggested that his audience should develop feelings of colonial pride, urging them to 'cultivate and cherish that feeling of patriotism... which it is the first duty of a citizen to acquire and the last possession he must relinquish'. Intrigued by the prospect of a distinctive colonial race, he speculated on alterations in physical characteristics:

> The typical John Bull of the mother country; the ruddy, rotund, marrowy, plump, and brawny emblem of our race, into whose rich blood have been distilled the juices of an infinite number of stall-fed beeves, of innumerable tankards of nut-brown ale, and of multitudinous hogsheads of "fine old family port," whose eye twinkles with the cheer of fifty jovial Christmases, and upon whose mottled cheeks frost and sunshine have set their crimson mark—will not suffice as the representative man of the Anglo-Australians. Spare and bright of eye, oval in countenance, quick in movement, with nerves more finely strung, and with a nature more impulsive than his British forefathers; with greater energy but less endurance; the national phlegm replaced by a vehement impetuousity; with—to borrow an illustration from the race course—more speed but less bottom than the old stock; with less reticence and morgue and a greater inclination to novelty and change; not so morose but much more excitable and mercurial with the home feelings less vigorously exerted, but the social sentiments more fully developed; less susceptible to profound impressions, but more alive to a sense of the ridiculous; a good hater, and a generous friend—such it appears to me, are the more prominent features of the character and person of Mr. Kangaroo Bull.[12]

Speculation such as this was a common colonial preoccupation, inspired in part by the need of the immigrants to re-establish a sense of national identity. Most of those who were of British stock retained their alle-

The immigrant

giance to Britain through ties of loyalty and affection as well as by right as members of the British Empire. But, as expatriates, they were in the ambivalent position of having made a deliberate decision to move away from their homeland in order to lead another life in a different environment. Under these circumstances, the development of a specifically colonial patriotism was an important factor in successful emigration. Comparisons between traditional British characteristics and those that appeared to be developing as a result of the colonial environment were also influenced by the impact made on scientific and other circles by Charles Darwin's *On the Origin of Species*, published in 1859. Darwin's theory of the evolution of animal species by natural selection stimulated a great deal of popular interest as regards its application to the human race. For the immigrants who were themselves undergoing a process of adaptation, it was an especially pertinent subject for discussion.

Smith's use of John Bull as a representative type of Anglo-Saxon allowed him to treat the topic on the theoretical basis best suited to speculation of the kind. Even though few members of his audience may have shared them, John Bull's characteristics are easily recognisable as those of a typical country squire. At middle age, secure in his awareness of the stability of succeeding generations whose lives had been little different from his own, he is symbolic of the mother country that the colonial Kangaroo Bull had rejected for the benefit of new experience. John Bull's solidity, however appropriate in its traditional context, seems less praiseworthy, by comparison, than the spirit of enterprise that had induced the immigrants to leave home. The beneficial effects of a more temperate climate, together with those of a freer social environment, might be expected to further influence the separate development of Kangaroo Bull, allowing the growth of characteristics that owed more to the new life than the old. There is an implied moral judgment in the fact that Kangaroo Bull is presented as the superior character of the two national types. Most of the modifications that Smith proposes are improvements, in a favourable assessment of the process of natural selection, as demonstrated in the colonies, that must have been a source of gratification to his listeners.

However satisfying the prospect of advancement through evolution may have been, the figure of Kangaroo Bull still belonged to the future. The immigrants might turn away from the old towards the new, but there was cause for immediate concern in their present life as potentially successful colonists. Smith struck a rare personal note in this lecture with an expression of confidence in the benefits of enterprise, while at the same time reaffirming his satisfaction with life in Melbourne:

> ...speaking as a man of the world, not utterly unacquainted with the social and intellectual enjoyments of European capitals; not wholly indifferent to the fascinations of art, the attractions of antiquity, and the glories of nature; not altogether insensible to the special advantages which attach to life in old and highly civilized

> societies; and not a native of Australia, I am bound to declare my belief, that in no part of the world are so many elements of well-being combined as present themselves here, and that to the man of moderate desires, and with a capacity for reasonable enjoyment, life presents as many opportunities for happiness as are to be found in any other portion of the globe.

In this statement of belief in the future of his adopted country, he took pains to publicly convey his awareness of himself as a person whose cultural affinities transcended geographic locations. There is a calculated use of negatives in the passage, which, acting as disclaimers, have the effect of suggesting a wider knowledge of Europe and its culture than he actually possessed at that time. Though presenting himself as a man of 'moderate' and 'reasonable' attitudes, he nevertheless succeeds in conveying a strong sense of his own self-importance because of the fact that he 'feels bound to declare [his beliefs]' as well as the manner in which he does so. However, without this strong feeling of personal appreciation of the best of British and European ideas and institutions, it is doubtful whether he or many of his fellows could have settled down in a remote colonial possession, whatever its potential. It was a feeling that would inform Smith's attitude to life in the Australian colonies and provide the means for setting standards by which he was able to proceed.

Early in 1861, he was invited to give two public lectures at the Ballarat Mechanics' Institute. The first of these, delivered on 15 February, was the now often-repeated 'England and Australia Contrasted and Compared'; the second, on the following evening, consisted of the popular readings from Dickens in which he was becoming a specialist, this time from *David Copperfield*. Towards the end of the first lecture, attended by 'the largest audience that ever assembled in Ballarat',[13] Smith had something to say about the very noticeable changes in the town since his first visit to the goldfields district in 1855. These remarks stimulated a wider interest in the topic, leading to an additional lecture, 'Ballarat Past and Present', which he gave on 18 February. Because of the short time available for its preparation, this lecture was briefer than either Smith or his audience might have wished. After his return to Melbourne, he extended the topic for publication, using his impressions of Ballarat as the basis for consideration of the phenomenon of Victorian colonial development. During the course of the article, published in the *Victorian Review* in the form of a lecture report, he elaborated upon the reasons for the constant activity in which he and many of his fellow colonists were engaged:

> I think it must be conceded that we live at a rapid pace in this colony; that the flow of thought and action, and the hurry of events, are wonderfully rapid, so that five years in Victoria are equivalent to fifty years in Europe. Having taken possession of a virgin soil, we find there is an infinite amount of work to do, in order to render it

productive and habitable, and to assimilate it to the country we have left; so we apply ourselves to the task with the characteristic energy of our race, and crowd the effort and the enterprise of half a century into a few short years.[14]

Here Smith extends his views on colonial enterprise by stressing the urgency of the work of consolidation if the immigrants were to gain the rewards they expected during their own lifetimes. There was also the question of the passage of time as it affected personal advancement. Smith and a good many of the immigrants who had arrived at around the same time were approaching middle age. Those who, like him, were anxious for public recognition, had to work quickly as well as assiduously, seizing each opportunity for self-promotion and, whenever possible, involving themselves in community affairs.

Although journalism was to remain the major focus of Smith's working life, he began searching for an alternative career during the 1860s, attracted by the prospect of diversification as well as the demands of ambition. His decision to seek nomination as a candidate for election as an independent member in the 1862 Legislative Assembly by-election for Brighton was a step in that direction. The vacancy had occurred through the resignation of pastoralist William Brodribb, who was planning a trip to England. Brodribb had defeated George Higinbotham, a barrister and former editor of the *Argus*, at the general election held in November 1861. In his letter to the electors of Brighton, published in the *Argus* on 28 March 1862, Smith pledged his support for the governing O'Shanassy ministry and made the following statement of his approach to colonial politics:

> I think the time has arrived when men of moderate views may combine in an honest effort to promote, by practical and well-considered legislation, the welfare of the colony; and when the mischievous class prejudices which have hitherto impeded this good work will be replaced by a salutary conviction that no actual antagonism of the interests exists, but that the prosperity of the farmer, the flock-holder, the miner, and the merchant rests upon the same foundation—wise laws, good government and stable institutions.

In presenting himself as a man 'of moderate views' in this context, Smith is implying that he would be free from involvement in political faction fighting if elected. But, however reasonable his approach, he was being unrealistic in expecting that the various elements of colonial society were about to be reconciled. It was inevitable that there should be antagonisms of interest between immigrants who adopted different methods as the means of becoming successful colonists. The four elements of the population that Smith refers to as 'the farmer, the flock-holder, the miner, and the merchant' are significant as being the main groups of colonists that sought representation in parliament. The pastoralists were part of the establishment by right of comparatively old wealth, while the merchants claimed position through the acquisition of newer money. The settlers wanted some of the land that the pastoralists had taken and the miners, some of whom wished to become settlers, looked for a democratic form of government in which all colonists would have a voice. Although some of these divisions overlapped, allowing areas of common interest, major differences of opinion meant that it was impossible to ensure stable government in Victoria at this time, even allowing for the combination of various factions in the temporary pursuit of particular objectives.

The traditional divisions of class may have been less obviously apparent than they had been in England becasue of the less rigid colonial environment. However, they still existed and wealth and position were as much a guarantee of privilege as they had been at home. Smith had achieved a certain prominence through the practice of his journalistic skills and, in the course of his lectures on colonial affairs, he had demonstrated his ability to act as a public-minded citizen. His election to parliament would mean added status, though not increased wealth; legislation allowing the payment of members was not passed until 1874. He would have had to continue working as a journalist as well as undertaking the duties required by the electorate. As it happened, his ambition to become recognised as a political figure remained untested. Almost immediately, he retracted his proposal for nomination because W. J. (later Sir William) Clarke had presented himself as a ministry candidate. Smith announced his retirement on 29 March , giving as his reasons the advisability of one of the candidates retiring in order to avoid dividing conservative interests in the electorate, and that he should be the one to step down because Clarke was likely to have more free time to devote to public duties.[15] It is obvious that Smith wished to appear unselfishly public minded in making this retraction. His motives in withdrawing his nomination are also likely to have been self-protective in that he was unable to count on success against Clarke, the eldest son of a wealthy landowner, who was himself to become one of the wealthiest men in the colony.

If Smith had remained in competition with Clarke, he would have had to stand as well against George Higinbotham, who was to contest the seat as an independent candidate and become the eventual winner of the by-election. Higinbotham's address to the electors at the time of his first decision to contest the seat consists of a more detailed statement of political belief than is contained in Smith's letter. Some of his views were radical—for instance, his support of universal suffrage in the colonial situation—but the changes he advocated were tempered by moderate provisos that both anticipated and accepted the likelihood of opposition. Reasonableness of this kind is a quality that Smith lacked, despite his claims of moderation. His political views, though less well documented, appear to have remained firm throughout his life: for instance, his continued opposition to protective tariffs long after protection had become accepted government policy, or his absolute rejection of the concept of universal (or manhood) suffrage. It is possible that he may have modified some of his attitudes in accordance with political alignments if he had been elected to parliament. However, he made no further attempt to enter politics.

After withdrawing from the nomination contest, Smith returned to work at what he had described as his 'arduous profession'.[16] But, still attracted by the prospect of change, towards the end of 1862 he began negotiating with Spiers and Pond, proprietors of the Café de Paris at the Theatre Royal, for their sponsorship of a lecture tour of England, which would involve him in a prolonged absence from the colony. Under these arrangements, he would have his passage home paid first class. On tour, he would receive a salary of £10 a week for six months, plus travelling expenses outside London.[17] This must have seemed a worthwhile project for a number of reasons: he was now an experienced lecturer with a wide repertoire; though not speaking in an official capacity, he would have been able to tell his English audiences much of what they wished to know about life in Victoria; he would also have had the opportunity of travelling about parts of England both familiar and new to him. There was another important factor in his wish to undertake the tour: it was to be a twelve months' contract with the possibility of extension, allowing him the flexibility of postponing any decision as to whether his visit to England meant permanent rather than temporary removal from the colony.

As it happened, the tour was not to go ahead. The reasons for the breakdown in arrangements are unknown, but certainly Smith must have been disappointed, even more so had he not almost immediately been given another opportunity for self-advancement in Victoria. On 10 January 1863, he was approached by the government statistician William Archer, on behalf of the Premier, John (later Sir John) O'Shanassy, in connection with undertaking the office of Parliamentary Librarian.[18] Appointments such as this were under the patronage of the minister responsible, in this case O'Shanassy himself. Smith's qualifications were those of a literary man: he wrote articles and delivered lectures on literary topics and he was known to have a substantial private library. He had also made a public declaration of support for the O'Shanassy ministry at the time of the Brighton by-election, making his appointment under that government an appropriate one. However, there was a serious obstacle to be overcome in that Charles Ridgway, the current Librarian, who had held the office since 1856, had to be induced to retire before Smith could take up the position.

Archer and Smith were on friendly terms and it seems most likely that the matter had been aired between them before any formal discussion with O'Shanassy. Archer acted as an intermediary throughout the negotiations with Ridgway, advising Smith and keeping O'Shanassy informed. Acting on O'Shanassy's suggestion that Smith and Ridgway should arrange the matter between them, Smith decided to make a direct approach to Ridgway. He went to Ridgway's house on 10 January and, as recorded in the private diary that he had recently begun keeping:

> Had a long chat with him on the subject, & offered him £200 a year for his life, conditionally on his resigning, and my obtaining the appointment. He received the proposition very favourably, but said it had taken him by surprise. He wished to have a few days to think it over, & is to give me an answer soon.

O'Shanassy's cognizance of the manner in which Ridgway's retirement was to be arranged is an indication that jobbery of this kind was not uncommon in the securing of government appointments. It is obvious that Smith was anxious to obtain the position, but, not surprisingly, Ridgway was reluctant to be removed from office in this manner, even though retirement might bring him financial security. On 13 January, Smith recorded that he had received a letter from Ridgway declining the proposition. Ten days later, Archer called to tell Smith that O'Shanassy had made 'an absolute promise of the reversion of the appointment'.[19] Archer, who seems to have been almost as anxious for the favourable conclusion of the matter as Smith, had then seen Ridgway and, managing to overcome the 'conscientious scruples' that had prevented the Librarian from accepting the previous offer, persuaded him to retire on condition of payment of a fixed sum as compensation.[20] After further discussion with Archer, Smith arranged to pay Ridgway £500: £250 in cash and £250 in discounted bills. This, of course, was a private arrangement between the two men and Smith's broker.[21] The next step, to be taken through official channels, was the organisation of Ridgway's retirement and Smith's subsequent appointment. On 26 January, as recorded in the diary, Smith went to see O'Shanassy in company with Archer. The Premier had 'pointed out the proper course to pursue': Ridgway should see the Chief Medical Officer to obtain a certificate to the effect that he was 'inadequate to the performance of his duties'. He would then offer his resignation and, if this was accepted, Smith would be appointed in his place. Ridgway appears to have been unwilling to retire under these circumstances. But, after a further visit from Archer, he finally agreed to the arrangement and, on 31 January, Smith heard that Ridgway's resignation had been accepted and his own appointment decided upon.[22] The official notification appeared in the *Victorian Government Gazette* on 6 February, together with the reasons for Smith's selection:

> The said appointment has been made without examination or probation, because Mr. Smith's known ability, extensive knowledge of books, experience as a literary man, and general acquaintance with literature, peculiarly qualify him for the discharge of the duties of librarian.

The immigrant

This explanation of Smith's informal entry into the public service was insufficient to forestall criticism of the appointment by opposition members. William Frazer, the member for Creswick, was 'horrified' at finding that the Librarian was actually installed.[23] Frazer strongly supported Mark Pope, the member for North Grenville, who gave notice of a motion to the effect that Smith 'as editor of *Punch* newspaper, leader writer to the *Argus* newspaper, and professionally a theatre critic', had been appointed 'in direct violation of the provisions of the Civil Service Act and [was] personally obnoxious to a majority of the members of this House'.[24] Smith described Frazer, a former miner, as being 'very drunk and extremely offensive' at the time.[25] He dismissed Pope, a journalist and mining manager before entering politics, as 'a fair sample of the democratic members of the Assembly'.[26] In any case, Smith was not then to become the subject of acrimonious parliamentary debate. Other business before the House was satisfactorily concluded and, during the subsequent adjournment, Pope's motion fell through. Officially secure, Smith was gratified to note that 'twenty or thirty members of the Legislature' had congratulated him upon his appointment.[27]

On his first official visit to the Parliamentary Library, he made a careful survey of the contents and decided that the classification was 'not sufficiently minute'.[28] He began work immediately on the preparation of a new catalogue, reclassifying the books already in the Library and ordering new books in the areas he found deficient.[29] Although his efforts at reorganisation were obviously influenced by his determination to succeed in his new position, he was genuinely appreciative of the benefits to be gained from well-stocked shelves. As he wrote in the article 'The Secret of Happiness':

> Books make us the contemporaries of all time, and citizens of every country. They enable us to live in the past as well as in the present. They are the sustenance of the mind, as food is of the body. They confer upon us the friendship of the splendid illustrations of our race. They are, when rightly chosen, the best of companions and the wisest of councillors.[30]

Smith's private library, brought out to the colony with him and augmented through frequent book-buying from new and secondhand booksellers,[31] was a source of such pleasure. It was also a considerable asset; it could provide reference material for professional use as well as reading matter for leisure hours and its resale value was a form of insurance against future need.

It is a measure of Smith's ambivalent attitude towards remaining in Melbourne at this time that, twice during the 1860s, he put large numbers of his books up for sale. In January 1863, in anticipation of the proposed lecture tour of England, he decided to sell the whole of his private library. Although there was a possibility that his return might be permanent, he was apparently unwilling to take it with him and may, perhaps, have expected that it would not be difficult to replace once he had settled back at home. As advertised in the *Argus*, the sale would include items of furniture and art work:

> LIBRARY.—FOR SALE by PRIVATE CONTRACT, in one lot (the owner revisiting England), the LIBRARY of Mr. James Smith, comprising about 2000 volumes of the best works in the English, French, Spanish, and Italian languages, many of them elegantly bound.
>
> As no pains have been spared in the formation of this library, the proprietor is desirous of seeing it pass into other hands intact, confident as he is that it will be a great acquisition to any gentleman wishing to obtain a really choice and valuable library.
>
> With it would be also sold, if desired, the whole of the carved oak furniture, oil paintings, and water-colour drawings, bronzes, statuettes, and works of art collected by Mr. Smith, and forming an assemblage that is perfectly unique in Victoria.[32]

Either there was no immediate buyer, or, as seems more likely considering Smith's change of plans, the library was withdrawn from sale. However, although he seems to have become quickly settled as Parliamentary Librarian, he was apparently determined to dispose of at least some of these books. About 1500 of them were selected for auction by Alfred Bliss on 23 and 24 July. According to Smith's diary entries for those dates, the first day's sale raised £228, and the second £160.

During the first period of his employment as Librarian, Smith appears to have maintained his enthusiasm for the position. However, as the years passed he found that there was insufficient work to keep him occupied. Because of the effort he had made, the Library was in good order and its operation largely a matter of routine. In 1866, he wrote to Spiers and Pond, who had left the colony, to ask their advice on whether he should himself return to England to earn his living. Their conclusion that the rewards available to literary men in London were not large enough to take the risk might have ended that particular speculation.[33] But, obviously disappointed, he approached Edward Wilson, then living in Kent, for another opinion on the opportunities for writers in England. Wilson's reply confirmed what Spiers and Pond had already told Smith, that without firm guarantee of adequate financial reward, he would be foolish to leave Melbourne and the security of his present well-paid position.[34] Apparently still expecting to go home in spite of this advice, he decided to sell the theatrical section of his library, comprised of histories, biographies, plays, dramatic criticism and other works relating to the theatre.[35]

In view of Smith's interest in the drama, his decision to sell these books is surprising, although it is probable that, as may have been the case in 1863, he intended to make replacements in England. What is more remarkable is the catalogue description of the books as 'the theatrical library of a gentleman leaving the profession', which implied that the library belonged to an actor who was about to leave the colony, rather than a drama critic. But it is evident from the corresponding details in Smith's library register that he was the gentleman in question.[36] While the library might have gained in value if its provenance had been known, it is probable that Smith chose anonymity because he preferred not to disclose his future plans until he could announce his retirement as Parliamentary Librarian. At the same time, it is doubtful that anonymity could have been strictly maintained, when the booksellers with whom he dealt had records of previous transactions respecting some of the books that were for sale. His friends and associates might also be expected to have some familiarity with his pursuit of desirable titles. In addition, it would have been difficult to find an actor who fitted the catalogue description of the owner; few actors of the period had the opportunity to lead a stable enough life with sufficient income to build up this 'perfectly unique' collection.

The sale of '700 volumes of choice, rare and valuable works'[37] realised a total of £106/15/6 before expenses, which was rather less than that for an equivalent number of books at the 1863 auction, although the value of individual titles may affect direct comparison. In the absence of other convincing reasons for these sales, apart from Smith's recurrent attempts to go back to England, it appears likely that he may have wanted to raise money. He was still writing occasional articles on a freelance basis and the payment for this work together with his government salary of £800 per annum should have been sufficient to make him financially secure.[38] However, book collecting on the scale required for the maintenance and extension of a large private library involved consistent expense and it is probable that he used at least some of the proceeds of both sales to defray the cost of new and currently more desirable titles. He could, of course, have required money for capital outlay or investment. There were now five children in his rapidly-growing family and, in 1864, he had bought a ten-roomed house in Abbotsford, which had increased in gross annual value from £100 to £180 by 1866.[39]

Towards the end of 1868, still anxious to go home and convinced that the Parliamentary Library could be managed without him for the next two or three years, he attempted to arrange matters through official channels by applying for the position of Secretary to George (later Sir George) Verdon, Agent General for Victoria in London. In an application dated 21 November, he proposed taking leave of absence, during which he would be paid an annual salary of £1000. He was prepared to combine the position with activity as a writer and lecturer in promotion of emigration to the colony. He was also willing, while in England, to undertake Library business, including the selection and purchase of books and other publications.[40] Unfortunately for his careful plans to return home, not as a failed immigrant, but in a position of colonial authority, his application had the effect of assuring James (later Sir James) McCulloch, who was now Premier, that his services could be dispensed with altogether. McCulloch had taken office in 1863, six months after Smith's appointment, when O'Shanassy resigned because of dissension over the provisions of the Land Act prepared by Charles (later Sir Charles) Gavan Duffy. Although the change in government had no immediate effect on Smith's position, his was an opposition appointment and, as such, less favourably viewed by McCulloch than it might otherwise have been. In February 1869, the post of Parliamentary Librarian was abolished. Officially, *Argus* leaders on the disadvantages of protection were to blame; the McCulloch government, then involved in setting up protective tariffs, could not countenance public criticism that might be attributed to an employee. Smith denied writing the articles, although it is possible that they may have been his work, given the determination of his support for free trade. Recalling the incident in later years, Henry Gyles Turner was inclined to think that a more important reason for Smith's dismissal was the fact that, as Librarian, he had 'filled the shelves with French, Italian and other foreign books' that were of little use to the general run of members. At the same time, Turner conceded that 'there [was] no doubt that he often lampooned his employers in Punch and other papers'.[41] Whatever the relevant importance of the factors that hastened Smith's departure from the Library, it seem obvious that McCulloch welcomed the opportunity to abolish the post of Librarian.

The matter was discussed in the course of the Legislative Assembly debate on supply, when the estimates for the Parliamentary Library for 1869 were assessed. McCulloch explained that 'the office of Librarian could be dispensed with, without any inconvenience, as a paid office'.[42] It was planned that, as an alternative, the duties might be performed by the Clerk-Assistant of the Legislative Assembly, effectively saving the Librarian's salary. Since the dismissal was in line with a general reduction of the civil service on economic grounds, McCulloch's proposal appeared perfectly reasonable: the Librarian had done the job required of him to the extent that it no longer existed. However, other speeches in the *Hansard* report indicate divisions of opinion. David Blair, now member for Crowlands, supported McCulloch by confirming the wisdom of the Premier's decision to abolish the post, complaining that the Library lacked books that could be used for practical legislative purposes and questioning the practice of allowing the Librarian to select new acquisitions without recourse to members. He also deplored the delay in the compilation of supplementary catalogues and suggested that records of borrowings were inadequate. Blair's remarks undoubtedly had some substance. Even so, his attitude was suspect because of previous disagreements with Smith, causing the next speaker, George Kerferd, member for the Ovens district, to modify and correct what he believed to be unfair accusations and mis-statements.

Butler Cole Aspinall, then member for St Kilda, took the opportunity of paying a tribute to his friend:

The immigrant

...Mr. Smith, the librarian was a gentleman of whom they might be proud. He possessed great qualifications for the office. He was a scholar and a gentleman; he was a student, and he knew what books it was desirable to procure, either for political or for literary purposes. He loved books for their own sake, and he took charge of the Library as a man would take charge of a family of children. He knew the value of the Library, and he knew how to classify it. He had classified it, and got it into such order as no person of inferior capacity could have done. His misfortune had been that he had fulfilled his duties too well. He had got the Library into such order that he had made the work which his successor would have to perform little more than mechanical.

Aspinall went on to refer to Smith's application for the position of Secretary to the Agent General and to recommend that, if Smith must leave the Library, he should be appointed to that position. Charles (later Sir Charles) MacMahon, the member for West Melbourne, supported Aspinall's recommendation, as also did the Attorney General and member for South Bourke, George Paton Smith. Edward Langton, the member for Dundas, suggested that Smith would have been treated with more courtesy if the matter of his position had been referred to the Library Committee before being aired in Parliament. However, despite the efforts of Smith's supporters, McCulloch's decision was final: the Clerk-Assistant, Mr. A. G. Dumas, was directed to undertake the duties of Librarian from 1 March 1869 and Smith's career as a public servant came to an end.

Making the best of the matter, Smith went back to the *Argus*, feeling, 'in no way discouraged, but...greatly renewed in health and vigor'.[43] Journalism was a profession that, on the whole, he found congenial and, in the absence of other opportunities for diversification, it was the one in which he would remain. From then on, he appears to have become more settled in the colony. His vacillation during the 1860s may be due, in part, to the stress of competition with other ambitious immigrants caught up, like himself, in the effort to take a leading place. The main cause, though, seems to have been his homesickness, his longing for English society, despite its restrictiveness, and his nostalgia for places that were still dear to him. Homesickness such as this was common to most colonists, although it varied in degree according to their adjustment to immigrant life. There is no record of his wife's feelings, but, for Smith, it was at times almost overwhelming. However, so far as is known, he made no further attempts to arrange for overseas employment as a colonial representative until the early 1880s, when he was at last to be successful in his ambition to return home in that capacity. But, at that time, when he had been almost 30 years in Victoria, he would return as a visitor, rather than a comparatively new immigrant.

4
INSTITUTIONS

Clubs and societies founded on English and European models were an important feature of immigrant society. They served as meeting places for those with like interests; they provided the security of familiar institutions in the colonial situation; and, for those who wished to combine social and cultural activity with personal ambition, they presented opportunities for leadership. Some of these institutions were socially based. Others were established for cultural, recreational or educational purposes. Committees formed for fund raising for various causes were also inclined to develop into club-like organisations during the most active periods of their existence. But, despite the dedication of the founders, few of these clubs and societies were able to sustain their membership for long. The proportion of the population with an active interest was insufficient for the support of each new institution. Some of the colonists joined two or three clubs and societies with related interests, leading to divisions in loyalty and, eventually, the closure of opposing organisations. Other clubs and societies were weakened by factions that broke away to reform in different guise. However, while they continued in operation, colonial institutions were the means of interaction between people of frequently varied occupation, allowing the extension of acquaintance and the development of particular interests.

James Smith was enthusiastic in the formation of many such clubs and societies. He popularised new organisations through newspaper columns, enjoyed founding membership and frequently accepted executive office. The following table shows the clubs, societies, councils and committees to which Smith belonged and on which he served, including the fund raising organisations that, in part, are the subject of the following chapter. They are arranged in order of the beginning of Smith's involvement, whether at foundation or a later stage, together with a representative selection of other known friends and associates.

This table covers the period from the foundation of the Garrick Club in 1855 through to the foundation of the Dante Society in 1896. Smith's continued membership of some of the later organisations extends the scope of the table until the time of his death in 1910. Because

Table 4.1 Clubs and other organisations with which James Smith was associated

Name	Year of arrival in Melbourne	Occupation	Garrick Club	Victorian Club	Victorian Society of Fine Arts	Fêtes Champêtres	Press Cricket Club	Royal Society	Shakespeare Memorial Fund	Garibaldi Memorial Fund	Acclimatisation Society	Melbourne Elocution Society	Brooke Memorial Fund	Athenaeum Club	Yorick Club	Victorian Proprietary College	Public Library	Kalizoic Society	Melbourne Shakespeare Society	French Literary Club	Alliance Française	Working Men's College	Caxton Fund	Dante Society
AKHURST William	1850	Music critic, dramatist	X			X								X											
ARCHER William	1852	Statistician, public servant		X							X														
*ASPINALL Butler Cole	1854	Barrister, politician		X			X							X	X										
*BARRY Redmond	1839	Judge					X	X									X								
BIRNIE Richard	1859	Barrister, journalist							X					X											
BLAIR David	1852	Journalist, politician																			X				
BLEASDALE John	1851	Roman Catholic priest					X							X	X										
BRIGHT Charles	1853	Journalist, lecturer												X	X									X	
BROOKE Gustavus	1855	Actor	X	X																					
CHEVALIER Nicholas	1855	Artist	X	X	X			X																	
CLARKE Marcus	1863	Journalist, novelist												X	X										
¶CLARKE William	1850	Landowner, philanthropist									X										X				
COPPIN George	1851	Comic actor, entrepreneur				X						X	X	X					X					X	
ELLERY Robert	1852	Astronomer, public servant					X						X	X	X							X			
GILLBEE William	1852	Surgeon	X	X			X							X											
GUERARD Eugene von	1852	Artist			X		X																		
HADDON Frederick	1863	Journalist											X	X					X		X				
HORNE Richard	1852	Poet	X					X			X														
KNIGHT John	1852	Architect, administrator			X								X	X											
LANGTON Edward	1852	Politician														X	X								
MACADAM John	1855	Physician, politician		X			X																		
MICHIE Archibald	1852	Lawyer, politician	X							X	X														
MOTHERWELL James	1857	Physician		X			X							X											
NEILD James	1853	Pathologist, drama critic	X				X						X	X	X			X	X						
SHILLINGLAW John	1852	Public servant, historian	X	X										X											
SMITH James	1854	Journalist, critic	X	X	X	X	X	X	X	X	X	X	X	X	X	X	X	X	X	X	X	X	X	X
*STAWELL William	1842	Chief Justice	X				X	X																	
TURNER Henry	1854	Banker, historian												X		X			X		X				
¶WALCH Garnet	1872	Author, dramatist												X						X					
WILSON Edward	1842	Journalist, philanthropist		X		X					X														

* Also members of the Melbourne Club
¶ Colonial-born

of the range of his activities, it is possible to trace the development of immigrant culture as expressed through colonial institutions.

Some of Smith's friends and associates were members of the exclusive Melbourne Club, founded in 1838 by military officers and other gentlemen resident in the Port Phillip district of New South Wales. Well before Victoria was established through separation from the older colony in 1851, the Melbourne Club had as many members as its committee could have wished. There were occasional vacancies through death or resignation, but these were soon filled by eligible gentlemen. A rival club, the Port Phillip, founded in 1841, lasted for only two years before it was forced to close because of outstanding debts. A few of the Port Phillip Club's members were absorbed into the Melbourne Club. The rest remained without a special place in which to meet and enjoy the social amenities that a club of the kind could provide. Although at the time of Smith's arrival at the end of 1854 the population had increased far beyond the expectations of the early colonists, there was still no other club in Melbourne that he and his fellow immigrants might join. Some of the better hotels, such as the Argus, where Smith became a member of a regular circle of drinking companions, served as a substitute. But an informal gathering at a hotel, however congenial, lacked the status provided by membership of a good club.

Within his first twelve months in the colony, Smith became involved in the formation of the first of the Melbourne institutions with which he was to be closely associated. The Garrick Club, founded in September 1855 in response to the interest in the theatre stimulated by the visit of the actor Gustavus Vaughan Brooke, was modelled on the London club of the same name that had been familiar to many of the members of the colonial club prior to emigration. As Smith described it in later years, they were 'drawn together by common sympathies and by a common love of Shakespeare and the stage'.[1] The writer R. H. Horne, something of a celebrity in the colony, was elected President at a general meeting held at the Argus hotel on 5 September, when the club's objectives were defined as 'the cultivation of dramatic literature and art, and the occasional production of dramatic representations in aid of charitable purposes'.[2] Smith was the Vice President, and James Edward Neild, a medical practitioner and drama critic, was the Honorary Secretary.

Through his position as a journalist on the *Age*, Smith was able to provide publicity for the club while elaborating upon its composition. The following extract is taken from a leading article that is obviously his work:

> Without any preliminary flourish of trumpets, elaborate preparation, or grandiloquent promise of magnificent impossibilities, an association has been planned, organized, and launched into vigorous existence, with a title borrowed from the name of the English Roscius,[3] and objects more comprehensive than the merely histrionic purpose denoted by its title. Its President is a gentleman honorably

and conspicuously identified with the literature of Great Britain; its Vice-President is also a laborer in the same field, and its Honorary-Secretary, we can testify of our own knowledge, is one whose versatility of mind is as admirable as his geniality and *bon hommie* of manner. Its committee includes an able dramatic writer, who is also the skilful dramatic critic engaged in the service of one of our contemporaries[4]; and the Club already numbers amongst its members many of the most distinguished members of two of the learned professions, and several intelligent representatives of the educated classes in this city.[5]

Smith's executive membership was probably the result of the reputation that he had achieved as a drama critic during the Brooke season. As evident from the tone of the article, as well as the linking of himself as Vice President with the much better-known Horne, he was now intent upon presenting himself as an important figure among the others for whose 'cultivated minds and refined tastes' the club was designed.

Unfortunately, all was not as harmonious as the founders could have wished and there were soon to be changes in the executive. In the *Second Half-Yearly Report*, dated 1 July 1856, the committee expressed regret at the lack of 'cordial co-operation' among members, which had inhibited plans for monthly soirées and weekly dramatic readings. Smith had resigned, depriving the club of 'the honor of possessing for its Vice-President a gentleman of such sterling worth, such amiable qualities, and such intellectual merit as are comprised in [his] character'. Neild also resigned as Honorary Secretary and, in November 1856, Horne as President. Smith then took over as President. It is possible that this was his original ambition and that dissension over the question of leadership may have provoked the series of resignations. Whatever the truth of the matter, the Garrick Club appears to have continued its operations without further serious problems of the kind. Smith's tenure as President is unknown, but the club itself remained in existence under various executives until 1870.

The production of amateur performances was a specific objective of the Garrick Club and, although professional actors gave assistance with female roles, club members were responsible for most aspects of the plays that were a regular feature of the year's activities. Theatrical addresses in the form of prologues, epilogues or other incidental pieces were popular additions to the performances. Smith shared the writing of some of these addresses with Horne and Neild. At the performance of *The School for Scandal* at the Princess's Theatre on 23 May 1866, on the occasion of comic actor J. C. Lambert's retirement from the stage, Neild was the author of the prologue, for instance, and Smith the epilogue.

Although he appeared in some of the early productions, Smith was not an accomplished actor. Henry Gyles Turner has recalled being surprised that this should have been so:

> It was rather curious that so attractive on the platform and so well seasoned a critic of the stage he had no real histrionic gift. I saw him in some amateur performances in those days [the 1850s] and was astonished at his want of ease. Probably it was partly due to his difficulty in memorising his part, which left him anxiously thinking about it all through.[6]

There might well have been more than one awkward actor amongst an amateur group such as this, but those less skilled played to tolerant audiences that usually accepted faults in the production. Smith's indifferent acting was more noticeable; it was incompatible with his function as a critic of professional actors and, although he retained his association with the club, his name soon ceased to appear on the cast lists.

The Garrick Club provided satisfaction for its members through involvement in its activities, but it was not a social club as such and its link with the theatre, which had certain disreputable associations, prevented it from attaining the standing in the community that its founders had desired. Smith and some of his fellow immigrants were resentful of the fact that they were unable to join the Melbourne Club. If they were to perpetuate social tradition of a more formal kind, the solution appeared to be the foundation of a similar club of their own. In May 1856, Smith was associated with Edward Wilson, then proprietor of the *Argus*, in founding the Victorian Club. Its objectives were clearly stated in the propectus:

> The promoters of this club believe that an institution facilitating friendly intercourse among the members of Victorian society is likely to be conducive to public benefit, and that a very large number of gentlemen have long felt the want in Melbourne of a place of resort which should offer the various advantages presented by the leading clubs in the British metropolis.
>
> The peculiar circumstances under which this colony has become peopled seem to add to the usual necessities for such an institution, inasmuch as the great bulk of our community consists of men who have arrived as strangers to one another. The heterogenous manner of our collection appears to point strongly to the propriety of the establishment of some place of rendezvous in which new and old colonists may have an opportunity, hitherto unsupplied, for becoming acquainted with one another.
>
> It is proposed, therefore, to found a Club upon a basis of respectability, combining the objects above alluded to with that of supplying to its members all the conveniences of hotels of the very best class, and at a more moderate rate of charge than that usual at such places.[7]

Smith was named as Honorary Secretary, *pro tem*. The provisional committee consisted of men who were achieving prominence in their chosen field, including among others the government statistician W. H. Archer, Professor W. E. Hearn, George Higinbotham, the artist Ludwig Becker and W. F. (later Sir William) Stawell, the Attorney General. With the exception of Stawell, who belonged to both clubs, these men were ineligible, unwilling, or unable through lack of vacancy, to join the Melbourne Club. The list of members published with the *Rules* in 1857 totals 288 members, 181 of whom were original. They paid an entrance fee of fifteen guineas and an annual subscription of five, which was considerably less than that of the Melbourne Club subscription of twelve guineas. However, membership of a rival club did not necessarily mean social satisfaction and the Victorian Club appears to have declined during the 1860s. The last newspaper report of its activities is an account of the opening of a new club-house in the *Argus* of 7 October 1859.

Smith's involvement in the formation of the Victorian Society of Fine Arts was the result of his appreciation of the arts and their value as a moral and ethical force, as well as his interest as a professional critic in the development of a society of the kind. The Victorian Society of Fine Arts was an ongoing association that provided encouragement for colonial artists as well as the stimulus for critical appreciation of their work. The earlier Victorian Fine Arts Society, which had held an exhibition in August 1853, had lapsed as an organisation. Public interest was re-stimulated by Frank Newton, editor and publisher of the *Australian Builder*, who arranged an exhibition in December 1856, preceded by regular publicity in his journal. A group of exhibiting artists and interested friends had met at the premises of printer William Baker on 20 October to discuss arrangements for the exhibition and form an association. At the public meeting that followed on 29 October, John Pascoe Fawkner proposed the formation of the Victorian Society of Fine Arts. Smith seconded the resolution, 'feeling certain', according to the *Argus* report, that 'no community could with impunity neglect the culture of the fine arts' because of the close relationship between taste and morals.[8] When the first meeting of the society was held on 17 November, Smith was named a member of the committee, with artists Nicholas Chevalier, Eugene von Guerard, architect J. G. Knight and sculptor Charles Summers included among others. Smith was also selected as one of the jury of reward for the exhibition, which opened on 5 December with 'every artist of note in the colony' being represented.[9]

The main objective of the society was 'to advance the cause of the Fine Arts in Australia' by means of lectures, *conversaziones* and the foundation of schools of design. It proposed to hold an annual exhibition, to organise an art union and to form a permanent collection of art works and a library.[10] In later years, Smith was proud to have been the prime mover in the foundation of a National Gallery, as suggested in his inaugural address at the *conversazione* held on 15 December 1856. He pursued this suggestion in a leading article that appeared in the *Argus* on 5 December 1857, during the first exhibition by members, at which he, Professor William Wilson and artists Ludwig Becker and William Strutt formed the hanging committee. Further exhibitons were held in 1860 and succeeding years, but the Victorian Fine Arts Gallery was soon shown to be inadequate for the purpose. The need for a National Gallery was by now widely acknowledged in cultural and government circles and, in October 1863, a Commission of the Fine Arts was appointed.[11] Smith was a member, with others that included barrister Archibald Michie, Professor Wilson, Charles Summers and the Chief Librarian of the Melbourne Public Library, August Tulk. The Commissioners were responsible for choosing paintings and sculptures for the new Picture Gallery, housed in the north wing of the Public Library, which opened on 24 December 1864 with an exhibition of British, European and Australian works of art.[12]

The Victorian Society of Fine Arts achieved a further objective in opening a school of design in June 1857, although it does not appear to have continued for long. The art union proposal was also put into operation. Under this scheme, used a means of promoting the work of local artists, numbered tickets were sold to group of art lovers on a lottery basis, with the winner receiving a specified work of art. Smith is listed as a council member in the report of the Art Union meeting held on 18 February 1863. The following year, with only a small number left in the union, the council met to discuss winding up, but postponed its decision. Cyrus Mason, the secretary of the Victorian Arts Union, organised other unions to raise funds for impoverished artists between 1872 and 1875.[13] By this time, the Victorian Society of Fine Arts was in decline. A new society, the Victorian Academy of Art was founded on 17 January 1870.[14] The Academy gained in strength and became the major association connected with the fine arts until, in 1886, a group of professional artists left it to form the Australian Artists' Association.[15] In 1888, the Academy and the Artists' Association reunited in the Victorian Artists' Society, an organisation that is still active.[16]

During the summer of 1856–57, Smith was one of the organisers of a series of outdoor entertainments. These were the fêtes champêtres modelled along the lines of French and other traditional country festivals. The first of the fêtes was held at Cremorne Gardens in Richmond on 1 November 1856, as a private function to which guests were invited by the proprietor George Coppin in celebration of the opening of his amusement park.[17] During the evening, some of those present discussed the arrangement of similar entertainments on a regular basis and, as a result, a committee was set up to organise 'six al fresco entertainments of an elegant and perfectly unexceptionable character'. Smith was elected Honorary Secretary, *pro tem*. Edward Wilson and the United States consul J. M. Tarleton are notable among other members of the committee. When the first fête of the series was held on 21 November to mark the opening of the first Victorian Parliament, attendance was less than anticipated because of unfavourable weather. The next fête was held on a night of full moon, when a sensational entertainment was provided in the form of a tight-rope act in which French acrobats Mademoiselle Delacasse and Monsieur Lalanne

Institutions

carried an infant across two ropes without a balancing pole, a performance that gained useful publicity through apprehension of criminal charges in case of accident.[18] However, the fêtes continued until the end of the proposed series in 1857, vice-regal patronage at the March fête having restored the original concept of a respectable evening's entertainment.

Smith appears to have enjoyed the stimulus of congenial company of many kinds, whether at private gatherings, social clubs, cultural societies or other focuses for meeting. The Press Cricket Club was one of the more leisurely associations in which he found relaxation.[19] This club was organised for the purpose of arranging friendly matches and social occasions for members of the various sections of the Melbourne press, most of whom knew each other through professional connections. At the inaugural meeting of the club on 14 August 1859, Smith was elected President, with W.M. Akhurst as his Vice President. Accustomed as a boy to watching cricket matches on the village green that bordered the churchyard near his home, Smith retained a keen interest in the game, even when played on a ground cleared out of a colonial paddock. He was re-elected President at the first annual meeting on 16 September 1860, presiding at the dinner that followed the annual match between the married and single members of the club on 6 October. He was again elected President at the annual meeting on 13 September 1862. But, by then, the club appears to have been in decline. There are no further reports of its meetings, its matches or its social activities.

Smith was an active member of the Royal Society, formed as the Philosophical Institute in 1855 through the amalgamation of the Victorian Institute for the Advancement of Science and the Philosophical Society of Victoria, both of which were founded in 1854. The title of the Institute was changed to that of Royal Society on 8 November 1859. Its objectives were 'the advancement of science, literature and art, with especial reference to the development of the resources of the country'.[20] Smith was an unsuccessful candidate for election to a vacancy on the council in April 1860.[21] He was, however, invited to become a member of the Exploration Committee responsible for the Burke and Wills expedition into the interior, so becoming involved in some of the vital decisions surrounding the expedition and its tragic conclusion.[22] The choice of an expedition leader was a major task for the committee. Fourteen candidates responded to public advertisements and, from these, five names were chosen for further consideration. One was Robert O'Hara Burke, a police superintendent from Castlemaine. Another name added to the list at the discretion of the committee was that of the South Australian police commissioner and explorer, Major Peter Egerton Warburton, who, though not an applicant because of his official position, was willing to act if appointed.[23] The final choice lay between Burke and Warburton and, when the ballot was taken at the committee meeting held on 20 June 1860, Burke was successful with ten votes to

Warburton's five,[24] even though he lacked experience in exploration. Smith was later to hear that the choice was the outcome of the prior selection of Burke as leader, a fact that was not made known to the dissenting voters at the time of election.

As Smith reported in his diary on 6 February 1863, railway contractor J. V. A. Bruce had told him the 'secret history' of Burke's appointment. Bruce had met Burke at Castlemaine while supervising the progress of the Melbourne to Bendigo railway. Impressed with the police superintendent, he advised him to apply for the leadership of the expedition and, on Burke's acquiescence, took him to Melbourne for a private meeting with some members of the Exploration Committee who had promised to support the application. Smith made the following comment on Bruce's information:

> His [Burke's] appointment, therefore, was a "foregone conclusion," & the advertising for a leader all a sham. I suspected this but never knew it till now. When the candidates were narrowed down to two— Major Warburton & Mr. Burke, the minority of the Committee who voted for the former, consisted of the Governor, Dr Mueller, Captain Cadell & myself.

The minutes of the committee meeting on 20 June 1860 are confused to the extent that the list of the seventeen present does not include all the names of those reported as taking an active part in the discussion.[25] Clement Hodgkinson and John Watson made no formal contribution to the meeting. Doctor (later Baron Sir Ferdinand) von Mueller is neither listed nor reported as being active, but Smith has named him as a dissenting member. According to the committee's records, he assisted Doctors Wilkie and Macadam in drawing up the progress report announcing the choice of a leader 'after much anxious enquiry and careful deliberation'.[26] The fifth dissenting member (not named by Smith) may be assumed to be Doctor Richard Eades, who had proposed that Warburton be requested to act as leader at the committee meeting held on 21 May 1860. Allowing for the five who voted against Burke, thirteen other names are mentioned in the minutes. Ten of these voted for Burke, leaving, as it appears, three abstainers. As well as Hodgkinson and Watson, the names are those of the Chairman, Sir William Stawell, Professors Georg Neumayer and Frederick (later Sir Frederick) McCoy, Doctors William Mackenna, David Wilkie, Solomon Iffla, Thomas Embling, John Macadam and William Gillbee, the Reverend J. J. Bleasdale and Sizar Elliott. J. V. A. Bruce was not a member of the Exploration Committee, but the firm of Cornish and Bruce had given £100 to the exploration fund, providing him with some preliminary influence.

With hindsight, the appointment of Burke as leader could well be regarded as an unwise decision. Bruce's information, revealed after the bodies of the explorers had been brought back to Melbourne for a public funeral, allowed Smith the self-justification of confirming his own good judgment as one of the dissenting voters. However, there appear to have been other factors at work as well as the effect of the prior influence that Bruce claimed to have exerted. Even though Smith's name appears in the minutes as the mover or seconder of some of the motions passed during the discussion of the appointment of a leader for the expedition, the Exploration Committee was not one in which he played as important a part as he might have wished. The institutions that had combined to form the Royal Society had begun meeting before his arrival in Melbourne and he was a comparative newcomer besides some of the other members. As is obvious from the number of those on the committee qualified in medicine and science, he was outclassed there as well. This does not necessarily mean that the ballot was decided on establishment and professional grounds: the dissenters included the Governor, Sir Henry Barkly, who was a founder and the current President of the Royal Society; von Mueller, who was the director of the Botanic Gardens, and Cadell, an experienced navigator. But, at the same time, there was an undeniably large majority in favour of Burke, suggesting that, whatever the degree of prior knowledge of his capabilities, there was a combined weight of influential opinion behind the decision.

Smith belonged to another colonial institution with a scientific basis and, in this instance, he was one of the foundation members. The Acclimatisation Society was established at a public meeting held on 25 February 1861, with Edward Wilson acting as the first President. Wilson, who had collected some animals for the purpose in Ceylon while returning to Victoria after a recent trip to England, was enthusiastic for community support for the practice of acclimatisation. As agreed at the inaugural meeting, the main objectives of the society should be

> the introduction, acclimatisation, and domestication of all innoxious animals, birds, fishes, insects, and vegetables, whether useful or ornamental;—the perfection, propagation, and hybridisation of races newly introduced or already domesticated;—the spread of indigenous animals, &c., from parts of the colonies where they are already known, to other localities where they are not known.[27]

Smith provided publicity through the *Argus* and other journals with which he was associated, enlarging upon these objectives and encouraging widespread support. Many of those immigrants who found much of the surrounding countryside featureless and unattractive joined him in welcoming the prospect of the transplantation of English and European trees and shrubs and the importation of live animal, bird and insect species.

Other members at this time included Professor McCoy, Dr Thomas Embling, W. H. Archer and Archibald Michie. The society held regular meetings at which business matters were discussed and papers given by members. Smith gave a paper on the topic, 'England's Debt to Acclimatisers' on 19 July 1864.[28] Otherwise he seems to have had little real involvement with the society. He attended only a quarter of the meetings during his first year on the committee and, in February 1865, he resigned. It is not known whether his declining interest was due to the pressure of other work, or, perhaps, to his growing awareness that an amateur interest in natural science was an inadequate qualification for active membership against the professional expertise that was becoming more frequently available in the colony. He may also have come to realise that the Australian landscape would retain its individuality, whatever exotic elements were added to it. In any case, it was eventually to become obvious to the members of the society that acclimatisation, while desirable in some respects, could be successful only at the expense of native flora and fauna, some of which might be entirely eliminated if importations continued on the present scale. Zoological activities began to take precedence and the society changed its name to the Zoological and Acclimatisation Society in 1872, becoming the Royal Zoological Society in 1910.

There were, of course, areas of expertise where Smith could be more certain of his ability. On 17 April 1863, he recorded in his diary that he had been invited to become President of the newly-founded Melbourne Elocution Society. An elocutionary and dramatic entertainment at which he presided was held at the Mechanics' Institute on 20 July.[29] His inaugural address at the meeting on 23 November was on the topic 'Some Thoughts on the Tragedy of King Lear'.[30] There do not appear to have been intervening records of the society's existence, but it, or another of the same name, was still in existence in September 1884, when Richard Birnie is reported to have given an address on Charles Dickens.[31] The continuity of Smith's involvement is unknown.

Two clubs combining social and cultural objectives were founded in Melbourne in 1868. The first was the Athenaeum Club, formed for the purpose of

> providing a suitable place of resort for gentlemen belonging to the various professions, the civil service, and those connected with trade and commerce, who are recognised as having literary or artistic tastes, or who may be otherwise considered eligible as members of such an association.[32]

Smith was one of the founders, with the special aim of the promotion of 'social and kindly intercourse between persons of kindred tastes and dispositions' and the establishment of 'a common ground on which gentlemen of intelligence and character [might] meet together irrespective of class distinction or personal wealth'.[33] This club, though founded with similarly high objectives, was a less ambitious venture than the now-defunct Victorian Club, setting its entrance fee at two guineas and its annual subscription at three. It was also designed as an alternative to, rather than a substitute for, the Melbourne Club, which remained exclusive. Those who might wish to join the Athenaeum Club belonged to a different category of gentlemen, who, like Smith, were becoming increasingly respectable through the diligent practice of trades and professions which, in themselves, were less important as social indicators than in the early years of settlement. The further qualification of 'literary and artistic tastes' is also an indication that the objectives of the club were intended to be distinct from those of the Melbourne Club, even though each club had some members in common.

The Athenaeum was formed as a proprietary club, with architect J. G. Knight as the first owner/manager. It opened with 215 members, increasing to 326 by November 1868. Included among them were Butler Cole Aspinall, J. E. Neild, Marcus Clarke and H. G. Turner. The office of President was not established until 1884, when it was filled by Sir William Clarke. Early programmes catered for a wide range of cultural interests, with music on Wednesday evenings, literature on Thursdays and science on Fridays. Smith's part in these activities and the length of his membership are unknown. However, the club continued to attract new members, allowing it to maintain its numbers throughout the nineteenth century and on into the twentieth. After going through several changes in proprietary, the committee in office in 1918 arranged for the purchase of the lease of club premises, together with furniture and goodwill.[34] The club is still in existence; it now operates from its own premises in Collins Street.

The Athenaeum Club shared some of its early members with the Yorick Club, also founded in 1868, which reputedly took its name through allusion to a skull that rested on the mantelpiece of its premises in a room at the *Punch* office.[35] This club, formed by a group of journalists that included F. W. Haddon, the editor of the *Argus*, and Marcus Clarke, then a member of Haddon's staff, soon became established as a popular meeting place. Many of its members were connected with the press in some way; others followed different occupations or professions, but all of them maintained the interest in literature that had stimulated their association. In time, however, the club was to lose its appeal for some of its members, including Marcus Clarke and Garnet Walch, who, with Richard Birnie and others of similar inclination, broke away to form a new and less formal circle that they called the Cave of Adullam. The Yorick Club continued, strengthened by the addition of new members, such as Henry Gyles Turner, who were more likely to appreciate its comparatively conservative basis.[36] Although there is no record of Smith's involvement in Yorick Club affairs, apart from his listing as an original member, it may reasonably be assumed that he remained in the club for at least the first years of its existence.

Always interested in education for its own sake as well as its capacity for moral improvement, Smith was a member of the provisional committee formed in November 1869 with a view to the establishment of the Victorian Proprietary College Company. The prospectus was published as an advertisement in *Touchstone*, which he was then editing. George Rolfe, a member of the Legislative Assembly, is named as President, with Smith as Treasurer. Other members of the committee included the government astronomer R. L. Ellery, surgeon Solomon Iffla, and industrial chemist J. Cosmo Newbery. The objectives were, as stated:

> This company has been formed for the purpose of offering the advantages of a first-class education, on a scale of charges which it is hoped will bring these advantages within the means of a large section of our community to whom they are at present unattainable. The institution will be entirely unsectarian in its character, and the moral and physical will be so combined with the educational training of the public, as to offer to parents not only instruction of high class for their children but also the discipline of a select home.
> ... The course of study will be more varied than that of the existing Victorian educational establishments, and it is intended to adapt it as far as practicable in every instance to specially qualify the pupils for the occupations they are intended to pursue in after life.[37]

Since the college would be in competition with established educational institutions, there were special provisions designed to attract both parents and investors with independent views on proper methods of education. One was its non-sectarian basis, a condition perhaps imposed upon the committee by Smith. Although he professed to maintain belief in a divine Creator,[38] he was opposed to the practice of formalised religion, preferring the application of moral training as a self-evident value. The vocational nature of the college was another provision. At the conclusion of their education, the students would be capable of taking up worthwhile occupations that should ensure their livelihood. The training that they had received would also be of wider benefit because of its emphasis on personal responsibility.

The identity of the prime mover in the project is unknown. However, Smith's influence in deciding its objectives may be assumed because of the reliance on Ruskinite principles that is evident in the prospectus. The project must have seemed a viable one to the committee: many of the names listed are those of men who, while not in themselves educationalists, were leaders in their particular fields and, as such, likely to have the ability to establish and control a college that would reflect their own attainments. They certainly expected to make money out of the project. The Victorian Proprietary College was to be a business venture, with an anticipated net profit of over 30 percent, paying a dividend of 10 percent, the remainder being set aside as a reserve fund for future developments. But, although the promoters were convinced that their prospectus offered educational opportunities for students whose parents wished them to pursue occupational courses under strict supervision, there are no further reports of the committee's activities. In the absence of information concerning the establishment of the college, it appears likely that there was an insufficient number of investors prepared to give financial support to the scheme.

Following Smith's conversion to spiritualism in 1870, there was a long period during which his intense activity as an exponent of belief in spiritual communication prevented him from participation in the cultural life of Melbourne. It was not until the end of the following decade, when his initial fervour had subsided into a more temperate acceptance of the existence of the spirit world, that he was able to resume some of his former interests. In 1880, he was appointed a Trustee of the Public Library, Museums and National Gallery of Victoria. He was a regular attendant at committee meetings and a member of several sub-committees. His knowledge of literature and his experience as Parliamentary Librarian also made him a useful adviser on matters of acquisition. When Henry Gyles Turner resigned the office of Treasurer in 1887, Smith accepted the position, which he retained until his retirement in 1909.[39] Turner continued to serve as a Trustee and, in 1892, he and Smith were appointed the Public Library representatives on the Council of the Working Men's College. This Council of sixteen members, under prime founder and benefactor Francis Ormond as President, included two nominated by the President, one by the Governor-in-Council, two by the Council of the University of Melbourne, two by the Trustees of the Public Library and two by the Trades Hall Council. The remaining six members were drawn from two grades of subscribers, according to amount.[40]

The Working Men's College (now known as the Royal Melbourne Institute of Technology) had been founded in 1887 with the objective of improving the education of the working classes. The project was first discussed between the Public Library Trustees and Francis Ormond at a meeting on 12 May 1882, when Ormond offered to provide the sum of £5000 (or more, as required), subject to community support and the observance of certain conditions regarding the type of building and its amenities.[41] Further discussion with members of the Trades Hall assured cooperation with the development of the plan[42] and, at a public meeting in the Town Hall on 26 June 1882,[43] financial support was promised in the form of public subscription.[44] After some delay, during which additional financial responsibility was assumed by Ormond, the College was established in May 1887.[45] In full agreement with the concept of the benefits that might be derived from further education, Smith was active as a Council member: he was a Trustee from 1903–04, Honorary Treasurer in 1903 and 1904, Vice President in 1905 and 1906 and President in 1907.[46] As described by F. A. Campbell, the first Secretary and Director of the College, the Council was 'a singularly business-like body which, without time or inclination for petty disputes, worked for the welfare of the institution with the greatest unanimity and zeal'.[47]

Smith's appreciation of the complementary beauty of nature and art, both for its own sake and as a force for moral improvement, was basic to his involvement in the formation of the Kalizoic Society, named from the Greek *kalos*, meaning beauty, and *zoe*, life. The initial proposal came from Louis Henry, a Melbourne surgeon, who wrote to the editor of the *Argus* on 2 January 1884, suggesting that a society such as the Kalizoic could encourage and cultivate beauty in Melbourne by planting trees and flowers along the roadsides and in reserved land. Doctor Henry's letter was followed by another from Doctor J. E. Neild, with the further suggestion of beautifying suburban back gardens and educating school children in the need for conservation of trees and plants.[48] The writer of an *Argus* leader, who, judging from the tone and style, appears unlikely to have been Smith, was appreciative of the proposal, though sceptical of the prospects for success of an 'akalizoic brotherhood'.[49] However, further encouraging letters appeared on succeeding days and arrangements went ahead for the foundation of the society. As established, it had similar objectives to the Kyrle Society of England, founded in 1874 with the aim of brightening the condition and improving the taste of the working-class.[50] The Melbourne society took as its main objective 'the encouragement and cultivation of the beautiful', by means of endeavouring 'to get trees and flowers planted in promenades and places of public resort, and to promote the laying out of reserves and the diffusion of correct principles of decoration in all its branches'. It was also concerned with the need for trying 'to bring about the purification of the back slums and the removal of all dwellings unfit for habitation'.[51]

Smith accepted the office of President and gave the address at the inaugural meeting on 16 March 1884. After acknowledging the benevolence of the founders, he expressed a universal sense of beauty:

> "Man doth not live by bread alone," was the impressive declaration of "the best of men that e'er wore earth about him;" and the truth of these memorable words is indisputable; for when we have made provision for the satisfaction of our physical wants, we must all feel that there is a considerable number of faculties and desires, mental and spirtual, craving to be supplied with their appropriate and adequate aliment. A beneficent Creator has bestowed upon all men, no matter how low down they may be in the scale of humanity, a sense of the beautiful and a capacity for its enjoyment, and at the same time has surrounded us with endless and ever varying means for its gratification.[52]

The address continued with the presentation of a moral argument for the love of beauty, and the suggestion that the best way for the society to function in 'a crusade against ugliness', was through individual subscriptions and personal efforts, with the added support 'of property owners, of municipal bodies, and of artists and architects'.

Institutions

Despite the idealistic attitude of the President and executive, the Kalizoic Society does not appear to have received sufficient public support for sustained existence. As a substitute for the beautification of streets and gardens, its activities seem to have been confined to the presentation of pictures to deserving institutions, such as the Melbourne Hospital and the Benevolent Asylum.[53] At the executive meeting on 22 March 1885, with Smith in the chair, a sub-committee was appointed to discuss the suggestion that the Kalizoic Society should amalgamate with the Australian Health Society, an organisation founded in 1875 to improve the sanitation of the city and the general health of its inhabitants.[54] Smith was one of the Health Society's panel of lecturers, speaking, for instance, on the topics 'Light and Health' on 19 June 1877[55] and 'Nature's Scavengers' on 28 August 1878.[56] In the absence of further reports of separate activities, it seems likely that the Kalizoic Society was absorbed into the Australian Health Society, which was still in operation in 1900,[57] with Louis Henry as President.[58]

Smith was an active member of the Melbourne Shakespeare Society,[59] originally founded by Professor E. E. Morris as a students' reading and discussion group at the University of Melbourne. Stimulated by intimations of wider public interest, Morris accepted the invitation of F. W. Haddon to publicise his views on the formation and operation of a Shakespeare Society in Melbourne through the columns of the *Argus*. In an introductory article that appeared on 24 May 1884, Morris explained that the society had been established primarily for the reading of plays aloud, thus not only assisting the students' understanding of their meaning, but also improving the quality of elocution, a matter of special importance in the colonies, where opportunities for hearing good Shakespearean actors were fewer than had been the case in the 1850s and 1860s.[60] A secondary though also important aim was the presentation of papers on topics concerning the plays and poetry. Morris went on to discuss the formation of a society that would be open to the general public:

> Let it be understood that the desire to form a Shakspeare Society in other than University circles means something very much more than merely gathering parties of an evening to read the plays. In many of the suburbs around Melbourne such gatherings are by no means uncommon now, and can be got together either with a strict or a loose formation by those who wish for them. But this proposal means critical study, the production and publication of essays on Shaksperian subjects, critical and aesthetical, together with meetings for discussion of these papers. For such a society to be worthy of the name it should not be on a small scale, and its members should be prepared to work. In such a case as this two difficulties always present themselves—first, we must face the question whether there is something more than a vague desire, a real readiness for work; secondly, granted that we ought to have a society, who will take the needed steps to initiate one?[61]

Morris answered his own question by offering to organise the first meeting, provided a dozen gentlemen sent him their names within one week of the publication of his article. There was no lack of sufficient response. Morris was himself a member of the New Shakespeare Society and the gentlemen to whom he appealed were sympathetic to the objectives of that and other English Shakespeare Societies and anxious to emulate their activities.

Smith became a foundation member of the society, which was formally constituted at a meeting held in the Town Hall on 4 June 1884. Morris was elected President, F. W. Scrivenor Honorary Secretary and Smith a member of the committee. Because it was founded on a specifically literary basis, the Melbourne Shakespeare Society attracted members from diverse occupational backgrounds, who were linked by a common purpose. Some were university men; others, like Smith, were not. But familiarity with Shakespeare's work could equally well be acquired by an enthusiastic amateur and the opportunity for study and informed discussion was especially welcome to those who belonged to the latter group. The society met monthly, expanding its activities into occasional entertainments for charitable causes and holding annual prize examinations in Shakespearean recitals. Doctor J. P. Wilson replaced Scrivenor as Honorary Secretary in 1885. As he recalled, the prize examinations began with a gift of £25 from J. C. Williamson in 1887.[62] However, the first recital, at which Smith and David Blair were the judges, was actually held in conjunction with the Shakespeare Fair at the Town Hall in 1885.[63] Members' papers were published in the *Victorian Review* from 1884 to 1886 under the general title 'Transactions of the Shakespeare Society'. In a total of 30 papers given during this period, there are three by Smith, who continued writing for the society until advanced old age. Henry Gyles Turner, also an active member, noted that Smith 'was so absolutely fond of writing and so prodigal of his capacity, that, up to his 90th year he was always ready to offer a paper for the Shakespeare Society, when outside contributions fell short'.[64] A further indication of Smith's activity is the fact that he was Vice-President of the society in 1910, the year of his death.

Although there are no records extant, Smith was probably a member of the French Club, founded in Melbourne in 1884 as a social and patriotic club for French colonists and their friends.[65] He was certainly a founding member and first President of the French Literary Club, a separate organisation founded two years later with the main objective of imparting 'a thorough knowledge of the French language in a novel, amusing, and interesting manner'.[66] There were 80 foundation members, twenty of whom were women. Garnet Walch was Honorary Secretary, while Monsieur Gustave Le Roy, a language teacher who had devised his own methods of instruction,[67] was responsible for conducting the *soirées littéraires* that were a dominant feature of club activities. Walch enlarged on the club's objectives in his address at the inaugural meeting:

Institutions

> Let those of us who already know something of French, and those of us who wish to open up an acquaintance with this beautiful language, meet together on a common ground to read and talk French, with here and there a veritable Frenchman in our midst to give an artistic "high light" to the picture, and with, above all, a mutual understanding to help each other and the good cause we have at heart.[68]

Members of the club were to meet weekly at the Athenaeum (the former Mechanics' Institute) for reading and conversation, enabling them, as promised in the preliminary notice published in the *Argus*, 'to acquire fluency, confidence and purity of pronunciation, while at the same time rendering themselves familiar with the current literature of both France and England.'[69] The cost was one guinea per quarter, plus about five shillings for library material. Free lessons in grammar were available for those who required them.

In his inaugural address as President, Smith discussed some of the advantages that members of the French Literary Club might derive from a knowledge of the French language. For instance, its value for social and cultural purposes:

> To speak it fluently is to be qualified to feel yourself at home—other things being equal—in the most elegant *salons* of St Petersburg, Vienna, Rome, and Madrid, as well as those of Paris and Brussels. It is to have at your command the resources of a form of speech that seems to have been specially designed for conversation; one that has grown out of the national characteristics, the individual wants, and social needs of a race of people among whom courtesy was cultivated as one of the fine arts, and with whom the constant interchange of ideas and opinions seemed to be a necessity of daily life—at any rate among the educated classes.[70]

He continued with some remarks on the logical nature of the language, stressing the growing importance of its use for business purposes and, in conclusion, commending the knowledge of foreign languages—whether German, Italian, Spanish or French—as an antidote to ignorance and, in consequence, racial prejudice.

Smith was well qualified to share in the club's activities. He reviewed French and other foreign language books in his capacity as a literary critic and he translated articles for publication in newspapers and periodicals. As Oscar Comettant remarked, '[Smith] spoke [the] language fluently enough to grasp the finer points of [the] most vivid, subtle and stylistically refined writers'.[71] His wife Eliza, who was also a fluent French speaker, seems likely to have been one of the members of the club, which, by extending its membership to both sexes, gave her an opportunity for mutual public involvement. While the club appears to have become established, there are no records of its progress and it is not known for how long it remained in existence.

Two more foreign language societies were formed in Melbourne in the 1890s and Smith, such was his interest, became involved with both of them. The Alliance Francaise, modelled on the parent association founded in Paris in 1883, superseded the functions of the French Club and the French Literary Club.[72] The local branch was established by two sisters, Madame Mouchette and Mademoiselle Lyon, who were stimulated to emigrate, together with Madame Mouchette's husband, on hearing a lecture about Australia in Paris.[73] Madame Mouchette worked as a drawing teacher in a studio in Collins Street, while Mademoiselle Lyon taught the French language.[74] The first public matinee of the Alliance, which consisted of readings of short stories by Guy de Maupassant, accompanied by musical items, was held on 9 September 1893. Regular meetings continued with entertainment provided by members. Smith served on the committee, giving readings and taking part in the presentation of dramatic scenes from the work of French novelists and playwrights. Eliza Smith was an active member, being Vice President for 25 years. The numbers in attendance at meetings grew steadily, and the library established for the use of members was improved by donations, including a valuable present of books from Lady Clarke, who, with her husband, Sir William, was also a member. Mademoiselle Irma Dreyfus was another benefactor, giving the proceeds of £70 raised by her 1897 course of lectures on French literature to the association. These lectures, which were a regular feature in Melbourne from 1895 to 1899, were not restricted to French speakers; Smith translated a selection from the series for publication.[75]

In June 1896, the Dante Society for the study of Italian language, literature, music and the fine arts, was founded in Melbourne by Cavalier Count Corte, the Italian Consul General.[76] There were almost 100 foundation members,[77] including James Smith and, most probably, his wife Eliza.[78] Smith had acquired a particular liking for the Italian people and their culture as a result of his tour of northern Italy in 1853. Since then, he had travelled through that country more extensively and become fluent in the Italian language. He was elected President of the Dante Society, a position that he retained for eight successive years of active involvement.[79] For his services to Italian literature, he was honoured by the Italian government with the decoration of 'Cavaliere dell'Ordine della Corona d'Italia' in 1901.[80] Similarly, for his services to French language and literature, he was honoured on 1 March 1902 by the Ministry of Public Instruction and Fine Arts of the French Republic, in being named an 'Officier d'Academie'.[81] The Alliance Francaise and the Dante Society (now known as the Dante Alighieri Society) are still active in Melbourne.

The motivation behind Smith's pursuit of involvement in colonial institutions depended upon the objectives of the clubs and societies that he joined and the committees on which he served. Some of them had a particular appeal to personal and professional interests. Membership of others offered a diversity of cultural action, while still others promised a certain social status. One of the most important factors of his enthusiasm for the foundation of many of these institutions was his desire to replicate in the colony the English and European clubs and societies that he might have aspired to join if he had remained at home. To some extent, these new institutions were branches of the parent organisations; even though they were usually autonomous, they were linked through common aims and objectives that promoted a sense of continuity. Another factor was his awareness of privilege as an educated member of colonial society and the responsibility he believed such privilege carried for the elevation of less well-informed people through further education and exposure to the arts. Membership of societies whose objectives included an appreciation of the benefits to be derived from the extension of knowledge allowed him the satisfaction of instigating Ruskinite ideology in practice. But his purpose in acting as a leading figure in forming institutions or taking executive office was more than a matter of congeniality or a desire for public service. His involvement in so many organisations over long periods of time brought him into a network consisting of a recurring series of important colonial figures. This enabled him to extend the limits of his acquaintance and achieve recognition as a cultural activist.

5
PUBLIC HEROES

The formal observance of major events in the lives of prominent people was an important aspect of Victorian culture. Royal births and marriages gave cause for loyal celebrations, both at home and in the colonies, while other notable events, such as a special anniversary or a victory in the field, were frequently marked by lasting memorials. Whatever the occasion, the organisation of festivities, testimonials and memorials provided opportunities for remembrance in which friends and admirers might share. Death, with its accompanying solemnities, was the ultimate occasion for remembrance. An appropriate memorial might take the form of an elegy, such as the 'In Memoriam' that Alfred Tennyson wrote for his friend Arthur Hallam. It could also be a stained glass window, an endowment, a statue, or, when conceived on a grand scale, the Albert Memorial that Queen Victoria had erected in Hyde Park after the death of the Prince Consort. In the Australian colonies, newspaper reports of appeals for contributions to testimonials and memorials linked with events in Britain and Europe were often followed with particular interest because of their association with famous people, or with places that had been familiar prior to emigration. At times, the colonists responded with direct financial support. On other occasions, they arranged specifically colonial tributes or organised related celebrations of their own. Through their participation in movements of this kind, the immigrants were able to lessen the isolation that prevented closer involvement. Their activities as fund raisers also had the effect of widening circles of friendship and acquaintance through membership of committees similar to those formed by the clubs and societies.

The Garibaldi Testimonial Fund was the first of the memorial movements in which Smith took an active part. Many Melburnians, especially those of Italian descent, were stirred by the exploits of Giuseppe Garibaldi as the leader of the struggle for Italian independence. Members of the French community were equally appreciative of the general's heroism in attempting to overcome the Austrian oppressors. On 8 August 1859, a group of Italians and Frenchmen met at the Café des Étrangers in Spring Street to celebrate the victory of the allied armies in Italy and to drink a toast to Garibaldi.[1] Prominent among the Italians that evening was Alexander Martelli, an ex-officer of the Sardinian army and a former member of the Sardinian parliament, living in exile because of his revolutionary activities. Martelli and his compatriot B. Dardanelli were fervent admirers of Garibaldi and active members of a committee set up for the relief of families of Italian patriots.

Garibaldi was also extremely popular in England. The movement towards a united, independent Italian state had the support of Lord Palmerston and the British government, while the imagination of the people was stirred by the individualistic approach adopted by Garibaldi in his determination to succeed. When the news reached Melbourne that the Italian hero had been proclaimed dictator of Sicily and that he had defeated the Neapolitan troops at Catalafimi and Milazzo in May 1860, colonial admiration became widespread. With Dardanelli in the chair, a group of Victorian supporters met on 20 August to decide upon an appropriate testimonial.[2] Martelli proposed that subscriptions be collected for the presentation of a ceremonial sword and Smith, who was a friend of Martelli's, moved a resolution of sympathy with 'the heroic exertions now being made by General Garibaldi, for the liberation of Italy from the yoke of its brutal oppressors'. At the public meeting that followed on 28 August, it was decided to call for one shilling subscriptions for the purchase of the sword and the relief of widows and orphans.[3] The Melbourne Club was one of the institutions canvassed at this time, but, although individual members may have been sympathetic to the cause, the club was unable to give official support because demonstrations of a political tendency were not recognised under its rules.[4]

Public interest in keeping up subscriptions was stimulated by the presentation of the play *Garibaldi*, the first performance of which was announced in the *Argus* on 8 September:

> An original three-act drama, of which Garibaldi is the hero and Sicily the scene, is to be produced this evening at the Prince of Wales; and from the interest manifested by all classes in the achievements of this heroic soldier, no doubt the production referred to will meet with an encouraging reception, if its dramatic merits are such as to satisfy the public expectation. We believe it is from the pen of a local author, and that the scenery has been painted expressly for the occasion, so as to give spectators a vivid idea of the localities which the fame of Garibaldi's exploits has rendered once more famous.

The text of the play has been lost, but, according to an *Argus* review, it combined the story of two Australian gold diggers from Kingower with the history of the Italian hero in a drama that was a 'decided success'.[5] At the end of the week's run, public curiosity as to the identity of the playwright was satisfied by the announcement that *Garibaldi* had been 'the major effort' of James Smith.[6]

Despite the hopes of the organisers that all classes of Melbourne society had been excited by the accounts of Garibaldi's activities, a meeting of Italian working men called at the Trades Hall on 25 September was poorly attended. However, substantial offers of support had been received from other sections of the community that were obviously better able to contribute. By that time, the committee had about £300 in hand and the members were optimistic that they could raise £500.[7] At the meeting held on 8 October, Smith was appointed treasurer of the fund and he and Martelli were commissioned to form a sub-committee to confer with local artists on the design of the sword to be presented to Garibaldi.[8] Five designs were submitted and that by Nicholas Chevalier was chosen. As described in the *Argus* of 30 October:

> The hilt, which will be composed of Victorian gold, represents enfranchised Italy, her brows encircled by a mural crown, her right arm raising aloft the short Roman sword wreathed with laurel, and her left resting on the guard, in which a bruised serpent and a broken chain are skilfully combined, to typify the overthrow of despotism. At the junction of the guard with the hilt, the lily of Florence, a couple of shields inscribed 'Garibaldi' and 'Victoria' and emblems of Justice, Truth and Patriotism, are introduced; and on the blade will be engraved in English and Italian, a concisely worded and appropriate inscription. When completed, the sword will cost about 200 guineas.

The sword took six months to complete, at a cost of £225. Part of Martelli's sword was incorporated in the design. The hilt, made of gold, valued at £123 and decorated with a diamond presented by an anonymous donor, bore the inscription 'Victoria to Garibaldi', and the blade, 'Giuseppe Garibaldi 1861'.[9] Clothed in a scabbard of green velvet ornamented with gold, the sword was placed on exhibition with the joint objects of demonstrating the standard of colonial art and raising additional funds.[10] Printing, advertising, postage and other charges had brought the cost of the memorial up to £343/9/6,[11] much of which had already been raised by subscription. Donations received during the following weeks made the total subscribed £358/10/1.[12]

It now remained the task of the committee to despatch the sword to Garibaldi. They sent it to the British Embassy in Turin on 25 May 1861, accompanied by a letter written on behalf of the subscribers, signed by Smith, Martelli and Dardanelli. It read, in part:

> Men of all nations, and of all creeds, have spontaneously contributed towards this tribute to the military genius and the sterling worth of the first patriot and the first soldier of his age... Remote as they are from the theatre of those great exploits in which you have played so noble and beneficient a part, the subscribers desire to assure you of their deep and earnest sympathy with your illustrious and unselfish efforts, and of their exultation at the brilliant and glorious results achieved; while it is their fervent hope that the great work in which

you are engaged will be consummated by the addition of Rome and Venice to the Kingdom of Italy.[13]

Receipt was acknowledged by the consul Sir James Hudson on 8 August and the sword forwarded to Garibaldi at his home on the island of Caprera. The memorial was graciously received by the Italian patriot and his letter of thanks was published in translation in the *Argus* on 10 October 1861.

Though pursued with what seems to have been commendable vigour by its promoters, the Garibaldi testimonial was the cause of some dissension in Melbourne. The official Roman Catholic attitude was to condemn Garibaldi because of the danger presented to the Holy City of Rome by his campaign, together with the threat to the authority of the Pope. A letter that the Reverend J. J. Bleasdale had written to the London *Tablet* was reprinted as part of an *Argus* editorial on 27 November 1861. It began:

> Among the Victorian news by this mail likely to make a noise, will be the address to Garibaldi and the presentation sword. I have no doubt that a clever attempt will be made to convey an impression that this colony has taken an interest in the matter. Of course the little committee who have worked up the little affair have a great idea that all Europe is interested in their doings, and deeply concerned about the attachment of a handful of popularity hunters at the antipodes to the person and cause of an Italian rebel, who ought to have been hanged long ago, if every man had his deserts...
>
> This beggarly tribute of what will be trumped up as Victorian admiration, this sword of honour is not paid for. A whole year and more has been spent by a committee in getting together as much money for this sword as I could collect for a pious purpose. At the end of the time they are £34/6/8 in debt. So much for the hero worship at the antipodes! It is hoped that Garibaldi may help them out of this difficulty.

The writer of the editorial, most probably Smith, took exception to the slight on 'the name which all the civilised world has agreed to place among the very highest in the catalogue of heroes'. On the following day, a letter to the editor from James Smith was published in the *Argus*, deploring Bleasdale's 'lack of Christian charity'. Smith described as 'false and calumnious' the charge that Roman Catholics had not supported the appeal, since two of the committed (Martelli and Dardanelli) belonged to that faith. He used figures taken from the balance sheet to prove that the committee was not in debt and concluded that

> the greatness of Garibaldi requires no vindication at the hands of so humble an individual as myself, confident as I am, that his name will be honoured and revered for centuries after the temporal power of the Pope has become a tradition of the past, and when, I am afraid, the mildew of ages will have obliterated all trace of Father Bleasdale's contribution to the scientific literature of Victoria.[14]

Bleasdale was a seminarian with a particular interest in science. He was well respected as a writer and lecturer on the subject and Smith's disparaging remarks are more an indication of the polarisation of opposing views in the context of sectarian mistrust than a justifiable reflection on Bleasdale's ability. It is not known whether there had been any previous differences between the two men. But, whatever the case, each now adopted a derogatory public tone concerning the activities of the other. However, Smith's confidence in the propriety of the undertaking was reinforced with the publication of letters to the editor of the *Argus* from 'Mentor', 'A Catholic', 'Anti-Jesuit' and 'Truth', all of whom supported the committee. Then, on 14 April 1862, it was reported in the *Argus* that Dardanelli had received a letter from Garibaldi, thanking him for 'vindicating the Italian cause from the slanders of Father Bleasdale'. So the matter ended, with religious direction overcome by feelings of popular outrage. Bleasdale was effectively silenced and the honour of the Italian hero reaffirmed, together with the credibility of the organisers of the appeal.

Smith himself was the subject of a testimonial appeal when, in January 1863, it became known that he was about to leave the colony for an extended visit to England. At this time, he had been associated with the Melbourne press for eight years and the proposed testimonial was 'in recognition of his services to the colony as a journalist'.[15] Many of those who had already subscribed when Smith's appointment as Parliamentary Librarian was announced believed that his 'past labours in the field of literature [might] with equal propriety be publicly recognized on his entering the office'.[16] The appeal continued and, on 28 February, Smith was given a complimentary dinner at Menzies Hotel. The Chairman, Doctor Richard Eades, proposed the toast to the guest of honour. According to the *Argus* report of the event:

> Dr Eades expressed the high gratification which he in common with the bulk of his fellow citizens felt that Mr. Smith's departure from the colony had been stayed by the opportune offer of an appointment for which he was so peculiarly well qualified, and which must be so congenial to his habits and feelings; adding that the Government could not have made an appointment more credible to themselves, or more satisfactory to the community, Mr. Smith was emphatically "the right man in the right place."[17]

Smith was then presented with an inscribed silver tea and coffee service. His response was not recorded, but there can be little doubt that he was gratified by this public expression of the value of past work at a time of new employment.

He was much in the public eye during the early part of 1863, when, as a member of the Exploration Committee of the Royal Society, he was involved in the arrangements for the funeral of Robert O'Hara Burke and William Wills, the remains of whose bodies had been brought back from the interior of Australia for ceremonial burial in Melbourne. In his diary entry for the first day of the year. Smith recorded his visit to the Royal Society's Hall for a private viewing of the remains:

> Last night the bones of Burke & Wills were deposited in their metallic coffins. The skull of Wills & the hands & feet of both had disappeared. Burke's skull a very fine one. In taking a cast of it some of the teeth dropped out which I procured. The woollen shirt of Wills still hung in tatters round his ribs. Mrs. Dogherty (Burke's nurse) who had "stretched" his father and his mother, performed the last sad office for her darling, wrapping the cere-cloth round his bones & placing a little pillow beneath his skull. The room (the Royal Society's hall) hung with black & dimly lit, with a catafalque & baldacchino in the centre, had a sombre and solemn effect.

In spite of his eagerness to obtain a personal souvenir once the remains of the explorers were lying in state, Smith had not at first been in favour of disturbing the little that was left of the bodies after native dogs had scavenged around the camp. However, he had failed to attend the committee meeting where the matter was discussed and plans made for a public funeral.[18] Alfred Howitt, sent out in search of the explorers, had found John King the sole survivor at Cooper's Creek, where Burke and Wills lay dead from hunger and exhaustion. Howitt buried the two men, reading appropriate Biblical verses and carving their initials together with his own on nearby trees. There the bodies might have stayed, but for the decision of the Exploration Committee to try to salvage some measure of the enthusiasm which, initially, had accompanied the venture.

It was customary for funerals of distinguished persons to be extremely formal during the Victorian era. Few women attended, apart from heavily veiled members of the immediate family. All those present wore appropriately plain black clothing and, after what was usually a long service of religious consolation interspersed with eulogies, the solemnity of the occasion was further marked by the slow procession of invited mourners that followed the coffin on foot from church to graveyard. In the colonies, where few, if any, family members were likely to be available, friends and acquaintances were asked to be pall-bearers. Among those for whom Smith performed this last act of friendship were W. S. Lyster and W. Jardine Smith. At a public funeral of the kind arranged for Burke and Wills, formalities were magnified to meet the importance of the event. As Smith described it in the diary entry for 21 January:

> All business suspended. The procession, about a mile in length, started from the Hall of the Royal Society, passing through Spring Street, Bourke St & Elizabeth Street to the new Cemetery. The footpaths lined with spectators, who also clustered on the housetops, on the awnings, at the windows, on cars, coaches, carriages & wagons, & wherever a view of the cortege could be obtained. From all the suburbs of Melbourne, and from the country districts people had been pouring in all the morning, & I should compute the num-

ber of persons who witnessed the imposing spectacle at not less than one hundred thousand. I rode in the same mourning coach with Bourke's [sic] foster mother, Mrs. Dogherty, & the survivor of the Expedition, John King.

The procession moved slowly through the city towards the Melbourne Cemetery, where the burial service was read by the Dean of Melbourne and the coffins, inscribed with approximate dates of death, were lowered into the prepared vault. The firing party gave three volleys and, according to an *Argus* report, 'the last chapter of the mournful history of the Victorian Exploring Expedition was closed'.[19]

Since the remains of the explorers were properly interred at last, the *Argus* reporter could write with some assurance that the funeral was indeed the conclusion of the matter. However, the expedition had been plagued both by misfortune and mismanagement and the Exploration Committee was the target of public criticism. A Royal Commission had been held from 18 November 1861 to 31 January 1862. While critical of Burke and William Wright, his third in command, the Commissioners found that the Exploration Committee had 'committed errors of serious nature'.[20] Now, in the evening after the grand funeral that had helped to assuage collective guilt for the tragic outcome of the expedition, a public meeting was held at St George's Hall with the Governor, Sir Henry Barkly, in the chair. At this meeting, the main purpose of which was the extenuation of the Exploration Committee, the Chief Justice, Sir William Stawell, spoke in justification of the committee's actions when faced with unforeseen circumstances. The Governor then presented illuminated addresses written by Smith to three notable Victorians: Ambrose Kyte, who had donated £1000 towards the cost of the expedition; William Norman, commander of HMCS *Victoria*, which had escorted William Landsborough in the brig *Firefly* to search for Burke and Wills; and Alfred Howitt, who had found and returned the bodies of the explorers to Melbourne. Dr John Macadam, the Secretary of the Royal Society, was given the task of further conciliating the audience. As Smith wrote in his diary:

> Dr Macadam made a successful speech vindicatory of the Committee. He was denied a hearing at first; but eventually carried the audience completely with him, & was congratulated by the Governor, the Chief Justice & the Bishop on having rehabilitated the reputation of the body to which he had acted as the Secretary.[21]

The meeting concluded in an atmosphere that appears to have been more favourable to the Exploration Committee than that with which it had begun. While admitting its mistakes, the committee had reaffirmed its intention of acting in the best interests of the community that had entrusted it with control. And, even though the unfortunate outcome of the expedition had not been anticipated, its supporters believed that there was still some glory to be derived by Victoria as the colony that had sponsored the first crossing of the continent from south to north.

On the same evening, Smith's 'Requiem Ode' was performed after the opera at the Theatre Royal. This ode, set to music by Anthony Reiff, musical director and conductor of the Lyster Opera Company, was sung by the whole company in mourning, with the principals—Henry Squires, Lucy Escott, Georgia Hodson and Henry Wharton—as soloists. In an atmosphere of public sorrow tinged by censure, it was important that the ode should praise the explorers' achievements without emphasising their failure to complete the expedition. Smith, obviously confident in the role of public poet, combined what he considered to be the right note of sadness for the deaths of Burke and Wills with the glorification of their exploits. In his opening chorale, he transformed the 'poor relics' into 'sacred dust' and the 'lonely graves' into a 'heroes' tomb'. The narrative, as given in the solo parts, progressed through the various stages of the expedition until, as described in the contralto solo:

> There came a day desired by all,
> Life's brightest hour perchance, for each,
> When Burke and Wills—their goal achieved,
> The Flinders' tidal waters reach;
> Oh! noble exploit, well fulfilled!
> Oh! splendid honor, bravely won!
> Turn, southward, turn, your wayworn feet,
> Heroes, your glorious work is done.

The bass solo, the last of the quartette, described the moment of death, not as it might have happened, but in terms of fantasy:

> The story in its pathos tells
> How fell these lion-hearted men—
> Calm, cheerful, steadfast, kindly, true,
> Surrendering their latest breath,
> With gentle words upon their lips,
> And smiling in the face of death.[22]

The audience applauded, apparently satisfied by hearing what it wished to hear. All was glossed over, and sadness relieved by admiration for heroic action, preparing the way for the final patriotic hymn of praise, and the repetition of the opening chorale. Then followed a *tableau vivant*, consisting of a group of figures arranged in the form of a monument, in the centre of which a single figure held a laurel wreath in each hand.

The events of the day had undoubtedly made it a memorable one, but much of what had been organised was calculated to turn public attention away from the Exploration Committee and its responsibility for the conduct of the expedition. It was not to be long before self-congratulation turned into communal defence. An editorial on the subject was published in the *Argus* the following day. The writer, who, because of his attitude, could not have been Smith, was severely critical of the Exploration Committee for allowing 'the great day of national mourning' to become 'the final triumph of the committee'. Dr Macadam's defence had misfired, after all, and the actions of the organisers of the expedition were again the subject of public controversy. As the writer complained: 'It is true that we have spent £23,000, that the expedition was a failure, and the leaders are dead; but we are assured that the fame of the colony has been very much increased by the proceedings of the Exploration Committee'. The editorial continued with a reminder of the most serious charge brought against the committee, that it had delayed arrangements for William Wright and his relief party to be sent to Cooper's Creek. Because of their negligence on this account, the writer declared the members of the committee to be responsible for the deaths of the explorers, the 'heroes...who were performing their glorious task in all singleness of heart and with a loyal trust in those they had left behind'.[23]

The whole tone of the editorial is one of rhetorical appeal to public outrage. An answer was called for from any member of the committee. Dr Macadam had already defended its actions and there seemed to be no point in the repetition of his speech. Apparently Smith decided that he was the most appropriate person to act as spokesman. He countered the charge in a long letter to the editor of the *Argus*, citing Burke's correspondence on the matter and insisting that the committee had sent the relief party as required, even though it had failed to reach Cooper's Creek. He was speaking as a member of the committee and not as a private citizen, but it is obvious from his conclusion that, despite his disclaimer, he had been hurt personally by the implied reflection upon himself:

> Much as I have been pained by the obloquy unjustly heaped upon the committee, I have never shunned from bearing my full share of it, confident as I am that when the decision of the public press of this colony is appealed against, and the merits of the case dispassionately sifted by my countrymen at the other end of the world, the verdict hastily pronounced upon us here will be reversed. I deeply regret the tone of the Victorian press in reference to this subject, because I conceive it must have this effect: that no man occupying a respectable social position, no man valuing his own peace of mind and self-respect, will henceforth consent to "shun delights, and live laborious days",[24] for the sake of carrying out, in a spirit of disinteredness and with singleness of purpose and perseverance of effort, a great public object, since he can anticipate no other reward but calumny, misrepresentation and reproach.[25]

Here he also demonstrates the imperial basis of colonial pride by deferring to the British verdict as the ultimate judgment. His letter was published with a commentary, presumably by the writer of the editorial that had sparked the controversy, and another letter to the editor by George Landells, the former second-in-command of the expedition. An article criticising the Exploration Committee also appeared in the *Weekly Review*,[26] but neither Smith nor any other committee member made further comment. The expedition came to its final conclusion when the Victorian government launched a public appeal with the gift of £4000 towards a suitable memorial to the explorers.[7] Smith was a member of the selection committee that commissioned sculptor Charles Summers to prepare an heroic-sized statue of Burke and Wills mounted on a granite pedestal, with bronze panels in bas-relief on each side depicting various stages in the expedition.[28]

On 19 May 1863, large crowds again filled the city. The news of the marriage of the Prince of Wales and the Danish Princess Alexandra was an occasion for exuberant loyal activity. As Smith described the scene in his diary:

> Festivities in honor of the marriage of the Prince of Wales to the Princess Alexandra of Denmark. A steady rain until 2 p.m. when it cleared up until midnight. The city and suburbs gay with garlands, triumphal arches, flags, banners and greenery. At night a brilliant illumination, the streets thronged with spectators, & the general effect impressive if not imposing. Transparencies innumerable were exhibited, & tons of Chinese crackers must have been exploded in the Chinese quarter, in Little Bourke Street, so incessant was the discharge that it resembled a sustained fire of musketry, & was accompanied by the beating of gongs, tom-toms, and all sorts of discordant instruments. From the roof of the Library, the *coup d'oeil* was magnificent. All Melbourne & its belt of suburbs, was visible. Bonfires were kindled on Mount Macedon, the You Yangs, Plenty Ranges, and at other points on the horizon, & showers of rockets were sent up from the Botanical Reserve. Coloured fires were burnt on the roof of the Melbourne Club, the Bank of Australasia & other elevated sites; two huge A's flamed in front of the University; a gigantic cross of light sparkled in front of St Patrick's & St Francis's Cathedral; & a huge cresset blazed at the unfinished tower of the former. Looking down Bourke St, the sight was very animated. The yellow light gleamed upon a dense mass of upturned faces, reaching from Spring Street to Queen Street, and through the midst of the crowd slowly wound a serpentine line of carriages, each with its pair of lamps, & looking, in the mass, like a monstrous snake with luminous scales. In most of the suburbs, oxen were roasted whole, & barrels of beer set flowing; while the poor and the inmates of the charitable institutions were universally regaled.

Celebrations on this scale were a demonstration of the intensity of colonial loyalty to the throne. They were also important to the immigrants as a means of sharing in distant national events, secure in the knowledge that festivities appropriate to the occasion would be taking place wherever there were British subjects.

In the evening, a loyal address written by Smith was given by actress Rose Edouin during the interval between performances at the Haymarket. He commenced his tribute with an historical account of the

Danish invasion of England, going on to stress the advantages to be drawn from the intermixture of Danish and English blood and concluding with a tribute to the Princess and an invocation for blessings on the Royal couple. The last lines are especially expressive of his feelings of loyalty:

> Wher'er our mother tongue is heard, wher'er our name is known,
> We breathe a blessing on the pair who stand beside the throne.
> Long may the widowed Queen, who sways the sceptre of our land,
> Continue in the exercise of that benign command.
> And when, amidst a people's tears, she passes to her rest,
> May Albert and his Danish bride be, like her, loved and blessed![29]

This was a sentiment that would have been shared by most of the people who had spent the day in celebration. As recorded in the diary, Smith was paid £5 for the address, presumably by the proprietor of the theatre.[30] By expressing popular community views in this manner, he was also acting as a public spokesman and, in effect, adopting the role of an unofficial poet laureate. This placed him as a central figure in the celebrations, both in the evening at the theatre and on the following morning, when his address reached a wider audience with its publication in full in the *Argus*.[31]

The colonial celebration of the Shakespearean tercentenary in 1864 marked the culmination of deliberations over the choice of a suitable memorial that had been going on since 1860. Although the Australian colonies had been invited to contribute towards an English memorial, it was decided, at a public meeting held in the Town Hall on 24 April 1860, that Victorians should erect their own memorial in the form of a statue of the poet.[32] Smith, elected to the committee of management with Sir William Stawell, Sir Redmond Barry and Professor Martin Irving, among others, was one of the most vocal supporters of the statue. But there were soon indications that the decision to erect a statue was less than unanimous. At a committee meeting held on 28 May, the possibility of a Shakespeare scholarship at the University was raised as an alternative.[33] Members were divided and the Shakespeare memorial became the subject of opposition between supporters of one or other of the projects.

Those who wanted the statue, initially the majority of the memorial enthusiasts, went ahead with arrangements for an amateur performance of *The Merchant of Vencie* by the Garrick Club, which raised £40.[34] Encouraged by the successful launching of its fund raising programme, the committee began the search for a suitable sculptor. English and colonial artists were invited to compete for the commission and an English tribunal consisting of Thomas Carlyle, John Ruskin and William Mulready was appointed to decide the winner, in cooperation with the Victorian committee.[35] However, time went on without a decision. Public interest declined and the tercentenary drew closer with little prospect of the erection of the Shakespeare statue. The memorial was the subject of an *Argus* editorial in which the writer, probably Smith acting as publicist, began with a description of the public meeting at which the choice of a statue had been accepted. He went on to deplore the shift in support for that form of memorial:

> More than two years have gone by, and brought us no nearer to the accomplishment of the Shakespeare statue. Our orators were too flattering, and our writers too hopeful. The scheme of the Shakespeare monument has miscarried, and April, 1864, will find us still without a sculptured effigy of the poet in Melbourne. The committee which was formed to carry out the resolutions adopted at the general meeting in April, 1860, has failed to raise a sufficient sum of money for the projected memorial. A minimum of £2000 was required before anything in the shape of a decent statue could be got, and, towards this amount, the committee has only been able to raise something like £500 or £600.[36]

One of the reasons for the committee's difficulty in raising sufficient money for the statue was the comparatively small section of the community upon which it could call for interested support. Another reason was the natural tendency of all but the most enthusiastic organisers to procrastinate when the event to be celebrated was still some time off. Probably the most important reason of all was the dissension among the committee as to the best memorial.

The statue faction continued its efforts towards fulfilment of what it believed to be the leading objective. As a compromise, Charles Summers offered to prepare a plaster model that could be cast in bronze for £1000.[37] This was a feasible alternative to the original plan, although obviously disappointing to a committee that had been prepared to spend twice as much. Summers went ahead and the model was displayed at the fourth annual Fine Arts Exhibition held in Melbourne, commencing on 1 March 1864.[38] It was then placed outside the Public Library and formally unveiled by visiting actor Barry Sullivan on 23 April, the date of the tercentenary. An *Argus* writer described the model in the following terms:

> The 'immortal bard' is represented in a sitting posture, with his head resting on the left hand, and some open manuscripts on his lap. The countenance is marked with thought, the attitude and disposition of the drapery manifest repose, and the entire treatment of the subject is consistent with the idea that the poet is giving form and shape to some piece of gorgeous fancy.[39]

This report appears to have been written by Smith, who, after seeing the model at a private viewing on 23 June 1863, wrote in his diary: 'Subject poetically treated; the pose easy, graceful and dignified, and the expression meditative'. The plaster model was certainly impressive, but it could be no lasting monument unless further funds could be raised to ensure that the statue was to be the Shakespeare memorial and not the scholarship proposed by the other faction in the committee.

On 22 April, the evening before the unveiling of the model, the amateur actors from the Garrick Club had given another performance of *The Merchant of Venice* in aid of the fund.[40] With their enthusiasm revived both by this performance and the unveiling of the plaster model, the supporters of the statue determined to make further efforts to achieve success. Meetings of those who wished to see the statue completed in bronze were held at Charles Summers's studio on 12 May and 17 June. At the first of these meetings, it was decided that circulars should be issued in the form of a photograph of the model, with space beneath for the receipt of subscriptions.[41] Sixty of these circulars were sent out, but, disappointingly, only three or four had been returned by the date of the second meeting, and the sum of £1 was the total donation.[42] Still not discouraged altogether, the committee arranged a series of lectures, to be given by James Smith and Doctor J. E. Bromby, among other speakers. As a further attraction, it organised a Shakespearean musical festival, to be held in St George's Hall on 1 September.[43] But, despite the efforts of this section of the committee, public response was inadequate for the purpose. The lectures were poorly attended and the festival received limited support,[44] diminishing any hope of a large addition to the statue fund.

The supporters of the scholarship had been active in the meantime. On 23 April 1863, a year before the tercentenary, a meeting of subscribers had decided that the funds in hand were more compatible with the foundation of a scholarship than the erection of a statue.[45] Additional subscriptions were called for and, as reported in the *Argus* on 18 March 1864, the visiting actor Charles Kean was one of those who responded, donating £25. A series of lectures was arranged, the first on the subject 'Falstaff' being given at the University on 31 March by G. W. Rusden, the prime mover for the scholarship.[46] Other lecturers included Archibald Michie and T. T. à'Beckett. Michie's Lecture, 'Shakespeare: his influence and his interpreters', was given at St George's Hall on 11 April. The Governer, Sir Charles Darling, in the chair, explained that his appearance in support of the scholarship was simply because that project was more advanced than the one for the statue.[47] At this stage, £600 to £700 had been subscribed for the scholarship,[48] while the statue fund stood at around £450.[49] Speaking to a large audience, the lecturer expressed the views of his supporters in decrying the need for a statue while the works remained as an adequate tribute. This was the view that gained final acceptance in Melbourne; the scholarship was within reach of its subscribers and the Shakespeare memorial eventually took that form.[50]

Although the factional operation of the Shakespeare Memorial Fund reflects the separation of the professional and amateur elements in the committee, these divisions were not rigid: involvement as a fund raiser in this context was largely dependent upon a knowledge and appreciation of Shakespeare's works that was not necessarily confined to university men. Both groups, in any case, would recombine in the formation of the Melbourne Shakespeare Society in 1884. However, at the time of the tertencentenary, it seems likely that the diversion of a small proportion of the funds was influenced by the frustration of the statue faction's objectives. In a letter to the editor of the *Argus*, the Garrick Club secretary J. M. Forde retracted the sum of £21/13/0 raised by amateur performances and announced the decision of the club to allocate this amount towards a memorial to the late actor Gustavus Vaughan Brooke, who had drowned in the shipwreck of the *London*, while on his way to Australia for a return season.[51] Forde's letter brought an immediate reply from Rusden, denying the right of the club to withhold the money, when it could be added to subscriptions received towards a second scholarship.[52] But it was not only disappointment over the outcome of the Shakespeare memorial controversy that had inclined the Garrick Club to transfer its funds to the Brooke memorial. The club owed much of the reason for its foundation to the interest in the theatre stimulated by Brooke's first successful season. Apart from the personal charm and undoubted ability that had made friends and impressed theatregoers in Melbourne, the actor's greatest appeal to those who now remembered him arose from the words he is supposed to have spoken when close to death. According to the account of the shipwreck in W. J. Lawrence's biography, Brooke called to a crew member manning one of the few lifeboats able to leave the ship: 'Goodbye. Should you survive, give my last farewell to the people of Melbourne'.[53] Whether or not this story was apochryphal, it stirred the imagination and provoked a sympathetic response to the project of a local memorial.

Smith had enjoyed the close friendship of Brooke and the American actress Avonia Jones, who became Brooke's wife after leaving Australia. Brooke's non-arrival for the planned 1866 season under tragic circumstances was, therefore, cause for personal as well as professional regret. On hearing the news of Brooke's death, Smith was inspired to create his own memorial in the form of the poem 'In Memoriam. G. V. B.':

"Give something to the dead!" Across the drear
And dread expanse of the remorseless sea,
Comes a faint echo of the words which he
Uttered so often in the gen'ral ear.

"Give something to the dead!" What can we give
Save vain regrets and unavailing tears,
And mem'ries of irrevocable years
Wherein we thought not, "He will cease to live?"

In him a hundred noble lives went down,
Gulf'd in the dark unfathomable deep;
With him a hundred gracious creatures sleep,
And "RICHELIEU," "ELMORE", and "THE HUNCHBACK" drown.

> Mute, mute, for evermore, the magic tongue
> Which thrill'd us with "OTHELLO'S sad farewell;
> While list'ning thousands, subject to its spell,
> In silent rapture on its accents hung.
>
> Closed are the eyes which flash'd electric light,
> Or blazed with hate, with sunny laughter gleam'd,
> Or radiant with warm affection beam'd—
> Closed in the darkness of an endless night.
>
> Vanish'd the noble and majestic mien,
> The graceful bearing and the lordly port,
> The dignity which might become a court,
> The stately presence which could fill the scene.
>
> Gone the rich promise that his life enclosed—
> The mellow fruitage of its perfect prime—
> The ripe result of art matured by time,
> And all its golden autumn had disclosed.
>
> That child-like loving heart will beat no more,
> It rests beneath the never-resting wave;
> And boundless as his fame, his world-wide grave—
> We stand upon its brink on every shore.
>
> O, brave in Death, as thou wast great in life,
> Facing thy doom with calm untroubled eye,
> And scanning wistfully the storm-rent sky,
> At peace within, while all without was strife.
>
> How we shall miss thee in the years to come!
> How blend thy voice and features with the past!
> But while the language SHAKSPEARE wrote shall last,
> Thy name will live in every English home.[54]

Smith was following the tradition of elegaic memorials in paying this private tribute to the life of a dead hero. Through the poem's publication in *Melbourne Punch*, he was also providing a focus for the commencement of fund raising activities in support of a more tangible memorial.

George Coppin, who had been responsible for arranging Brooke's return tour, was the first to suggest the erection of a monument, calling for the formation of an appropriate committee in a letter to the *Argus* published on 17 March 1866. Coppin then initiated fund raising by organising a benefit performance at the Theatre Royal. Other programmes of assistance were also planned. A special meeting of the Garrick Club was held on 23 April, with Smith in the chair, to make arrangements for an amateur performance by club members.[55] In addition, Smith was involved with another group of Brooke supporters, consisting of a number of men connected with the Melbourne press, who had become known as the 'press amateurs' because of their theatrical performances. Since entertainment of the kind was a popular form of fund raising, this group set about arranging amateur performances of its own.

Public heroes

A marble bust of the actor was the most favoured choice of memorial, provided sufficient money could be found. But the Brooke Memorial Fund committee, made up largely of Garrick Club members, succeeded in raising only £50.[56] Since this was an inadequate amount, they decided to invite the press amateurs to confer as to the best method of disposal of the memorial funds. However, the press amateurs had given more performances and raised more money than the Garrick Club players and, in consequence, wished to have more control over the manner in which their funds were used. Press amateur committee meetings were held on 21 July and 12 December without definite conclusion.[57] Over £200 had been raised by their performances but more money was required for a good memorial.[58] The next meeting was, if only temporarily, more conclusive. On 9 March 1867, the press amateurs decided to make the £200 the nucleus of a fund for a dramatic college of 'deranged and indigent members of the profession', modelled on a similar English college.[59] But, at the meeting held on 23 March, this resolution was cancelled, as being of a 'crude and impractical character' and 'alien to the objects which the press amateurs had in view'. It was then decided that a bust of the actor should be placed in the Public Library.[60]

Charles Summers left the colony in May to further his career overseas, first in London and then in Rome. On 10 April 1868, it was reported in the *Argus* that he had been commissioned by the press amateurs to furnish either a bust or a statue of G. V. Brooke. It was at this stage that the Garrick Club members decided to transfer the money raised by them for the Shakespeare statue into the Brooke Memorial Fund. But, following the objection of the Shakespeare scholarship supporters to the dispersal of the money in this way, the club decided at a general meeting on 10 October to give £20 of the money in hand for the Brooke fund to charity and to place the £60 raised for the Shakespeare statue on fixed deposit for twelve months. The members of the club also recorded 'a strong wish to see the Brooke memorial carried out'.[61] This left the way clear for the press amateurs to go ahead with their plans. Although there had been differences of opinion as to who should have the credit for the memorial, many Garrick Club members were associated with the press in some professional capacity, involving less dissension between the two groups of fundraisers than might otherwise have been expected. Even so, there were to be factional disagreements over the unveiling of the completed bust, which took place at the Duke of Edinburgh Theatre on 12 December. The writer of the *Argus* review of the evening's entertainment, perhaps Smith, writing in support of the press amateurs, claimed that the unveiling was premature and the arrangements made without the approval of the members of the press who had raised the funds.[62] This was confirmed when the trustees of the 'Press Brooke Memorial' announced that they had had no part in the 'so-called unveiling'. As they explained it, Charles Summers had consigned the bust to his brother, musician Joseph Summers, who, acting 'out of a misapprehension', had not handed it directly to the trustees.[63]

The official ceremony of presentation to the Melbourne Public Library took place in the picture gallery of the Museum of Art on 29 December, when the Attorney General, George Paton Smith, also a trustee of the Press Memorial Fund, presented the bust to the library trustees.[64] In the course of his address, he recalled the means by which the memorial had been obtained. He also acknowledged the debt owed to Brooke by the people of Melbourne for the stimulation of interest in the drama and referred to the actor's last words as 'Remember me to my friends in Melbourne'. Sir Redmond Barry, accepting the memorial on behalf of the trustees of the Public Library, expressed the appreciation of the fund raising efforts of the press, while still regretting their decision to act separately without the cooperation of other sympathetic supporters. But the bust was now securely placed in the library and Sir Redmond promised that the trustees would 'gladly give to those who frequent these walls an opportunity of renewing their remembrance of [Brooke's] lineaments, and also of being reminded of his great dramatic power'.[65]

The movement for the commemoration of the fourth centenary of the first printing in the English language by William Caxton in 1471[66] was another occasion for fund raising activities in Melbourne.[67] The Caxton Fund, modelled on the Royal Literary Fund, originated at a meeting held at the Criterion Hotel on 5 August 1871 to discuss an appropriate means of commemoration. A committee that included Charles Bright and George Coppin among others was elected for the purpose of establishing a Caxton scholarship in aid of 'decayed pressmen'.[68] At the following meeting, held on 12 August, it was decided that the proceeds of the commemoration would be better used for 'the establishment of a Caxton Fund for benevolent and educational purposes'. In an extension of the objectives of the Royal Literary Fund, all members of the press were to be eligible for assistance, whether 'writers, printers, or otherwise'.[69] A subcommittee was then appointed to enquire into means of raising funds. Its recommendations, made public at a meeting on 30 September, and recorded by government printer John Ferres in the souvenir pamphlet compiled for the occasion, included a course of popular lectures, to be given by the Rev. Charles Clark, Charles (later Sir Charles) Gavan Duffy and the novelist Anthony Trollope, who was visiting the colony at the time. A cricket match and a marine excursion were to be organised and members of the Yorick Club promised support in the form of a collection of papers for publication as a Christmas gift book.[70]

There were 2000 people in the audience at the Town Hall for Charles Clark's lecture on Oliver Goldsmith on 14 November,[71] with the net proceeds being £78/9/0. The promised lecture by Gavan Duffy seems not to have eventuated, but Trollope, speaking on the topic 'Modern Fiction as a Rational Amusement' on 18 December, attracted 3000 listeners[72] and added £177/15/1 to the fund. The cricket match between members of parliament and members of the press raised £31/2/6 and the excursion down the bay in the *City of Adelaide*, £4/0/5. The proposed Yorick Club Christmas Annual does not appear to have been published. Individual donations were payable to representatives of the daily newspapers and the Government Printing Office. James Smith is listed as having contributed two guineas, along with other donors, including Charles Bright, Marcus Clarke and George Coppin. According to the Balance Sheet dated 12 October 1872, £515/10/0 had been raised through organised activities and £261 through subscriptions, making a total of £776/10/0. Subscribers of one guinea upwards, on or before 6 November 1871, were made responsible for the administration of the fund. On 25 April 1873, George Higinbotham, David Syme and Frederick Haddon, acting as trustees, invested £500 in government stock, the dividends from which were to be added to the fund. An account opened at the National Bank of Australia showed a balance of £5/19/10 after withdrawal of the £500 invested and the payment of expenses connected with fund raising activities. The date of the last entry in this bank book is 24 December 1875.

On 24 July 1893, some of the surviving subscribers met to form a new committee. Of the 29 who had formed the original committee, 12 had died since 1875. Others were either known to have left the colony or were unable to be traced. Apart from the appropriation of small sums from the bank account in two or three instances, the administrators do not appear to have been called upon to make disbursements from the fund. This may have been because it was conceived at a time of growing prosperity, when, with few exception, the needs of impoverished pressmen were less obvious than they were to become during the early 1890s. There was good reason for the revival of the Caxton Fund in 1893. Members of all levels of society were affected by the bank crashes and depression that followed the end of the 1880s land boom and there were now many more needy members of the press. Smith himself suffered considerable financial losses, but he was more fortunate than some of his fellow journalists in being still in full employment. As the *Argus* representative on the committee, he was to be involved in the operation of the fund for at least the next ten years.

A further meeting was convened on 4 August 1893, with Smith in the chair, to determine the action to be taken for the disposal of the remainder of the fund, which then consisted of a total £492/0/10. No decision appears to have been reached until the meeting held on 18 November, when committee members agreed that the fund should be 'wound up and money divided and paid, in proportion, to representatives of the Melbourne Typographical Association and to representatives of the literary profession'. The literary representatives, who included James Smith, had claimed two-thirds of the contributions because of their initial organisation and control of the operation, but the decision of the meeting was to allot three-fifths to literary claimants and two-fifths to typographical claimants. The literary section of the fund became known as the Victorian Literary and Benevolent Fund, while the typographical section remained the Caxton Fund. As indicated by the reports of disbursements, Smith was active in the operation of the Benevolent Fund, to which journalists or their dependants could apply. Since the interest on the capital sum was used to provide the disbursements, only small amounts were available to claimants. For instance, in 1893, the sum of £10 was paid to the widow of James Harrison, an original committee member who had proposed the resolution on which the constitution had been based. With this payment went an apology for the paucity of the amount. There was little or no increase in the amount available for each claimant in 1904, when Emmeline Whitworth, the daughter of R. P. Whitworth, was given £10 for her mother. But, despite its financial limitations, the Benevolent Fund was instrumental in establishing a tradition of payment to writers. It is possible that its operation may have influenced Alfred Deakin, for some years a trustee, when, as Prime Minister, he was responsible for the foundation of the Commonwealth Literary Fund in 1908.[73]

Of all the fund raising activities with which Smith was concerned in Melbourne, the Caxton Fund appears to have been the least divisive of its supporters, probably because its purpose was clearly defined at the time of inception. Its administrators were inactive, rather than quarrelsome, during the early years of its existence, but those who were left when the fund was most needed appear to have rallied to give their services for as long as they were able. Factional differences affected the smooth operation of the other fund raising organisations. In a small cultural community, where interests and occupations often overlapped, personal preferences were likely to vie with professional jealousies to inhibit, delay and alter apparently viable decisions. So the Garibaldi sword provoked personal criticism based on religious bias, the Shakespeare memorial became a scholarship instead of a statue and the Brooke bust was twice unveiled. Even so, each of the fund raising committees eventually achieved one or other of its prime objectives and, despite the dissension encountered in the process, succeeded in honouring the hero of the moment.

Loose village, from the viaduct, c. 1875. This village, near Maidstone in Kent, was James Smith's fondly remembered birthplace.

On the river, Ware, showing the malthouses that provided the town with its main industry. James Smith lived at Ware during the 1830s.

View at Amwell, c. 1794. James Smith named his house in Burwood Road, Hawthorn, after this village in Hertfordshire.

High Street, Salisbury, c. 1850. James Smith lived in the High Street while working as editor of the Salisbury and Winchester Journal.

James Smith as a young man around the time of his arrival in Melbourne in 1854.

James Smith in old age.

James Smith's carte de visite. *From Mrs. J. E. Neild's photograph album.*

James Smith's memorial ode for Gustavus Vaughan Brooke, who died in the shipwreck of the London. *This ode, written in Smith's hand, was published in* Melbourne Punch *on 22 March 1866.*

The bust of actor Gustavus Vaughan Brooke by Charles Summers, which was presented to the trustees of the Melbourne Public Library by a group of Brooke's former friends and associates in 1868.

Collins Street, Melbourne, at the intersection of Elizabeth Street, looking west towards Queen Street, c. 1860.

Collins Street, Melbourne, at the intersection of Swanston Street, looking west towards Elizabeth Street, c. 1890.

The office of the Argus *and the* Australasian *in Collins Street, Melbourne, where James Smith worked as leader writer and critic for almost forty years.*

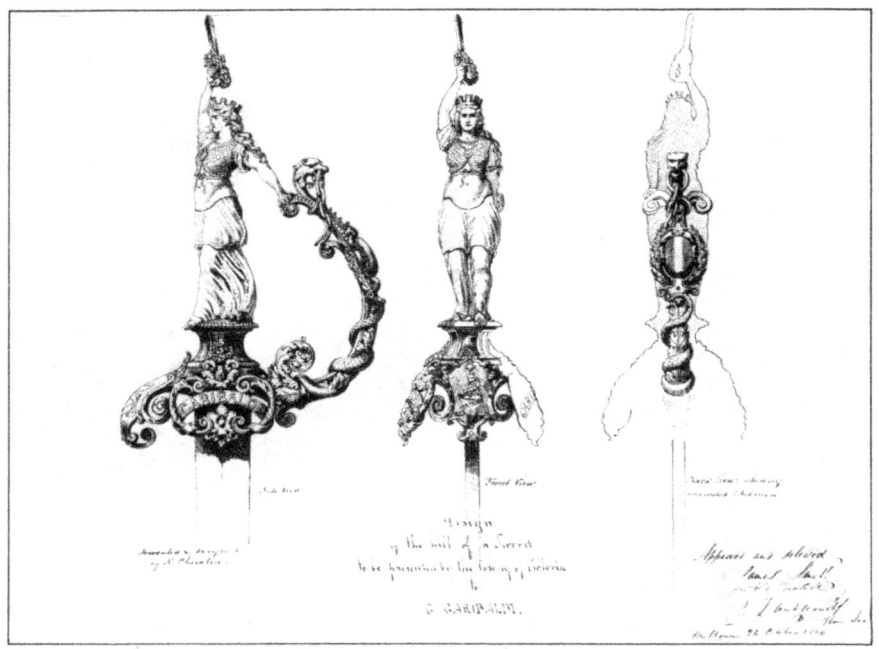

Nicholas Chevalier's design for the hilt of the sword presented as a testimonial to Giuseppe Garibaldi by his admirers in Victoria in 1861.

The subscription card for a memorial to mark the tercentenary of Shakespeare's birth in 1864, showing the plaster model for a statue by Charles Summers that was never completed.

The memorial to the explorers Burke and Wills, erected at the intersection of Collins and Russell Streets, Melbourne, in 1865, after the Victorian expedition to the interior of Australia that resulted in their deaths.

The interior of the Parliamentary Library of Victoria, where James Smith worked as Librarian from 1863–1869.

Henry Gyles Turner, who arrived in Melbourne in the same year as James Smith, and became a close friend. From Mrs. J. E. Neild's photograph album.

Annie Bright, a feminist and the editor of the spritualist magazine Harbinger of Light, *to which James Smith made frequent contributions.*

6
PERIODICALS

Although they often bore titles that signified local origin, colonial periodicals were closely modelled on the British and American prototypes with which the immigrants were familiar. Large quantities of these overseas periodicals were imported into the colony each month on private or library subscription or for individual sale. They served the important purpose of providing regular reading matter in the form of fiction and articles that varied in style according to the taste of the subscriber. For the informed reader of literary reviews as well as the worker who looked forward to the arrival of a favourite penny paper, the overseas periodicals had an added attraction because of their nostalgic appeal. However, there were disadvantages in that the latest magazines were already two or three months old when they arrived in Melbourne and the material they contained lacked immediate topicality. There was also no scope for local talent in an imported periodical. Those immigrants who were active in promoting the development of colonial culture while still maintaining traditional links with home soon became dissatisfied with the exclusive supply of imports and began to produce and edit their own periodicals.

The first colonial periodical was produced in Sydney in 1821. This was the monthly *Australian Magazine*, which lasted for thirteen numbers. It was followed by a great many others, few of which fulfilled the aspirations of the promoters in proving to be viable. There were problems in production that were peculiar to the colonial situation. In the early years of settlement, there was a shortage of suitable paper and type as well as efficient machinery and the labour to run it. These difficulties were gradually overcome when populations increased and conditions became more stable, but costs of production and distribution remained high. While adequate subscription lists were desirable as a means of continued production, in practice subscriptions were infrequently sustained beyond the first quarter. There were several reasons why this should have been so: the promoters and the subscribers often belonged to the same circle, acting as editors, contributors and supporters until one or the other broke away, either through the exhaustion of capital, diminished interest, or the desire to begin again with the foundation of a new periodical that might be in direct competition with the one they had abandoned. This was a pattern that would repeat itself through the end of the nineteenth century and into the twentieth. There were never enough actively interested people available to support more than a few of the hundreds of periodicals produced in the Australian colonies. These problems were aggravated by the intense competition provided by the overseas periodicals, which retained their popularity against the colonial versions and, being produced more cheaply and imported free of tariff, were able to be sold at the same price.[1]

Close to 200 literary or partly-literary periodicals were produced in Melbourne during the nineteenth century. They ranged from literary reviews and miscellanies, through humorous and satirical journals to family and other popular papers. There were denominational and institutional journals, social and political weeklies, illustrated newspapers and many more kinds of periodicals, including those in which various objectives were combined in order to attract a wider reading audience. A few appeared in country centres, such as Ballarat or Geelong, but the great majority were published in Melbourne. It was almost always a hazardous business. Melbourne promoters suffered from similar handicaps to those in neighbouring colonies, even though the rapid increase in population from the time of the gold rushes provided a larger market, encouraging proprietors and editors to continue producing new periodicals in the hope that the latest might be the best.

Several attempts were made to found local periodicals in the early years of settlement. The first of these was the *Port Phillip Magazine*, edited by the Melbourne coroner Doctor W. B. Wilmot and illustrated by drawing master G. A. Gilbert, which ran from January to April 1843. This magazine, designed to encourage the development of literary and artistic taste among the colonists as well as to convey information to friends in England, was a brave effort by its enthusiastic promoters. But the infant colony was caught up in financial depression and the magazine failed to receive adequate support. Other periodicals of a similar nature followed, including the *Illustrated Australian Magazine*, a monthly journal of 'Science, Art, Commerce, Statistics and General Literature', produced and illustrated by the enterprising Ham brothers, Thomas, Jabez and Theophilus. It first appeared in July 1850 and continued successfully until publication was suspended in February 1852, when 'engravers, printers, compositors, pressmen and even contributors' joined the rush to the goldfields.[2] The last number appeared in August 1852. In October of the same year, teacher and historian James Bonwick decided to capitalise upon the current colonial situation by producing the *Australian Gold-Diggers' Monthly Magazine*, which ran for eight issues, closing in May 1853 after the gold diggers and their families, for whom it was intended, had demonstrated their lack of interest in the effort Bonwick had made through his magazine for their enjoyment and instruction. Popular family papers also appeared during the early 1850s, but with little lasting success, and, except for church magazines and others of minor specialised interest, there were no colonial periodicals of any standing in production in Melbourne when Smith arrived at the end of 1854.

Table 6.1 contains the titles of the more important periodicals published in Melbourne during the remainder of the nineteenth century, together with the year of first issue and the names of some of those known to have been actively associated with their production. Apart from the artists Thomas Carrington and Nicholas Chevalier, these people were journalists either by profession or occasional inclination.

As this table demonstrates, James Smith played an integral part in the development of these periodicals, whether in the role of proprietor, editor or contributor. Marcus Clarke and J. E. Neild are also seen to have been involved in several different ventures. Overall, the table displays the manner in which groups of people formed and reformed in attempts to produce periodicals that might defy past experience and prove to be successful.

The first issue of the *Melbourne Monthly Magazine* appeared in May 1855. This periodical was modelled on *Blackwood's Magazine*, an English monthly review that also featured literary items contributed by well known writers. In Melbourne, where established talent was less freely available, there was nonetheless an enthusiastic and active literary team. The extent of Smith's involvement in the project is unknown, but he was a regular contributor during the six months that the magazine was running, writing articles on drama, literature and travel, as well as a series of literary and philosophical discussions. R. H. Horne, Butler Cole Aspinall and Sir William à'Beckett were prominent among other contributors. Although its promoters had believed that this periodical would meet an obvious need in Melbourne, its appeal was confined to educated colonists like themselves, of whom there were still too few to uphold for long the multiple roles required in production and support. The *Melbourne Monthly Magazine* closed with the first issue of the second volume in November 1855.

Although the failure of the magazine was necessarily disappointing, Smith was already actively involved in the production of a different kind of periodical that was destined to be far more successful. There were to be a number of colonial attempts to found a local version of the London *Punch*. *Melbourne Punch* was the first and the longest running of the colonial imitations. Like its English forerunner, it consisted largely of articles and sketches on social and political topics, short humorous and satirical pieces, satirical verse, jokes and cartoons. As it became established, more of the material was original, but, in the early years, the editors were often forced to rely on selections from its parent and other overseas publications in order to fill the pages. Founded by Edgar

James Smith

Table 6.1 Important Periodicals published in Melbourne between 1855 and 1888

Year	Title	ASPINALL, Butler Cole	BLAIR, David	BRIGHT, Charles	CARRINGTON, T. C.	CHEVALIER, Nicholas	CLARKE, Marcus	HEARN, W. E.	HORNE, R. H.	NEILD, J. E.	SINNETT, Frederick	SMITH, James	TURNER, H. G.	WALSTAB, George	WHITEHEAD, Charles	WILLIAMS, W. H.
1855	Melbourne Monthly Magazine	X						X				X				
1855	Melbourne Punch	X	X	X	X			X			X				X	
1856	Melbourne Leader					X					X	X				
1856	Illustrated Journal of Australasia					X					X	X			X	
1856	My Note Book		X					X	X	X	X			X		
1857	Examiner and Melbourne Weekly News	X							X		X					
1858	Illustrated Melbourne News				X						X					
1859	Victorian Monthly Magazine		X								X			X		
1860	Victorian Review (1)							X			X			X		
1862	Weekly Review	X							X							
1864	Australasian				X	X					X					
1865	Australian Journal		X		X								X			
1865	Australian Monthly Magazine			X	X			X	X	X	X	X	X		X	
1866	Australasian Monthly Review									X	X			X		
1867	Colonial Monthly		X		X				X		X	X	X			
1869	Humbug				X				X							
1869	Touchstone											X				
1876	Melbourne Review	X			X	X						X				
1879	Victorian Review (2)	X			X	X					X					
1888	Centennial Magazine	X									X					

Ray and Frederick Sinnett, who was also the first editor, *Melbourne Punch* attracted contributors which, during Smith's association with the journal, included Butler Cole Aspinall, R. H. Horne, Charles Whitehead and Edward Whitty, with Nicholas Chevalier as leading artist. James Stiffe, another noted contributor, had been responsible for the advice given to a writer to the London *Punch* who was contemplating marriage: Stiffe's answer was 'Don't!'[3]

Periodicals

Smith became editor of *Melbourne Punch* in 1857 and, two or three years later, one of its proprietors. He devoted much of his spare time to its successful operation until he retired in order to take up the appointment of Parliamentary Librarian in 1863. His remarks at that time illuminate the often thankless task of editing a colonial periodical:

> None but those who have served a seven years apprenticeship to such a task, can estimate the difficulties under which a publication of this kind is produced. Its quantum of illustrations must be furnished and the requisite amount of letter-press must be forthcoming, no matter how lamentable the dearth of subjects for pictorial treatment, no matter what may be the paucity of themes to write upon. In sickness, or in health, in cheerfulness or in trouble, in prosperity or in adversity, the artists, engravers, contributors and editor must, as Mr Snagsby says, "come up to time;" while there has frequently been no corresponding disposition in the part of subscribers to fulfil their share of the contract; as the heavy arrears due to the proprietor from persons in all parts of the colony will painfully testify.[4]

Nevertheless, *Melbourne Punch* continued to attract able editors. The *Argus* journalist Charles Bright was the next, followed in 1866 by W. Jardine Smith, another Melbourne journalist with whom Smith enjoyed a long and friendly association.

A new literary periodical was established in 1856. This was the *Journal of Australasia* (later the *Illustrated Journal of Australasia*),[5] the first issue of which appeared in July, published by George Slater and edited by William Sydney Gibbons. In January 1857, the printer and literary enthusiast W. H. Williams became the proprietor and Frederick Sinnett the editor. The *Illustrated Journal* took the form of a miscellany, consisting of articles on general and literary topics, serial and short stories, poetry, prose extracts, notes and queries and other minor features. A monthly news summary was divided into 'Journal' sections dealing with current events, politics, science and industry, literature and art. Thomas McCombie's serialised 'History of Victoria' is signed, but, as customary, many original contributions appeared without acknowledgment. However, Henry Gyles Turner is known to have been the author of 'The Captive of Gippsland', and Nicholas Chevalier was an illustrator. While Smith's name does not appear in the magazine, it is possible to recognise some of his articles through comparison with others on similar topics written later and signed either by name or initials. For instance, 'A Dream of Travel', published in the *Illustrated Journal* for September 1856, forms the basis for reminiscences of Italian travel, including 'Recollections of Padua', which Smith wrote for publication in the *Argus* on 1 January 1881. He may also have been responsible for some of the material printed under the 'Journal' headings, extracts from which were published in the monthly *Newsletter of Australasia*, printed on a double sheet of fine paper, with space for a personal letter to friends at home. The *Illustrated Journal of Australasia* continued through four volumes until June 1858; the *Newsletter*, embellished with illustrations by S. T. Gill and engravings by Samuel Calvert, ran from July 1856 to December 1862.

My Note Book began publication in December 1856, published by the firm of Shaw Hartnett and edited firstly by Thomas Lockyer Bright and, later by Charles Bright (who was unrelated). This periodical was designed to provide, 'in as small a compass as possible, a popular Epitome of news and passing events, as also reading of a light and amusing character'.[6] It was arranged in sections of varied interest, most of which were presented as a continuous series. The editor appears to have provided most of the content of the early numbers. However, he was soon to be joined by an able body of writers, including J. E. Neild as drama critic. R. H. Horne and Charles Whitehead were also contributors. *My Note Book* ran for five volumes, closing in June 1859. During this time, the same team was also largely responsible for the conduct of the *Examiner and Melbourne Weekly News*, 'a journal of politics, literature, art and social progress', published by the proprietors of the *Argus* from July 1857. T. L. Bright and Charles Bright were again consecutive editors, while Neild conducted the theatrical section under the pseudonym of 'Christopher Sly'. General contents included overseas news and intelligence, essays, serial stories, verse and extracts from other publications. The *Examiner* continued in this form until its incorporation into the *Australasian* in 1864.

Smith was an occasional contributor to *My Note Book* and the *Examiner*. In 1858, as editor, he was also associated with publisher and bookbinder William Detmold, artist Nicholas Chevalier and engraver Frederick Grosse in the production of the *Illustrated Melbourne News*, a weekly paper modelled on the *Illustrated London News*, which was published for the proprietors by George Slater. The contents included illustrated accounts of local news and events, dramatic criticism, notes and queries and other short miscellaneous items, including a good deal of material selected from other publications. The venture was short lived; the *Illustrated Melbourne News* ran for only six issues, suffering from competition with its English model, which, besides proved excellence, had a nostalgic appeal that could not be matched by a colonial production. As acknowledged by a reviewer for the *Illustrated Journal of Australasia* (possibly Smith himself), 'The illustrations were excellent, the literary matter good, and the general conduct able.'[7] But, once their initial capital investment had been absorbed without profit, there was little option for the proprietors except closure.

The first issue of the *Victorian Monthly Magazine*, a more ambitious literary periodical than those that had preceded it, appeared in June 1859. Though produced in Melbourne, this periodical was published simultaneously in Sydney, Hobart, Launceston and Adelaide, in the hope of attracting inter-colonial subscribers. Like most of the literary periodicals of the time, it consisted of a miscellany of articles on local, general and literary topics, fiction, drama, sketches, reviews and news summaries. Not all of the material was original: qualified writers were still too few. The identity of the proprietors is unknown. If not directly involved with the production, it may reasonably be assumed that Smith was a contributor. One article in particular in the second issue appears to have been his: 'On the different orders of intellect', attributed to 'A Literary Lounger', deals with the concept of an aristocracy of intellect. This was a subject of natural concern to Smith, who claimed colonial precedence on the ground of intellectual ability rather than the advantage of birth. He had, also, a reverent appreciation of the great minds of the past, and, in its concentration on the imperishability of the intellect, this article foreshadows an important tenet of spiritualist belief on which he was to write at length in later years. David Blair may also be identified as a contributor, writing over the initials 'D. B.'. Charles Whitehead was another: the first part of his verse drama, 'The Spanish Marriage', was published in the magazine, to remain unfinished at its closure in July 1859 after two issues.

Smith took on an additional commitment at the end of 1860 with the publication of the *Victorian Review*, the first of two Melbourne periodicals to be published under that title. It was published at the *Punch* office, a convenient arrangement for Smith, who was able to combine his duties as editor of *Punch* with the responsibility for the literary section of the *Victorian Review*. Modelled on the English *Army and Navy Gazette*, the *Victorian Review* was a composite publication in its colonial form, designed for the information and entertainment of the volunteer forces, the civil service, the bankers and the insurance officers. In the 'Volunteer Roll of Victoria', included in the first issue, Smith is listed as a member of the Collingwood Rifles, a group of soldiers who, together with other Victorian volunteers, were issued with rifles while providing their own clothing and accoutrements. The Collingwood Rifles, dressed drably at first in grey, were to be transformed by new uniforms of gold-braided scarlet jackets, red-striped blue trousers and tall, black peaked caps decorated with brass plaques. Volunteer forces were formed in Victoria in 1854 during the Crimean War, when there was a widespread colonial fear of Russian invasion. After the Maori Wars began in 1860, the volunteers took over the duties of the 40th Regiment, which had been sent from Victoria to New Zealand.[8] Involvement in military training as a volunteer was considered an important duty by many able-bodied colonists. Smith appears to have been especially concerned about the need for adequate defence forces. At a public meeting in July 1859, he had invited signatures to a petition to the Queen, descriptive of the defenceless condition of the colony, and seeking protection from its prospective enemies.[9] Involvement with the *Victorian Review* and its function both as stimulus and recreation for the volunteer forces was part of this concern.

Thirteen chapters of *Ralph Penfold*, Smith's autobiographical novel, were published in the *Victorian Review*. Céleste de Chabrillan's novel *Les Voleurs d'Or*, set mainly in Melbourne, also appeared as a serial story, titled *The Gold Seekers* and presumably translated by Smith. There was a large amount of original material in the *Victorian Review* in proportion to that selected for republication from other periodicals. Smith wrote much of the content himself, including regular columns of drama criticism. R. H. Horne was another frequent contributor, while Charles Whitehead's narrative poem 'Eustace' ran through a number of issues. However, support in the form of subscriptions was less readily available and, by the end of its second quarter, it was obvious that the *Victorian Review* was in trouble. As announced by the editor, it had been making a weekly loss for some time because of 'the insufficient support accorded by the members of the various Volunteer forces, to whose interests this paper was designed to be more especially devoted'.[10] A meeting called by Edgar Ray to discuss the future of the journal proved ineffective in preventing closure and the last issue appeared on 15 June 1861.

Other groups of writers were combining in the production of various kinds of periodicals. David Blair was editor and perhaps proprietor of the *Weekly Review and Christian Times*, a Presbyterian journal divided into sections of political, social, religious and literary interest, that began publication in October 1862 and continued, with an intervening change of title to *Weekly Review and Messenger*, until December 1864. J. E. Neild was a frequent contributor during the early part of this journal's existence. The *Australian Journal*, first published in September 1865 by the proprietors Clarson, Shallard and Company, was modelled on the English *Family Herald*. It contained serial and short stories by English and Australian writers, articles in series, poems and miscellaneous short pieces. George Walstab was first editor; Marcus Clarke and Robert Whitworth followed at a later stage. Clarke's *His Natural Life* was serialised from 1870 to 1872 and reprinted twice in the *Journal*. Other notable colonial contributors included 'Rolf Boldrewood' [Thomas Browne], Ada Cambridge and Charles Harpur. Originally published as a weekly paper, the *Australian Journal* appeared monthly from 1869. It was one of the few colonial productions to continue into the twentieth century, retaining its popularity as a magazine of light and varied reading through changing tastes until its closure in 1962.

The *Australian Monthly Magazine* began also in September 1865, founded by W. H. Williams, who had been one of the proprietors of the now-defunct *Illustrated Journal of Australasia*. As apparent from his introduction to the first issue, Williams was confident that the time was appropriate for the production of a distinctively Australian periodical:

> Many of the obstacles which long existed to the successful establishment in this part of her Majesty's dominions of a magazine,

worthy to be compared with any of the English monthlies, have been gradually removed during the last few years; and the projectors of this magazine may fairly claim the credit of being the first to take advantage of the altered state of circumstances to supply the blank which has long been felt in our periodical literature....[11]

Contributions were invited from all Australian colonies and, after the first two issues containing a large proportion of material selected from overseas periodicals, the magazine had a decidedly local content. The Australian serial story 'Mark Forrester's Trial' (by an anonymous author) commenced in the third number, while other new features were short stories, sketches, book reviews and further contributions from Australian writers, including J. E. Neild, writing as 'Cleofas' and Marcus Clarke as 'Mark Scrivener'.

Although, as Williams had suggested, shortages of labour, materials and machinery had largely been overcome, there were still difficulties in production with its accompanying high cost and there was a lack of sufficiently interested people to support both the *Australian Monthly Magazine* and the popular *Australian Journal*. Williams sold the magazine to Clarson, Massina (formerly Clarson, Shallard) and Company at the completion of the fourth volume. Since the new proprietors were also publishers and proprietors of the *Australian Journal*, the title was changed to the *Colonial Monthly*. After six months, the magazine again changed hands, being purchased by a group in which Marcus Clarke was a leading figure. The exact identity of the new proprietors is a matter of conjecture, but as Brian Elliott has suggested, it seems likely that they belonged to the same set of people as those who were to gather around Clarke in the Yorick Club,[12] which could include such club members and proprietors in common as George Walstab, J. J. Shillinglaw and Thomas Carrington. Smith and Neild, both foundation members of the Yorick Club, contributed to the *Colonial Monthly*, and Henry Gyles Turner, a later member, also made frequent contributions of topical articles.

The first requirement for the revised *Colonial Monthly* was an original serial story and Clarke, as editor, was ready to provide it. His novel *Long Odds* began in the issue for March 1868, to continue until July of the following year. When Clarke was injured in a hunting accident during the serialisation, George Walstab wrote two of the next instalments in order to keep it going.[13] Clarke also contributed the short stories 'Vox Populi' and 'Pretty Dick'. After the completion of *Long Odds*, he was unable to find a suitable Australian novel to take its place. George Walstab's previously published *Double Harness* and Victor Hugo's *Hans of Iceland* began serialisation in the issue for July 1869 in an effort to attract continued support, but the magazine was already in decline. Both proprietors and subscribers appear to have lost interest and, although J. J. Shillinglaw took over in September 1869, hoping to salvage what remained of the once-hopeful venture, the *Colonial Ma-*

gazine had suffered a fatal loss of collective impetus. The last issue appeared in January 1870.

Smith was actively involved in the foundation of the *Australasian Monthly Review*, which ran for two issues in March and April 1866. He referred to the possibility of a forerunner to this periodical in his 1863 diary:

> Discussed the project of an Australian Quarterly Review, drawing its contributions from the whole of the Colonies in this group, circulating among them all & endeavouring to build up a sound & healthy public opinion to discuss problems of political & social science with breadth and vigor, and to serve as a bond of union among the first class literary and scientific men in Australia. Woods,[14] Archer & I offered to give our services for a year.[15]

Nothing more seems to have been done at the time. But, in January 1866, Smith gave George Walstab, as prospective editor, a letter of introduction to W. H. Archer, who had maintained his interest in the establishment of such a publication. As a result, Walstab gathered around him a group of contributors which included, besides Smith and Archer, the Reverend J. J. Bleasdale, W. E. Hearn, Frederick Sinnett, H. E. Watts and the Reverend Julian Tenison-Woods.

As indicated by its prospectus, the *Australasian Monthly Review* was modelled on the English *Fortnightly Review*, devoting its contents 'solely to the various branches of Science, Art and Light Literature'. Smith wrote the article 'Impressions of Tasmania', based on a visit to the island in 1864, for the first issue published in March 1866. Archer's contribution 'Prudentia' was a sociological paper dealing with life assurance while Sinnett's article 'Earth as a disinfectant' was about earth-closet systems. Walstab wrote a good deal of the rest of the content, including the first of the series 'The Australians in India; or, Sketches of the Indian Mutiny'. His novel *Looking Back*, published in India in 1864, also began serialisation in this issue. Although neither Smith, Archer nor Sinnett was a contributor to the second issue, it was similar in style and content, with the addition of an article in series, 'Australian Bibliography', by Tenison-Woods. This series, one of the first of its kind, was left incomplete on the closure of the review, but continued in the *Australian Monthly Magazine*. Although intended to be a periodical of serious content, the *Review* catered to the popular demand for fiction with the serialisation of Walstab's novel. But, despite the efforts of the editor and proprietors to please a large enough group of people to make it viable, the *Australasian Monthly Review* could not compete successfully with the *Australian Journal*, based almost exclusively on fiction, or the *Australian Monthly Magazine*, which had a wider appeal because of the variety of its literary content. The second issue of the *Review* was also the last.

Two humorous and satirical periodicals were founded in 1869: *Hum-*

bug in September and *Touchstone* in October. Designed as imitators of the successful *Melbourne Punch*, these journals were rival publications. After his association with the *Colonial Monthly* had ended, Marcus Clarke joined Garnet Walch in the production of *Humbug*, assisted by contributors including Charles Bright, J. E. Neild and Henry Kendall. When James Smith began editing *Touchstone* from its first issue, there were three weeklies of a similar kind in circulation in Melbourne, with an appreciative audience large enough to support one at most. *Humbug* was the first to go under, ceasing publication in January 1870. Smith, obviously glad to be relieved of one of his rivals, published a black-bordered obituary notice on 22 January. In the next issue, *Touchstone* included a memorial that, as shown by the stanza that follows, owed a lot to Thomas Hood:

> The bleak want of "tin"
>   Made It struggle and quiver,
> Like a Lilliput twin,
>   Till It "shut up" for ever.
>   Bald is Its history,
> Now in Death's mystery
>   Safe It is hurled,
> Hooted and hooted, sirs,
>   Out of the world![16]

Humbug consisted largely of social and political commentaries, humorous and satirical sketches and verse. *Touchstone* was similar, though more comprehensive, including literary and dramatic reviews as well as sporting notes and other short, miscellaneous pieces. Much of the material published during the early part of *Touchstone*'s existence appears to have been written by Smith. Some of it is identifiable by the pseudonym of 'Touchstone', which he adopted as editor and used as the signature for some of the items, including a series of critical reviews of Daniel Bandmann, the Shakespearean actor then touring the Australian colonies. He also used 'Pleesman X', familiar from his years at *Melbourne Punch*, for some of his humorous verse. After the early months of 1870, there is less obvious indication of his contributions, and it is not known for how long he remained with *Touchstone*. Henry Kendall and W. Jardine Smith were later editors.

Smith's most important editorial position in Melbourne was with the *Australasian*, which had been published as a weekly paper by the *Argus* since 1864. Like the *Leader* and the *Weekly Times*, published by the *Age* and the *Herald* respectively, it was designed mainly for the interest of country readers, although a separate edition was sold in town. The *Australasian* had a diversified content. Its pages were divided into sections under headings such as 'The Church', 'The Yeoman', 'General News', 'Entertainments', 'Literature' and 'The Jurist'. The literary section that was a notable feature contained serial stories by English and

Australian writers, short stories, book reviews, original verse and items of news and general interest. In 1888, when discussing weekly papers of the kind, Alexander Sutherland made the following assessment of the literary importance of the *Australasian*:

> It made itself more distinctly a literary organ than the *Leader*, and soon attained an acknowledged position as the chief literary authority in Australia, occupying in regard to the colonies somewhat the same position as that occupied by the *Spectator* and *Athenaeum* in England.[17]

Concentration on the literary section of the journal was instigated by Frederick Haddon and extended by W. E. Hearn. When Hearn resigned as editor in February 1870, Smith was offered the position. The *Australasian* had a wide circulation and this was a valuable opportunity for him to confirm his reputation as a leading literary figure.

There is little evidence of Smith's direct control during the early stages of his appointment. He had the support of an able team of writers, including J. E. Neild, who acted as drama critic. Henry Kendall was another notable contributor. A native-born Australian, he had achieved distinction though little financial reward as a colonial poet. In 1870, while living in Melbourne, he desperately sought the work that might alleviate the poverty that was making his family life miserable. Surviving letters from Kendall to Smith are largely concerned with possible opportunities for casual publication, or, preferably, sustained employment.[18] In the first of these letters, dated 4 March, Kendall mentioned that he could be contacted at the *Touchstone* office, indicating that he was then acting as editor, or was, at the least, a regular contributor to that journal. But, in itself, this was a matter of small recompense. Encouraged by Neild, who had tried to help his unfortunate colleague, Kendall approached Smith for consideration as an 'all round' writer for the *Australasian*. He had already written occasional pieces for publication and hoped to extend his association with the journal. Smith appears to have been generally sympathetic towards impecunious writers. He had found work for Charles Whitehead on *Melbourne Punch* and other early periodicals and he also arranged the appointment of Richard Birnie as an essayist for the *Australasian*. He was in a position to give assistance of a similar kind to Kendall. But, according to the correspondence, Kendall's talents, as Smith saw them, were better suited to casual contributions than regular features. Kendall, glad to have work of any kind, submitted several pieces over the next few months. Two of those that Smith accepted were associated with another colonial poet. On 25 June 1870, Kendall's review of Gordon's *Bush Ballads and Galloping Rhymes* was published in the *Australasian*. The review, which Kendall had shown Gordon prior to publication, was a favourable one. But, the next morning, Gordon, who, like Kendall, had severe financial problems, shot himself at Brighton beach. Kendall wrote the 'In Memoriam' for Gordon that Smith published on 2 July.

In further correspondence with Smith, Kendall gave a detailed account of a dispute between himself and Marcus Clarke over payment for contributions to the *Colonial Monthly* and also to *Humbug*. As Kendall explained, he had offered to write for the *Colonial Monthly* without payment because Clarke had told him that, as part-proprietor, he was 'not making a fortune out of the magazine'. Although Clarke preferred to use paid contributions, the proprietors found it difficult enough to meet essential costs, such as those for printing and publishing, let alone payment for their contributors. When the *Colonial Monthly* closed down, Kendall made no claim for the money that he believed to be owing to him, even though he was 'desperately hard up'. Clarke, realising Kendall's position, advanced him £5, on condition that it be worked off on *Humbug*. This was done and, from then on, Kendall wrote regularly for *Humbug*, without further payment, even though he was assured by Clarke that the journal was being subsidised and he should expect to be paid regularly. Eventually, after several requests from Kendall, Clarke agreed to pay another £5, to be sent by cheque the following day. But the promised cheque failed to arrive on time and Kendall, deeply affected by the death of his child and threatened with immediate eviction, sought advances from other sources against Clarke's bank order. Clarke met the debt, but Kendall kept the money, hoping to find enough to repay the advances at a later date. Aware that his actions were dishonourable, he decided that he must write to Smith, to tell him all that had happened, in the hope of finding understanding and, perhaps, further work. As proven through his own unhappy experience, 'Poverty lies hard upon a man with the poetic temperament'. Clarke, trying to balance the requirements of family life with an inclination towards bohemian congeniality, found it equally hard to survive. Only those literary figures with secure and well-paid employment could pursue their careers without undue fear of failure or financial disgrace.

It is not known whether or not Smith felt able to support Kendall in the poet's efforts to restore his tragic situation. He may have helped to solve the immediate problem with some form of financial assistance, but, in the matter of influence, his authority had declined. Despite his apparent suitability for the position of editor, his conduct of the *Australasian* was proving unsatisfactory. One of the issues that caused his employers concern was his unfriendly relationship with Marcus Clarke. Kendall's disagreement with Clarke was based on incompletely documented financial arrangements that invited dispute. The disagreement that Smith had with Clarke while editor of the *Australasian* was an entirely different matter. Although so recently made aware of the futility of public dissension, Smith indulged in acrimonious comment on Clarke and his work, allowing the clash of different personalities, allied with mutual professional jealousy, to cloud his judgment. Clarke's 'Peripatetic Philosopher' column, written under the pseudonym of 'Q', was a regular feature of the *Australasian* and his stories of interesting people and exciting events in colonial history were beginning to appear frequently. He was a valuable asset to the journal and should, therefore, have been able to expect loyal support from his editor. But Clarke was successful in a way that Smith never would be; he was popular among his contemporaries because of his easy-going attitude to life and work, turning out with apparent ease articles and pieces that Smith, with all his fluency of expression, would have laboured over. What was even more a case for resentment, Clarke's work showed flashes of the brilliance that Smith, for all his careful cultivation of the literary art, was unable to capture.

Smith's attitude to Clarke and his work was, to some extent, controlled by professional jealousy. It was also a demonstration of the power of the critic over the artist in the contest between educated opinion and natural ability. A prime example is found in an unsigned comment in the *Argus* on the reaction of the English press to *The Peripatetic Philosopher* (a collection of essays from the *Australasian*) and Clarke's first novel *Long Odds*, which had been published in volume form after its serialisation in the *Colonial Monthly*. While the essays were well received, *Long Odds* had attracted mixed reviews. The one by the *Australasian* critic was favourable. There the reviewer, whose identity is unknown, described it as 'a capital novel', despite its faults, 'many of them brilliant ones'.[19] But Smith, obviously unimpressed by its slight nature and uneven quality, damned the novel with faint praise. In the *Argus* article (attributed to Smith by David Watterson, a later editor of the *Australasian*)[20] he reiterated the opinions of the English press, while indicating his own opinion of Clarke's ability:

> The English press has been pleased to compliment the 'Peripatetic Philosopher' of the *Australasian* in a way that must be gratifying to that gentleman's well-known vanity. Several papers received by this mail contain favourable mention of his writing. *Public Opinion* characterises the fragmentary essays as "full of point and cleverly humourous," and says that "those who read them will be glad to have met a writer whose humour is as original as his style is sparkling and powerful;" while the *European Mail* observes that "it is not a little to the credit of 'Q' that, week after week, he has been able to keep up the sparkle of his papers." We may congratulate Mr. Marcus Clarke on the favourable reception of his first novel, *Long Odds*, by the English press. The *European Mail* says that "the book is one of the most entertaining and brilliantly written novels we have ever read," and the *Spectator* concludes a long and critical review in which Mr. Clarke's many and obvious sins of commission and imitation are unsparingly commented on, by saying that "there is much that is readable in the book," and that, "while the plot might have turned on a more moral and less unhealthy subject than

combined bigamy and seduction, the writing shows talent, and gives promise of better things." We hope it does.[21]

Clarke referred to Smith's comments in the 'Peripatetic Philosopher' column, treating the reference to his own 'well-known vanity' in a light-hearted manner, while also suggesting that the *Argus* writer was apt to display an equal amount of self-assertion.[22] Apart from some irritation at Smith's use of personalities, Clarke had little reason to be much disturbed by the *Argus* article. He was himself aware that *Long Odds* had its faults; later, when revising *His Natural Life*, he described his first novel as 'the greatest trash'.[23] Even so, it had served the purpose of providing a major serial story for the *Colonial Monthly* and, after minor revision, been suitable for republication as a complete novel.

In February 1870, the first of Clarke's series 'Old Tales Retold' appeared in the *Australasian*. During the following month, the *Australian Journal* published the first instalment of *His Natural Life*. This novel was to be Clarke's greatest work and the one into which he put most effort: it took him over two years to write and, after serialisation, almost as long again to revise prior to publication in volume form. The proprietors of the *Australian Journal*, realising from the first few chapters that Clarke's story of the convict era had the potential for success, promoted it as a major attraction. But, on 8 June, obviously disappointed by the fact that there was no reference to the novel in the *Australasian*, even though its author was a noted contributor to that journal, they complained to the proprietors of the *Argus* that 'the editor of the *Australasian* was prejudiced against their publication because their leading story was contributed by a writer with whom he is personally unfriendly'. Smith replied evasively when asked to comment on this allegation. In consequence, he was reprimanded by Hugh George, the manager of the *Argus*, who told him, 'You have made a mistake, inasmuch as you have acted contrary to the well-known principles upon which the editorial function should be discharged'.[24]

Sensible to the warning conveyed by the tone of George's reprimand, Smith made a renewed effort to conduct the *Australasian* in a satisfactory manner. Apart from the articles that he wrote for the *Argus* as required, he appears to have done little outside work at this time. It is probable that, in view of this lack of further literary activity, he was prevented from direct involvement with other journals under the terms of his employment. If he had been consistent in his efforts, he may have been able to remain editor of the *Australasian* for as long as he wished. The paper was well established and its future as a successful country weekly seemed assured. Before long, however, he was again to be distracted from efficient functioning because of his investigations into spiritualism. The proprietors of the *Argus* were prepared to overlook some of the administrative faults that he had displayed as editor of the *Australasian*. Though concerned to the point of issuing a reprimand, they had also passed over the indiscretion of his attitude to Clarke. But public eccentricity of the kind that he began to display after his conversion to spiritualist belief was more than they were able to sustain. Smith remained editor until January 1871, when he was asked to resign. As David Watterson recalled, there had been a number of complaints at the way in which the *Australasian* was being conducted.[25] When the Council of Management of the *Argus* met on 12 December 1872, they discussed the 'careless and indifferent way in which the editorial duties of "The Australasian" were being performed'. The decision was made that, whenever the right man could be found to replace Smith, 'no time should be lost in securing him'. At the next meeting, held on 9 January 1872, the question of Smith's views on spiritualism was the subject of further discussion. The Council was unanimous in deciding that 'it was desirable in the interests of the paper to make a change'. Henry Gullett, a sub-editor of the *Argus*, was mentioned as a possible successor.[26] He took Smith's place, remaining with the *Australasian* until 1885.

Henry Gyles Turner was a leading figure among the group of enthusiasts that founded the *Melbourne Review*, a quarterly periodical that began in January 1876 and continued until October 1885. Conceived, 'not as a financial speculation, but purely in the interest of literary development',[27] the *Melbourne Review* was edited by a committee of three: Turner, A. Patchett Martin and A. M. Topp. The first number consisted of articles on general topics, many of which were of local interest. Subsequent issues followed a similar design, with the addition of literary articles and poems. So far as is known, Smith had no connection with the *Melbourne Review*. Although the name 'James Smith' was appended to the article 'Colonial literature and the colonial press', which appeared in the third volume, he denied authorship.[28]

The original editorial arrangements continued until 1880, when an item by Marcus Clarke caused something of a sensation in conservative Melbourne circles. Clarke had contributed the rationalist article 'Civilization without delusion' to the contemporary *Victorian Review*, causing the Anglican Bishop Moorhouse to reply in defence of Christian beliefs. Clarke's rejoinder was refused by the *Victorian Review* on the grounds of bad taste, but accepted for the *Melbourne Review* through the offices of Martin. When the other members of the committee saw this article, the issue was withdrawn from sale and the offending pages removed. The publisher, George Robertson, refused to continue with the magazine unless the editorial committee was reformed, with the result that Turner and Alexander Sutherland became joint editors, continuing in that capacity until the closure of the magazine.

The eventual falling off in subscriptions may have been caused, in part, by the fact that quarterly periodicals had become outdated. As George Robertson assessed future prospects in 1885, in response to Turner's suggestion that the venture be placed on a profitable business basis: 'In the process of the suns all literary quarterlies must die—they are out of harmony with the 19th century, and they will be impossible in the 20th'.[29] Competition with the *Victorian Review*, which began in November 1879 and continued until February 1886, must also have affected the circulation of the *Melbourne Review*. The *Victorian Review* was a monthly periodical, published by a limited liability company with H. Mortimer Franklyn, an American journalist then living in Melbourne, as nominal editor. Smith appears to have been the effective editor, or, at the very least, to have had an influential voice in the selection of content. His work is a feature of every volume excepting those published during his overseas trip in 1882, while Franklyn's articles appear in eight out of the thirteen volumes only. It is possible that Franklyn, even if editor, was not disposed to be a regular contributor. However, Smith's articles usually take the opening position. David Blair, Marcus Clarke and Edward Morris are notable among other contributors.

Initially, the *Victorian Review* courted popular interest with the publication of a serial story. This practice was discontinued with the novel's conclusion at the end of the first volume, and, from then on, the contents consisted of articles on a wide variety of subjects of local, general and literary interest, together with original poetry, book reviews and the transactions of the Melbourne Shakespeare Society. As described by a reviewer from the contemporary *Pacific Weekly*, the issue for May 1880 was 'generally...fully equal to the average issues of the monthly reviews of England and America'.[30] The *Melbourne Review* and the *Victorian Review* were the best and the longest running of any colonial periodicals to date. As rivals, they provided a stimulus for one another, and, while there were several contributors in common, the publication of two periodicals of this quality at the same time extended opportunities for literary discussion. The *Victorian Review* had certain advantages; it was a monthly periodical in opposition to a quarterly, and, as such, not only offered more frequently for sale, but also more able to display a topical approach. It had another important factor for success in that it appeared to have extensive financial backing. But Franklyn, encouraged by the magazine's success, launched a weekly journal, followed by a daily, and found himself in debt through overexpansion. As a result, the *Victorian Review* ceased publication.

Although the extent of his involvement is unknown, Smith was a contributor to the *Centennial Magazine*, which began in August 1888, combining the functions of a review, a literary periodical and a journal of popular fiction. The title was chosen in commemoration of the hundredth anniversary of white settlement in Australia, and, in line with the nationalistic sentiment that was spreading through the country, contributions were sought and accepted fron neighbouring colonies. It has been generally accepted that the *Centennial Magazine* was a Sydney publication. However, there is some evidence that it originated in Melbourne and was then transferred to Sydney to escape postal charges.[31] Victorian newspapers were charged one halfpenny and magazines either one penny or two, depending upon weight. In New South Wales, newspapers were carried free and any magazine registered as a newspaper (such as the *Centennial*) could be posted from any part of New South Wales to Victoria without cost.

Many other periodicals of various kinds were produced in Melbourne from the 1840s through to the 1880s, a decade of especially intensive production. There were more to come before the turn of the century, but, by the end of the 1880s, Melbourne had begun to lose the leadership in the production of colonial periodicals that it had maintained since the 1850s. The 1880s were also a time of increased production in Sydney, where a new weekly paper was provoking considerable interest. This was the *Bulletin*, an aggressively Australian socio-political and literary journal that was to inspire a number of imitations. Although no periodicals approaching the quality of the *Melbourne Review* and the *Victorian Review* were produced in Sydney until the foundation of *Cosmos Magazine* in 1894, lively cultural circles were formed, attracting writers and artists from other colonies. The loss of people with those interests and abilities was especially noticeable in Melbourne after the depression of the early 1890s. There was then little capital available for investment in literary projects; there was also a comparative scarcity of enthusiasts of the kind that had made Melbourne an acknowledged centre of periodical production.

7
THE DRAMA, THE OPERA AND THE FINE ARTS

Although Smith's closest connection with the theatre was through his work as a drama critic, he had some aspirations towards recognition as a dramatist himself. There are no surviving texts, but newspaper advertisements and reviews provide information about his plays, two of which were produced in Melbourne in 1860 and two more in 1863. Each of the earlier plays was written for a specific purpose: *Garibaldi* as a fund raiser,[1] and *A Broil at the Café* as the main feature of a complimentary benefit given to Spiers and Pond, the popular proprietors of the Café de Paris at the Theatre Royal, by G. V. Brooke, who was then managing the theatre. This farce, described in an *Argus* advertisement as 'an absurd trifle',[2] was played to a crowded and evidently receptive house on 22 September 1860. The *Argus* critic gave the following account of the plot and the action:

> ..."A broil at the Café"—that is the Café de Paris, [is] intended as a vehicle for the eccentricities of Mr. F. Younge, and the exhibition "for the first time on any stage" of certain other well-known individualities in Melbourne. Mr. F. Younge appears in his own person and gets absurdly jealous of his better half, whom he surprises with "a strange gentleman." In his wrath he rushes off to the café, and by his exceedingly wild behaviour excites a "broil" in that usually most correct and stylish establishment. Ultimately he discovers that the strange gentleman is his wife's brother, and so the fracas ends. Mr. Younge is perfectly at home in his role as may be easily imagined: and the appearance of Mr. Pond himself, *in propria persona*, raised the fun of the audience to the utmost.[3]

The critic for the *Age*, while more concerned with the excellence of the acting of Frederick Younge than the slight nature of the plot, agreed with the *Argus*'s assessment of the success of the evening.[4] Operatic selections and popular songs and dances made up the rest of the programme and, as it seems, a good time was had by all present, whether audience or performers.

The Duke's Motto was the first of Smith's plays to be produced in 1863. This was a translation and dramatisation of Frédéric Soulié's *Le Bossu*, for which Smith used the same title as in Paul Feval's translation, then playing in London with Charles Fechter in the lead. The play was presented at the Haymarket for five nights, from 6 to 10 July, with a cast that included Richard Younge, George Fawcett and John Edwards. It does not appear to have been a great success. Smith described the production as 'a failure' in his diary, blaming the actors for their 'incompetency' and inability to learn their parts.[5] The critics from both the *Argus* and the *Herald* placed the fault on the drama rather than the acting. The *Argus* review concludes:

> ...whatever incidents of character were to be found, these were lost in the mass of dullness and commonplace by which they were accompanied. It may be that the materials are sketchy, and the dialogue weak—for these the translator is not responsible; but it can scarcely be considered that Mr. Fechter's adaptation is not closer put together, and more vigorously rendered, unless the alternative conclusion is adopted, that it requires to be performed by a very strong company, stronger than that which appeared in our colonial adaptation last night.[6]

Considering his fluency in the French language, there should have been little to complain about in Smith's translation. But the accurate text that he may be assumed to have prepared appears to have suffered from his deficiencies as a dramatist as well as the inadequate preparation of the cast. *The Duke's Motto* was produced again in Melbourne in 1876, using the version in which Fechter had been successful in London. According to the brief *Argus* review of the later Melbourne production, 'the play was well put on the stage, and the principal characters were fairly sustained'.[7]

Smith was evidently commissioned to write the second of his plays in 1863, which was a dramatisation of *Aurora Floyd*, a new sensational novel by Mary Braddon. As he recorded in his diary, he agreed to adapt the novel 'as a three, four, or five act play (according to circumstances) for [the actress] Miss Quinn, at £10 an act, to be completed by the middle of February'.[8] According to the diary entry for that date, he began the dramatisation on 17 January, but progress was slower than expected because of other commitments at this time. The third act was finished on 23 February and the play as a whole on 20 March.[9] There was some further delay before it was produced and then, when the play was performed at the Princess's Theatre on 14 and 15 September, Rose Edouin and not Miss Quinn played the leading role opposite George Fawcett. Smith's diary entries for this period of the year are spasmodic and there is no record of his reaction to the play's reception. Long reviews in the *Argus* and the *Age* are largely taken up with details of the complicated plot. As the *Argus* critic wrote:

The title... and one of the leading features of the popular novel are all that the playwright has taken from his original; and only in these respects is there relationship between the novel and the drama. The early marriage of the heroine with her father's groom, and her subsequent union with Mr. John Mellish (from whom she conceals the false step taken in her girlhood), the unwelcome reappearance of her first husband, over whom she had been led to believe the grave had long closed, and his tragic death, form the groundwork of the play; and thus far the dramatist is indebted to the novelist for the idea which he has endeavoured to carry out. For the rest, he has depended very much upon his own skill and power of invention, and the result is not altogether a success. Literary merit the drama has none; but there is incident enough in it to render it effective from a stage point of view, with the help of good acting and good scenery. With improvement in these respects the drama would go better than it does at the Princess's; without them, it would be successful nowhere.[10]

The *Age* critic was more favourable. His review began:

A very fair house welcomed the producion at the Princess's Theatre, last evening, of the new sensation drama entitled 'Aurora Floyd', and compiled from Miss Braddon's popular work. The piece is not too lengthy to tire an audience, and throughout it engrosses attention from the 'thrilling' scenes which are represented in it.[11]

Apart from some comments on the acting, the remainder of this review consists of an account of the plot. As had been the case with *The Duke's Motto*, *Aurora Floyd* seems to have done little to advance Smith's reputation as a playwright. His plays appear to have been good enough to attract a sufficiently large audience for a short run, but it is obvious from their moderate success that they lacked the originality of approach that might have enlivened them further. Smith prepared translations for particular actors on occasion in later years. However, so far as is known, he made no more attempts at dramatisation, seemingly content to revert to the role of critic.

The English actor Henry Irving is reputed to have divided drama critics into three kinds: 'those who wrote their criticism before they had seen the play, and peppered their writing with erudite historical references; those who brought their preconceived ideas of Hamlet or Shylock to the theatre with them; and those who judged the play according to the night's performance, and interpreted the feelings of the audience'.[12] Smith's work as a critic reveals aspects of all three categories: he often included items of stage history in his reviews; he was a traditionalist, with definite views on proper methods of acting and interpretation; he also reviewed current performances on their own merits, but, rather than interpreting the feelings of the audience, he acted himself as interpreter, explaining the meaning of the action so that future audiences might understand it better. Most importantly, he had a firm belief in the capacity of the theatre for instruction in moral and ethical values.

Smith's critical judgment was derived in the first place by reliance on established authority. He was especially impressed by the Victorian concept of the morality of art and letters, as applied to criticism of the drama and the fine arts. William Hazlitt and John Ruskin were prominent among the English writers who propagated this concept. Smith's acceptance of their views is evident throughout his published criticism. However, although he retained his conviction of the elevating effect of cultural experience for longer than some of his contemporaries, he was not alone in his adoption of mid-Victorian criteria for understanding and benefiting from that experience. Hazlitt and Ruskin were authoritative figures whose works were widely read.

In order to provide his readers with the means for greater appreciation of a play, Smith often opened his drama criticism with descriptive material, including information about the playwright and recollections of London productions. For his assessment of the action, as presented to a colonial audience, he followed a similar approach to that advocated by Hazlitt in the essay 'On Actors and Acting':

> The stage not only refines the manners, but it is the best teacher of morals, for it is the truest, most intelligible picture of life. It stamps the image of virtue on the mind by first softening the rude materials of which it is composed, by a sense of pleasure. It regulates the passions, by giving a loose to the imagination. It points out the selfish and depraved to our detestation; the amiable and generous to our admiration; and if it clothes the more seductive vices with the borrowed graces of wit and fancy, even those graces operate as a diversion to the coarser poison of experience and bad example, and often prevent or carry off the infection by innoculating the mind with a certain taste and elegance.[13]

With Hazlitt, Smith held a strong belief in the elevating nature of the drama as an educational and moral force. In his work as a critic, though always appreciative of technical ability, he judged the absolute success of the actor's performance on how well that actor conveyed the moral inferences that could be drawn from the playwright's work.

After many years of critical experience, he made the following statement of what he continued to believe to be the proper function and ultimate value of the drama:

> It might, and should be, the people's university, I think, teaching those who resort to it for instruction and delight English and universal history, the richness, the majesty, the variety and the sweetness of our noble mother tongue; the persuasiveness and power of the human voice in elocution and in oratory; the manifold qualities, attributes, capabilities and mysteries of the human mind and character; the necessity and nobility of goodness, and the hatefulness and the miserable consequences of all manner of evil.[14]

Smith's tone here is more didactic than that of Hazlitt, in line with his firmly-held assumption of the role of the critic as educator. But it is obvious from the similarity of the views thus expressed that he had remained in complete agreement with the concept of the association of culture and morality.

He began work as a drama critic while employed by the *Age* in 1855. He was not the only one; J. E. Neild also acted as a drama critic for the *Age* at that time and there may have been other staff members who filled in on occasion. Since the reviews were unsigned, attribution is sometimes uncertain. However, Smith and Neild were noticeably different in style and attitude, and further evidence in the form of theatrical reminiscences and other related material assists identification. Much of Smith's criticism during his first year in the colony was directed towards the performances of Gustavus Vaughan Brooke, whose long tour of Melbourne, Sydney and the country districts commenced on 26 February. Prior to the gold rushes, Melbourne audiences had been entertained by local companies in the Queen's Theatre. New-found wealth attracted leading overseas actors and actresses to the colony, to perform in new theatres large enough to hold enthusiastic immigrant audiences. Brooke, who was one of the first of the imported actors, gave some of his greatest performances in the Australian colonies. His interpretation of the role of Othello was especially successful in Melbourne. Recalling the occasion of Brooke's original London performance as Othello in 1848, Smith wrote that he had been 'greatly impressed with his noble physique, his handsome face, his imposing presence, his rich and flexible voice, and his unquestionable dramatic power'.[15] In all, he was to see more than 50 of Brooke's representations of the Moor.

Smith's previous critical experience had been confined to reports of concerts and dramatic performances at the Assembly Rooms in Salisbury. Now an immigrant and relatively unknown, he found in Brooke's tour the means of establishing himself as a colonial critic. As reported in the *Age*, his work during this period was 'the subject of very general admiration'.[16] He was fortunate in having interesting material on which to work. Brooke was a well-known actor who had been at the peak of his career when Smith had seen him perform in London in a repertoire of Shakespearean tragedy interspersed with standard works such as Lytton's *Richelieu* and *The Lady of Lyons*, and representations of Irish gentlemen, including the popular part of Felix O'Callaghan in *His Last Legs*. A successful American tour from 1851 to 1853 was followed by further London appearances at Drury Lane. But, increasingly, Brooke was performing in the provinces at this time. The effects of excessive drinking combined with severe attacks of bronchitis almost ruined his voice, while financial difficulties aggravated by domestic problems added to the deterioration of his ability. However, George Coppin, in England in search of talented performers, was convinced that Brooke still had the power to attract audiences and fill the Olympic, commonly known as the 'Iron Pot', the prefabricated theatre that Coppin had arranged to have shipped to Melbourne for erection in Lonsdale Street.

Smith believed that English audiences never saw Brooke at his best. As he recalled:

> When he first appeared in the character at the Olympic Theatre, Wych-street, Strand, he took the town by storm, but it was only during his visit to Australia that his histrionic powers seemed to reach their highest perfection. They were stimulated in their development by what was at that time an exceedingly critical audience, composed chiefly of men drawn hither between 1851 and 1860 from all parts of Europe and America, where they had been accustomed to witness dramatic performances which reached a high degree of excellence in the capital cities of the old world, and were therefore somewhat exigent in their demands for choice entertainments in this new land.[17]

It was to this eager and receptive audience that Brooke's Shakespearean season opened. Since the Olympic Theatre was not ready until the end of July, the season began at the Queen's Theatre with *Othello* on 26 February 1855 and continued with productions of *Hamlet*, *Richard III* and *Macbeth* until 23 March. Performances of high standard had been extremely rare in Melbourne and the tour by the visiting company demanded serious critical reviews that attracted attention not only to the leading actors but also to the critics.

The first of the *Age* reviews of *Othello*—perhaps by Smith, though not directly attributable—was written in terms of general rather than critical appreciation. The critic noted 'a considerable improvement' in Brooke's voice and described the performance as 'a triumph' and a 'renewal of enjoyment' for the audience.[18] After a second season at the Queen's Theatre from 9 April until 4 May, in which the Shakespearean group of plays was augmented by others from the repertoire, Brooke opened at Coppin's Olympic with *The Lady of Lyons* on 30 July, in an extended season that concluded with *Love's Sacrifice* on 1 December. The *Age* review of Brooke's representation of Othello on 6 August appears more certain to have been Smith's work, because of its similarity in style and content to the sections of his theatrical reminiscences dealing with Brooke.[19] Here, in an analogy with an artist's sketch and the finished painting, Smith compares the first Melbourne performance with the latest, improved through 'study, observation and experience [and] a more thorough insight into the character pourtrayed'. The section of the review in which he describes the effect of Iago's innuendoes on the Moor is interesting both as an example of Brooke's power to convey rapidly-changing emotions and Smith's total critical involvement:

> The first suspicion seemed to drop into his mind like the weighty and pregnant agent of a submarine explosion, scarcely leaving a ripple on the surface, and only indicating its descent by the emission of an

> occasional bubble, but anon the mine explodes, the deep is broken up and all is weltering tumult and commotion, where lately all was calm and sunshine. The conflicting power of opposite emotions, love, jealousy, the fondest tenderness and the most agonizing suspicions, expressed itself in the tone of the actor's voice and in every gesture of his countenance; and the self-disparaging reference to his own swarthiness of visage and seniority in years, was given with true pathos.[20]

This passage also illustrates the extent to which Smith was dependent upon earlier critics at this stage in his career. His views on the arousal of Othello's jealousy reflect those of Hazlitt, who had written, 'Not only is the tumult of passion heaved up from the very bottom of the soul, but every the slightest undulation of feeling is seen on the surface...' Hazlitt also describes 'the doubtful conflict between contrary passions...of love and hatred, tenderness and resentment, jealousy and remorse...'[21]

In spite of their mutual regard and his appreciation of the actor's ability at his best, Smith was aware of Brooke's failings:

> Did Brooke never rant? Did he never disappoint an audience? I answer, often. Whenever what I have called, for want of a better name, his inspiration deserted him, he would endeavour to make his physical energies compensate for the absence of the *Mens divinior*. It was like seeking illumination from an empty lanthorn. There were "the contortions of the sybil," but nothing more. Obedient to his genius, he was a wonderful actor. Temporarily estranged from it, he would roar like Bottom, the weaver.[22]

Brooke's acting deteriorated considerably after he left the Australian colonies. When Coppin arranged a return tour for 1866, Avonia Jones asked James and Eliza Smith to undertake friendly supervision of her husband because of her concern about his ability to satisfactorily complete the coming engagement.[23] But Brooke was not to be put to the test. His heroic actions in the shipwreck of the *London* commended him to his friends in Melbourne. At the same time, those who knew him best felt some measure of relief that there could be no further risk to a once-great reputation. As Smith wrote, in a letter to W. J. Lawrence in 1892: '...I feel that for Brooke's sake it was better that he should have died like a hero, than have come out to show the audiences who idolised him only the relics of his former greatness'.[24]

The visit of the American comic actor Joseph Jefferson in 1863 provided Smith with another opportunity for notable critical reviews. As had been the case with Brooke, Smith soon made friends with the actor, meeting him for supper after the theatre and inviting him to his home. In a retrospective diary entry about a late-1862 dinner party, Smith gave his impressions of Jefferson off stage:

> Joseph Jefferson about 36; slight & consumptive, with a small, sharp, eager face; forehead very prominent above eyes, soft brown

hair, Napoleonic chin, & a quick bright eye, full of expression. One of the most unassuming men, charming companions and most finished comedians I ever met with; an admirable mimic & a no less admirable story-teller; his Yankee stories being the best. Nothing of the actor about him off the stage; none of the professional envy & jealousy; fond of hunting, fishing and sketching.

Jefferson had opened in the role of Rip Van Winkle on 31 March 1862. His was a revolutionary method of action. In a departure from the stylised mode in which actor and audience were constantly aware of the other's presence, he believed in an illusion of naturalism that was conveyed by art. As he presented the play in Melbourne, *Rip Van Winkle* was an adaption of actor Charles Burke's dramatic version of the old story of the Catskill villager who fell asleep for twenty years and awoke to find all about him had changed. Burke (who was Jefferson's half brother) had, in turn, refined and extended the work of earlier actors in the part. Jefferson collected three earlier versions of the play, all in two acts, which, by making the scene where Rip meets the ghosts of Hendrik Hudson and his crew into a separate act, he converted into three. When he left the colonies in March 1865, he took the play to Dion Boucicault in London for further alteration and revision. That version, and not the one used in Melbourne, was the one in which he opened at the London Adelphi on 4 September 1865 and which he continued to use in subsequent performances in England and the United States of America.

Despite his usual conservatism, Smith was properly appreciative of Jefferson's innovative style, describing it has having 'a finish and completeness about it which denote great artistic culture as well as innate ability'.[25] He wrote several perceptive reviews of *Rip Van Winkle* during the Melbourne season of the play. Then, in 1878, with these reviews as a basis, he made a comprehensive analysis of Jefferson's interpretation of the character as part of his 'Theatrical Reminiscences'. There, using an analogy of painting, Smith compared the effect of Jefferson's acting with that of one of Meissonier's pictures: 'It depended for its effect upon conscientious accuracy of drawing, minuteness of touch, nicely discriminated gradations of tint, a masterly balance of light and shade, a Flemish fineness of finish, and a perfect harmony of colour'.[26] He comments at greater length than was possible in the reviews, on every aspect of Jefferson's representation of the Dutchman, from the 'humour and tenderness' and the 'childlike gaiety' with which he had invested the character in the first and second acts, to the manner of his 'half-timid, half-audacious, and altogether propitiatory management of his shrewish wife', the 'careful study' or perhaps 'an intuitive perception of the phenomena of drunkenness' that informs the scene of the signing of the marriage contract, and the natural and sympathetic communication of pathos in the last act. He gives the following illustration of the effect of Jefferson's impersonation of the bewildered old man of the last act:

The drama, the opera and the fine arts

> To illustrate the naturalness of Mr. Jefferson's acting, it is worthy of mention that one night when a villager struck the representative of Rip sharply on the shoulder with the palm of his hand, I heard a person in the pit cry out "Shame!" with undissembled anger and generous indignation. To him, as to hundreds of other spectators, the actor had disappeared. Rip Van Winkle, in his forlorn old age, tattered garments, and pitiable decrepitude, stood there in his place—with a mute wonder looking from his dim eyes—a gesture of sorrowful inquiry conveyed by his outstretched hands; a sense of loss, loneliness, mystery, and mournfulness weighing on his distracted mind; and a feeling of hopeless perplexity clouding his perception of things present, and confusing his memory of things past.

Here Smith reinforces the accuracy of his first impressions of Jefferson's methods, in perceptive appreciation of the comic, yet equally pathetic, style that was the result of artistic effort applied to proven skill. Jefferson's portrayal of Rip Van Winkle was to become the definitive one, attracting enthusiastic audiences wherever it was presented.

So far as is known, Smith had no formal musical training. When the Lyster Opera Company began presenting Italian opera in Melbourne in the early 1860s, he treated the productions in much the same way as he did the drama, with the added dimension of music. There had been previous opera seasons, but none to equal those produced by the American entrepreneur William Saurin Lyster. In 1888, Smith recalled Lyster's colonial career:

> [The] institution [of opera in Australia] as a permanent source of enjoyment was due to the enterprise of Mr. F. S. Lyster,[27] an Irish American gentleman who came hither from California about five and twenty years ago, bringing with him a well-organized and remarkably efficient company, together with a skilful conductor, for the performance of grand opera. He produced the masterpieces of Meyerbeer, Mozart, Rossini, Donizetti, Bellini, Gounod, Flotow, Verdi, Auber, Balfe, Weber, and other composers upon the boards of the principal theatres in Australasia, with a completeness which may have been subsequently equalled, but has certainly not been surpassed; and he contributed in no unimportant degree to raise the taste of the play-going public in many instances, to educate it in some, and to provide an intellectual form of entertainment for all.[28]

The Lyster Opera Company opened at the Theatre Royal on 25 March 1861, in the first of a series of opera seasons that included, among others, Donizetti's *Lucia di Lammermoor*, Wallace's *Maritana* and *Lurline*, Bellini's *Norma* and *La Sonnambula* and Verdi's *La Traviata* and *Il Trovatore*. Lyster continued producing operas with other companies at intervals until his retirement in 1879.

Les Huguenots was the company's most ambitious production. Lyster gave a detailed account of the thoroughness of his arrangements in a lengthy *Argus* advertisement. As he explained to his prospective audience:

> The Director, in placing this great work upon the Australian stage, has undertaken a task of no ordinary difficulty. To collect and organize an orchestra and chorus of sufficient numerical strength and ability to enable him to produce this grand opera in a manner worthy of the genius of its great composer, has been his ambition ever since he arrived at the conclusion that there was sufficient musical taste in this country to appreciate the higher order of music. This opera has been in preparation for more than six months, and has cost the management in its production £1200 more than the regular expenses of the opera season. The orchestra will be increased by all the instrumental talent obtainable in the colony. The chorus numbering over 50 voices, has been carefully drilled, and will far exceed anything in the choral department ever attempted.[29]

The 'historical accuracy' of the scenery, the 'superb' stage property and the 'elaborate' machinery were added factors of attraction in a production that promised to be the biggest and the best to be seen.

Lyster's emphasis on the scale of the production and its cost was an obvious attempt to impress colonial opera-goers who had yet to experience anything of the kind. His flattering appeal to their intelligence was also a clever device to help ensure full houses for each performance in what was, undoubtedly, the company's most ambitious venture to date. This advance publicity appears to have had the hoped-for effect: when *Les Huguenots* opened on 15 November 1862, the Theatre Royal was 'crowded to excess, from pit to gallery one mass of faces'.[30] The opera ran for another 25 performances, nineteen of them consecutive, before the end of the season on 31 January 1863.

The *Argus* review of the first performance is attributable to Smith on the grounds of tone and style. It begins with the story of the opera, act by act, and continues with an account of the life and work of the composer. The criticism opens with an enthusiastic assessment of the production:

> High as expectation had been raised, and exacting and critical as the audience were, the result far surpassed the most sanguine anticipation. The execution, the smoothness, the finish, rendered it almost impossible to believe that this was a first performance.[31]

Smith goes on to review the work of each of the principals, following Henry Squires and Lucy Escott through their performances as Raoul and Valentine. He also comments on the acting and singing ability of the other members of the cast as well as the quality of performance shown by the chorus and orchestra.

Sixteen reviews of *Les Huguenots* appeared in the *Argus* during the season. It is unlikely that Smith wrote them all, although it might be expected that other *Argus* writers would consistently reflect his known attitudes. There is no sign in these reviews of a lessening in interest caused by repeated professional exposure. In each one, Smith (or his associates) found something to say about variations in the quality of individual performances.[32] Lucy Escott's acting and singing inspired constant praise, except on one occasion, when, 'evidently fatigued, she appeared to dread the exertion of the by-play, and considerable portions of the opera were omitted'. Henry Squires was also not always at his best: 'At times Mr. Squires seems to lack a little animation, not that he has not got it in him; he has established the contrary to demonstration, but he appears to be occasionally somewhat listless'. Similarly, with the minor parts, Wharton became 'much more successful as an actor lately than when he first appeared'. In those reviews that are more obviously his, Smith displays a growing confidence in his own judgment that was the result of experience gained as a colonial critic. He was, by now, well on the way to acquiring the reputation he sought as a knowledgeable writer on the theatre and each new major season provided the opportunity for further consolidation.

There was to be a break in Smith's work as a drama critic during his initial preoccupation with spiritualist belief. Adelaide Ristori's visit to Melbourne in 1875 was the means of renewal. Ristori was a member of the Italian Dramatic Company, brought out by Lyster for a season at the Opera House. A great tragic actress, Ristori took leading parts in plays that included *Medea, Elizabeth, Queen of England, Mary Stuart, Judith, Lucretia Borgia* and *Marie Antoinette*. Although, as might be expected, these plays were presented in Italian, the management provided bilingual texts for the assistance of a mainly English-speaking audience. The writer of an *Argus* article on Ristori's life and career, which, in style and arrangement of content, appears to have been Smith's work, promised that the use of a foreign language would provide no difficulty in communication: 'the experience of all who have seen Madame Ristori is to the effect that her acting is so inspired that her face and gestures are amply sufficient to convey her meaning'.[33]

Ristori's performance as Marie Antoinette was outstanding among many notable appearances during the season. The play by Giacometti, 'written expressly for and by request of Madame Ristori',[34] consisted of a prologue, five acts and an epilogue, in which the domestic and political aspects of the French Queen's life are presented in settings such as Versailles, the Tuilleries, the Prison of the Temple and the Conciergerie. The wider issues raised by the French Revolution appear to have had no place. As described by theatre historian Henry Knepler:

> It portrays nothing but the slow decline of the Queen who rises in fortitude and magnanimity with each downward step forced upon her by her persecutors. She is not the frivolous queen of the Trianon, but an anxious, responsible wife and mother, a strong argument in favour of conservatism and the *ancien regime*. The play is not a study of conflicts, but a set of effective scenes of pathos, in which an almost endless series of farewells provided ample employment for the handkerchief trade.[35]

Knepler's is, of course, a twentieth-century view. For audiences of the Victorian era, accustomed to the display of extremes of emotion on the stage, as well as the practice of writing plays designed to demonstrate the particular skills of leading actors and actresses, *Marie Antoinette* was an appropriate vehicle for a virtuoso performance in the Italian style.

While it is not possible to identify the *Argus* critic of the play with certainty because of the absence of corroborative material, it is reasonable to assume that it was Smith, not only for the tone and style, but also because of his knowledge of the Italian language and culture. That he was also interested in the personality of Marie Antoinette is evident from his lectures and articles on the subject. As demonstrated by the concluding paragraph of his *Victorian Review* article 'Marie Antoinette', his attitude was consistently sympathetic and his admiration for Marie Antoinette—the epitome of 'all that is highest and purest, truest and best in womanhood',[36] unqualified:

> As long as divine pity is capable of finding an entrance to the human heart, and the spectacle of a noble nature sustaining a sublime conflict with unparalleled sufferings can move us to love and sympathy, so long shall we continue to find a fascinating interest, a source of elevating and purifying emotion, and a lofty example of the rarest virtue and the most exalted courage, in the life and character of Marie Antoinette.[37]

There is no hint of sympathy for the French people in their desperate struggle towards independence, nor is there any acknowledgment of the aristocratic excesses that had contributed to Marie Antoinette's plight. Always wary of democratic movements, especially those that had the potential for mob rule, Smith obviously preferred to take the side of an idealised nobility and use its suffering and ultimate fate as a means of moral edification.

Marie Antoinette had eleven performances in Melbourne, each of which was favourably reviewed. In the first of the *Argus* reviews, Smith discussed the production act by act, with particular attention to Ristori's interpretation of the leading role. He described her acting in the fifth act, where the Dauphin is removed from his mother, as 'more than a triumph', and continued:

> It was so striking in its manner that it stilled the audience. They held their breath in reverence for the great grief of the mother, whose woes had reached the very summit of human misery. Maternal agony never surely had so perfect exponent as she in this scene. It seemed to fill the whole scene; there was nothing but this majestic grief discernible. It was stupendous and yet exhausting in its completeness. And then, when in despair she finds that no protest, no entreaty, no passionate denunciation can move her persecutor, and she must really give up her child, and take a last leave of him, her dignity was grand in the truest sense.[38]

The drama, the opera and the fine arts

There is a further reference to this scene in the second review that, in itself, is an assessment of Ristori's performance as a whole:

> We have here power in its most subtle expression. It is the very exaltation of art. It typifies what is meant by art in its most perfect uses. It teaches of how much the drama is capable when rightly employed, and it makes us wish that all acting were like this.[39]

Obviously able to become fully immersed in the action, despite his usual critical detachment, Smith shows in these extracts a receptivity to the faithful performance of the great passions of the drama. He also uses the inspired acting of Ristori as the means for reinforcement of his concept of the theatre as a moral and educative force, provided both the play and its actors were devoted to the purpose.

While Smith approached all branches of the arts in a similar manner, he was especially emphatic when writing on the fine arts. In 1857, he opened his *Argus* leader on the need for the foundation of a National Gallery for Victoria with the following sentence: 'The value of the Fine Arts, as instruments of civilisation, moral teachers, means of intellectual culture, sources of enjoyment, and adjuncts of industrial enterprise, is now fully realized by the most enlightened nations of Europe'.[40]

Here Smith is echoing the convictions of John Ruskin, whose *Modern Painters* was then appearing in volume sequence. Smith was eventually to have the whole work in his private library, as well as *The Seven Lamps of Architecture*, published in 1849 and *The Stones of Venice*, published in sequence from 1851 to 1853. In each of these works, as well as in lectures, articles, treatises and other avenues of propagation, Ruskin expounded his ideas on the relationship between art and morality. One of these ideas that Smith found particularly appropriate to the colonial situation was the link between the art and architecture of a country and that country's national character. More specifically, in the Preface to the second edition of *Modern Painters*, Ruskin suggested that each generation of every nation might possess a gift peculiar to itself. Smith's actions as a cultural activist in an immigrant society illustrate his sense of the importance of his position in place and time, even though the activities in which he engaged and the organisations he supported were, for the most part, modifications of a national culture that was already established.

Smith believed, with Ruskin, that the best artists had the facility of communicating basic moral and religious truths through art. The mere depiction of a subject, however thoroughly carried out, was inadequate unless something more of universal relevance was conveyed to the viewer. This had a special application in the case of landscape, where, as Ruskin declared, 'nothing can be beautiful which is not true'.[41] Smith consistently applied the criterion of the indivisability of truth and beauty to his fine arts criticism, using it as a standard of authority that was further reinforced by his conviction of the fortunate possession of taste in art.

Ruskin defined perfect taste as 'the facility of receiving the greatest possible pleasure from those material sources which are attractive to our moral nature in its purity and perfection'.[42] Smith believed that his ability to assess a work of art and respond to its subtleties of meaning was largely dependent upon that facility. Writing in 1908, when his career as a critic was past, he described taste in art as

> ...an inborn faculty or natural instinct, which exists in certain minds independently of artistic training, and cannot be taught or implanted by it, and is only occasionally, and not invariably, to be found associated with it; that it is largely influenced in the direction it takes by the temperament, sympathies and emotional tendencies of its possessor; that it is capable of being matured, strengthened, refined, purified, elevated and perfected by close and continuous familiarity with the masterpieces of art in the great galleries of the world; and that it is incommunicable to, and impossible of being acquired by, those to whom it has been originally denied by nature.[43]

Taste is thus shown to be an innate quality that, by association, was possessed by a critical elite to which Smith was proud to belong. Taste in art might, of course, be extended to cover taste in any cultural activity, and, although Smith was referring specifically to the fine arts in the article from which this extract is taken, he was also reasserting his belief in the validity of his position as a colonial authority.

The Australian landscape presented problems of interpretation for artist and critic alike. It was different in contour and vegetation from any other that they had known and, especially when compared with the picturesque and well-peopled countryside to be found in many parts of England and Europe, its vast areas of emptiness could be overwhelming. As new districts were opened up by exploration, landscape artists followed, recording new scenes in faithful detail, often using large canvases in the attempt to convey as much as possible of the grandeur as well as the strangeness of the landscape. The intensity of artistic interest in the new land was linked with the desire to meet the challenge of depicting an unfamiliar landscape. It was also caused by the need to produce a likeness for English and European eyes, so that those who had remained in the old countries might better appreciate the peculiar natural characteristics of the new. But, because their paintings were important as visual records of immigrant experience, the early colonial artists were inclined to paint idealised pictures in which the attributes of new landscape were conveyed from a European point of veiw. By working in this way, they were also able to feel more certain of conveying accepted moral truths.

It was the critic's task to give literal expression to the moral force of nature that the artist had presented as well as to comment on the methods used to meet the desired objective. To some extent, their work was complementary: the artist was interpreting the landscape through his painting, while the critic was interpreting the validity of the artist's view. But individual reactions were not necessarily the same and an artist's depiction of a particular scene, however praiseworthy in a technical sense, might be found lacking by a critic with a different point of view. Smith's approach to the work of Eugene von Guerard was the result of a conflict of this kind. Von Guerard had arrived in the colony in 1852, along with many other immigrants attracted by the prospect of instant wealth. After two unsuccessful years on the goldfields, he reverted to his occupation as a landscape painter. An Austrian by birth, he had trained in Italy and also at the Dusseldorf Academy in Germany. His response to the Australian landscape was, in part, dependent upon the German Romantic tradition in which realism was charged with emotion. He was also influenced by the more straightforward realism of the Biedermeir School. In Australia, he produced large panoramic landscapes, rendering the details of topography and vegetation with careful precision while still attempting to capture a distinctive atmospheric effect. For the artist, these paintings were an almost religious expression of the elevating power of nature when properly interpreted. Smith disagreed, finding in von Guerard's work an interpretation of nature that was at fault because of the artist's insistence on realism at the expense of spiritual values.

Lengthy descriptions of the subject-matter of the paintings usually formed the opening paragraphs of Smith's reviews. Writing in the *Examiner* in May 1860, he began his assessment of von Guerard's latest work, 'a transcript of a glorious forest scene in Illawarra, New South Wales', in this way:

> I like it better than any of its predecessors, for the subject is a happy one, and it is happily treated. We get into a new vegetation, and exchange the dingy greens and dirty browns with which we are painfully familiar in Victoria with a verdure as vivid and a foliage as luxuriant as those of old England. The scene is a forest clearing, and the time a summer afternoon. We stand upon the spur of a woody range, and look through an opening to a conical mountain (Kembla) rising in purple majesty beyond. Between it and the spectator are the densely-timbered flanks of the range on which he stands, touched goldenly by the westering sun. That winding bridle-path tempts you to trace its devious course, with the certainty of your eventually scaling an eminence from which you would command an outlook over a magnificent expanse of country; but there is enough in the objects immediately before you to arrest your attention and awaken admiration. Everything is new and strange. The cabbage-tree lifts its straight graceful plumage to the "caller air;" and the Bangalo palm, rivalling it in height, and excelling it in beauty, flings forth its exquisitely curved frondage with a haughty consciousness of its superb loveliness. The very parasites are touched with a weird fantastic grace, as though fashioned when nature was in a wayward,

as well as loving, mood. From the knots and boles of the forest giants jut out green antlers,—giant ferns assuming the exact similitude of a pair of elk's horns. What is that gorgeous blossom, that lurid apparition, which shines so luminously forth from amidst its dark environment of leaves? That is the "fire-tree", a blaze of glorious crimson, inconceivably rich, inconceivably effective in such a leafy neighbourhood... Underneath are pillared aisles, and dim arcades, and dark recesses; and high up, above the sunny summits of the palm and fig, flocks of cockatoos wing their careless flight and fleck the stainless blue with points of purest white.[44]

Here, as was his habit, Smith is responding to von Guerard's images of the natural landscape by writing about the paintings in a consciously literary style and an elevated tone. This, as he obviously believed, was the proper manner in which to communicate the impressions of an educated and idealistic observer. He was also acting as a direct interpreter of nature for the further benefit of his readers.

This review includes Smith's definition of the artistic function:

The true artist is he who, while faithfully reproducing the imagery of nature, selects that which inspires the mind with the most agreeable sensations, exhibits it at its best and most poetic aspect, and makes the form expressive of the sentiment of which that form is but the outward and visible sign.

In this he found von Guerard lacking. However faithful the components, the whole gave cause for adverse criticism:

His interpretation is faithful to a fault. He stands in such reverential awe of nature that he seems to be restrained from anything like a free translation much less a paraphrase—of the lessons which she teaches him. He is, it must be confessed, more intent upon conveying the form than the spirit; the symbol than the thing signified.

For Smith, with his strong belief in the essential beauty of the fine arts, the spirit of significance of the work was more important as communication between artist and viewer than the accurate depiction of natural scenery. Although in 1870, von Guerard became first master of painting at the National Gallery School of Art and curator of the National Gallery of Victoria, Smith remained adversely critical of his work, seemingly unable to appreciate that an opposing point of view might be an equally acceptable means of striving towards a similar goal.

He was especially critical in an *Argus* review of von Guerard's painting of a view of the Grampians in the western district of Victoria. Apart from some hardness in the colour, he had little to complain of in the technical quality of the picture. But, using dictums taken from Ruskin in support of his views, he accused the artist of failing to properly appreciate the sublime grandeur of the mountain range. Von Guerard, evidently upset at what appeared to be Smith's consistent misunderstanding of his approach to the natural beauty of the Australian scene, wrote a letter to the editor of the *Argus*, in which he justified his method of imitating nature, 'not only in the masses but also in the details'.[45] He claimed to have been 'inspired to the highest extent' by the landscape in question and suggested that paintings that could be used as illustrations of the botanical and geological features of the colony might be of higher value than those that were less distinctively Australian in subject.

Von Guerard's reply to Smith's criticism was not published in the *Argus*. It may have been omitted because the artist had difficulty in expressing himself clearly in English. It is possible that Smith himself had a hand in preventing the publication of a letter that could lead to the discussion of his qualifications as a fine art critic, or, as von Guerard put it, 'where he accumulated all his treasures of critic knowledge'. Smith's tone throughout the review was obviously that of one who, though a lay critic, considered himself superior to the artist. The important issue was one of selectivity: the artist must select the best things to paint and paint them in an inspiring manner; if he failed to do this according to the critic's design, he was a bad artist. There was another factor in the argument that could have influenced Smith in his dogmatic judgment. Von Guerard had been appointed to the National Gallery positions ahead of Louis Buvelot, whose work Smith admired. As one of the founders of the Gallery, Smith could expect to have his views considered when important appointments were being made. His refusal to allow the equal validity of von Guerard's approach to the interpretation of nature may have stemmed, at least to some extent, from the need to reconfirm the value of his own opinions.

Buvelot had arrived in Melbourne in 1865. A Swiss artist who had studied in Lausanne and Paris, he possessed the artistic qualities that Smith held most important. As Smith was to comment retrospectively, Buvelot was 'both a realist and an idealist',[46] capturing the 'distinctive characteristics of Australian foliage', while elevating his themes by a treatment that was 'at once poetical and realistic'.[47] His work had links with the French Barbizon School in its movement away from conventionally arranged scenes towards more naturalistic impressions. Unlike von Guerard, who had followed the pioneers into practically untouched bush, Buvelot painted scenes on the fringes of the settled areas. While his approach remained under the influence of his European background, he was sympathetic to the Australian bush in a way that von Guerard was not. Because of this affinity with the landscape, he was able to capture something of the colonial vision that combined a nationalistic sentiment with the growing awareness of a unique local beauty.

Smith assessed Buvelot's '[Road] near Fernshaw' for the *Australasian Sketcher* in November 1873. As usual, he opened his review with a long and detailed description of the work, written in deliberately poetic language. In doing so, he was further demonstrating his perception of the role of the critic as being similar to that of the artist in the proper interpretation of nature. Buvelot, he believed, was able to stimulate an appreciative response because of his particular skills:

> He combines the two great requisites of a *paysagiste*—the seeing eye and the facile hand. He instinctly discerns the most poetical aspect of a landscape, seizes upon it at the very moment when the position of the sun or the drift and shadow of a fugitive cloud are found to be productive of the most picturesque effects of light and shade, and fixes the transitory scene upon his canvas with an apparently careless freedom, which is, in reality, the result of a mastery of the *technique* of his art. He seems to be conscious that the function of a landscape painter is not to copy, but to interpret nature.[48]

Obviously, Smith thought Buvelot an imaginative artist, one who 'saw more than the ordinary observer could'.[49] This critical opinion was justified by popular appreciation of Buvelot's work. The artist chose scenes that might also be familiar to his viewers. Places such as Fernshaw, in the Dandenong Ranges east of Melbourne, were accessible to artist and excursionist alike and Buvelot's paintings could be recognised by others besides the artists attracted to the district by the picturesqueness of the scenery. But, although Buvelot succeeded in portraying the Australian landscape more accurately than any earlier colonial artist, he conveyed his impressions through a traditional approach to the art of landscape painting. He was a pioneer of 'plein air' painting in Australia and because of this, as well as his individual style, he might be described as a forerunner of Australian impressionism. However, he was not in any sense an experimental painter of the kind that inspired the later Australian impressionists, whose work would provoke Smith's angry disapproval.

8
LITERARY CONTROVERSIES

The public discussion of literary topics was a popular activity among the Victorians. Matters such as authorial identity or intention were the subject of lectures, followed by debates, or, in the hope of attracting a wider audience, through correspondence in the form of letters to the editors of newspapers. Other topics were also discussed in this manner, but, perhaps because the answers to questions relating to the interpretation of literature were often inconclusive, controversies of that kind attracted particular attention. The immigrants carried the tradition with them, using the platform and the press as vehicles for civilised arguments. Literary controversies in Melbourne, as elsewhere, were usually conducted in a gentlemanly fashion. There were, however, occasions when one or other of the participants took the opportunity of using personal innuendo in the course of refuting opposing opinion.

Smith was at the centre of the Hamlet controversy, which was conducted through the columns of the *Argus* in 1867. The question of the reality of Hamlet's madness arose after the arrival in Melbourne of Walter Montgomery and James Anderson, actors of a widely divergent style. The *Argus* published a special leader on the coming Shakespearean season, together with an introductory article about Montgomery and his acting methods. Smith appears to have been the writer; the leader includes a section on the moral and educational value of the theatre that reflects his known views. There is also a paragraph in the article that indicates his reservations as to the validity of Montgomery's interpretation of Hamlet:

> That Mr. Montgomery's Hamlet will be a production of a kind quite new to the colonial stage cannot be doubted. He has grafted, it is alleged, all the best innovations of the new school upon the traditional experiences of the old, and, while trusting to his own judgment for the rendering of many lines, has profited by the established rules and acknowledged standard of dramatic impersonation to preserve all the excellences of the old style, while discarding much that is incongruous and ungraceful. Whether such a reading of the character is suited to the taste of the Melbourne public tonight will decide.[1]

Anderson had played Hamlet at the Haymarket on 13 July. Since two productions of the same play were running concurrently in Melbourne, rivalry was inevitable. At the same time, comparisons between the methods of the actors who played the leading role were to provide a stimulus for lively discussion.

The role of Hamlet was an important one for the tragedian. Most critics had their own views on the way in which it should be played and any interpretation that moved away from the traditional one was certain to be the subject of comment. Anderson's reading was conservative. According to the *Argus* critic, it was 'not among those in which his most considerable success has been achieved'. This critic continued:

> His Hamlet is as far as possible from the ideal Hamlet which every genuine student of Shakespeare pictures to himself; but it is a tolerably good example of that artificial, though certainly unnatural, Hamlet to which your average playgoer is most accustomed, and which, probably, he believes in the main to be as near an approach to the true embodiment as the art of acting can bring about... The Hamlet of Shakespeare is dreamy, philosophic, fitful, uncertain of purpose, passionate and yet moody, impulsive and yet melancholy. The Hamlet of Mr. Anderson is a robust individual of naturally jocund proclivities whose assumed air of tristfulness is carried to an almost ludicrous excess, and produces in the mind of the thinking spectator an effect the reverse of what is intended.[2]

Obviously, Anderson's Hamlet was far from perfect. It must have seemed even less so in comparison with Montgomery's modern approach to the part. The *Argus* critic, who, on this occasion may be identified as J. E. Neild because of the similarity between this review and the one he wrote as 'Jaques' for the *Australasian* on 27 July, was enthusiastic about Montgomery's style of acting. He described it as being

> ...so new, so fresh, so pre-eminently natural, so remarkably free from that forced unreality of what is commonly understood as the traditional style that it occasions in the mind a curious blending of surprise and delight... It requires no knowledge of Shakspeare, and none of dramatic art, to understand Mr. Montgomery, but at the same time, to the Shakspearian student, and to him who can comprehend the wonderful skill necessary to the perfect interpretation of a purely poetic drama, his acting is delightful by its exact conformity to the conditions necessary to give effect to dramatic creations.[3]

More important than Neild's enthusiasm for the style, in the light of the controversy that was to follow, was his appreciation of Montgomery's conception of the character of Hamlet and his approval of the actor's presentation of the assumption of madness, in a theory of interpretation that, according to Neild, was one 'which the mass of argument most chiefly favours'.

Smith's opposing views were published in a letter to the editor of the *Argus*. He opened his discussion of Montgomery's Hamlet with a perceptive appreciation of the individualistic representation:

> Let me premise that every Hamlet of note I have ever seen has been largely affected by, if it has not faithfully reflected, the temperament of the actor. Mr. Montgomery's Hamlet is no exception to the rule. It is essentially lymphatic. The portrait he presents to us is that of an amiable, affectionate, self-indulgent, plaintive, and somewhat lachrymose Prince. He brings out in strong relief the vacillating, wayward, irresolute and half-hearted traits in Hamlet's character. He shows him to be as unstable as water, as variable as the clouds, as inconstant as the moon. His melancholy is not so deeply seated as to render him incapable of fugitive moods of cheerfulness. He can be diverted from his purpose by trivial incidents, and find a pretext for procrastination in dreamy reveries. His grief is the indulgence of a weak mind, and not an influential principle of action operating upon a strong one.[4]

Obviously, Smith gave Montgomery due credit for his original conception of the character. However, he disagreed, both on textual and traditional grounds, with Montgomery's portrayal of assumed madness:

> Mr. Montgomery's is an eminently agreeable Hamlet. It is most effective where other representatives of the character have been least so; and it is defectively unimpressive in those scenes—the interview with the Ghost, and the closet scene, for example—in which previous actors, and Mr. Anderson especially so, have made their strongest points, and produced their most powerful impressions. In both these instances, Mr. Montgomery presents us with a striking picture of mental abstraction when, as I think, it should be one of mental absorption. His mood of mind is subjective, when it should be objective. He is occupied with his own meditations when every nerve might be supposed to be strung to the highest tension, and every faculty wholly engrossed by the awful apparition, the hour, the place, and the astounding nature of the revelation made to him by the "dread corse." This much is obvious from the text; and it derives additional sanction from the traditions of the stage...

In support of his firm belief in Hamlet's madness, as displayed in an 'extravagance of conduct and language', Smith referred to other authorities, including J. C. Bucknill (the second edition of whose *Mad Folk of Shakespeare* had just appeared in London) and the critics Coleridge and Villemain.

His letter provoked a literary and dramatic controversy in the form of a series of letters to the editor of the *Argus* from Shakespearean scholars and theatregoers. The first, from 'John Brown', appeared on 31 July, and the second, from 'Thomas Jones' on 1 August. Smith replied in his own name, which, in fact, was as plain as those adopted by his fellow correspondents, on 1 August. Other letters followed, from 'Jack Robinson', Richard Birnie (writing under his own name), 'Jack Robinson, junior', and 'John Robinson', on 3 August. Smith replied on 1 and 6 August. A letter to the *Age* on the same topic, signed 'R. H. H.' was also published on 6 August. This collection of correspondence was republished in Melbourne in 1867 as *The Hamlet Controversy. Was Hamlet Mad? or, the Lucubrations of Messrs. Smith, Brown, Jones and Robinson*, edited by F. W. Haddon, editor of the *Argus*. Haddon made some minor alterations, omitting the second of Smith's letters as well as that of 'A.M.', published on 1 August, and those of Richard Birnie and 'John Robinson'. He also revealed that the pseudonymous writers were J. E. Neild ('John Brown'), Charles Bright ('Thomas Jones'), Archibald Michie ('Jack Robinson'), David Blair ('Jack Robinson, junior') and R. H. Horne.

With the exception of Horne who, as a correspondent to the *Age*, was outside the series of letters written to the editor of the *Argus*, the participants in the controversy disagreed with Smith on the important question of Hamlet's madness. Neild (as 'John Brown') gave as his opinion, 'Hamlet's own declaration of his motive—namely that he simulates madness the better to compass his purpose—is by far the most reasonable estimate to entertain of his mental condition'.[5] Charles Bright (as 'Thomas Jones') found Montgomery's representation of madness, as assumed by 'a Hamlet perfectly sane and consistent with human nature', his 'surpassing merit'.[6] Michie (as 'Jack Robinson') defended Montgomery's right to depart from traditional interpretation when motivated by his own conviction as to the proper method of presenting the text.[7] Blair (as 'Jack Robinson, junior'), basing his authority on the fact that he had not seen either production and was therefore unbiased, refuted Smith's claim to support from the critics, citing among his opposing sources Hazlitt, Schlegel and Goethe.[8] Smith's theory of the reality of Hamlet's madness was further expounded in another letter, where he affirmed his belief that the madness was originally feigned but became an intermittent malady when latent insanity was provoked by adverse circumstances.[9] Horne's letter was largely an appreciation of Smith's point of view.[10] Most of the letters cover other aspects of Montgomery's acting, the excellence of which was less a matter of dispute than his interpretation.

While the Hamlet controversy is an interesting example of literate communication between educated theatregoers, the argument was necessarily inconclusive because the proponents of either point of view claimed acceptance through reliance upon a particular interpretation of the text. In the words of a writer for the English *Home News*, who was relieved to find that 'such debates are carried on with equal skill and intelligence' in the colonies, 'the main question of the real and assumed madness of Hamlet [was] left pretty much where it was found'.[11] However, the outcome of the controversy was less important than the reasons for its having taken place. There had been an appreciative audience in Melbourne for previous Shakespearean seasons and the current revival provided the background for informed discussion. The controversy might have developed into an extension of the rivalry between the critics Smith and Neild if other interested correspondents had not been involved. But, despite the generally good-natured tone adopted by the participants, Smith's authority as a traditionalist was being challenged, especially by Neild, as the chief proponent of the validity of Montgomery's interpretation. The majority support of Neild's views is perhaps an indication that, in some respects, colonial cultural circles were becoming less firmly based on traditional values.

There had been a long-running feud between Smith and Neild, carried on mainly through the newspapers and periodicals for which they wrote. Although the two men had worked together on the *Age* and, later, the *Argus*, they were rival critics, with noticeably different approaches to the drama: both were concerned with the overall effect of performance, but, as was evident in the Hamlet controversy, Neild looked for innovative methods of stagecraft that might lead to better acting, while Smith preferred reliance on tradition. In many respects, each one's work was complementary to that of the other, since theatregoers might benefit, if they wished, from the provision of wider aspects of criticism than could have been gained by reading the work of one alone. However, professional jealousies had disrupted the close friendship that they had shared during the early years of immigrant life.

Derogatory remarks about each other's critical function became increasingly more acrimonious, until, in December 1862, Neild accused Smith of accepting bribes in return for favourable criticism. The actor in question was Joseph Jefferson, the American whose performances had attracted considerable attention following Smith's reviews. As Jefferson recalled his Melbourne tour: 'The audiences were numerous and fashionable, and the articles in the daily papers referring to our plays and acting was of the highest literary character; those in the "Argus," written by the accomplished critic James Smith, were models in style and strength.'[12] But it was these reviews that had given rise to a current rumour that Smith had been guilty of 'puffing-up' Jefferson for monetary gain. Neild had also appreciated Jefferson's performances, though apparently not to the same extent as Smith, who seems to have quickly realised that the American had the ability to become a great comic actor. Writing in the *Weekly Review*, Neild attacked Smith under the heading 'Theatrical Criticism to Order':

> Is it possible that critics, being also men, have like other men their price? Is there such a thing as a tariff of charges for current commentaries on theatrical matters? That popular dictum "they say" inclines to an affirmative in response to these queries; and it goes still further, and says that *the* critic of a journal, shall we say, the leading journal?—of this colony, does a very profitable business in this way. "They say," in fact, that the gentleman who does the theatrical criticism to order for the *Argus* journal, received some

little time ago, from a certain manager in this city, the handsome sum of one hundred pounds as a general retainer; the equivalent to be rendered in exchange for this honorarium, being the absolute and unconditional puffing of a "star" just then about to appear in the Victorian theatrical horizon.[13]

No names were given, but the implications were obvious and Smith could not afford to let them remain without challenge. Treating the matter as being too serious for refutation through the *Argus*, he sued David Blair, editor of the *Weekly Review*, for libel. The case did not go to court; Butler Cole Aspinall acted as an intermediary, with the result that Blair withdrew the charge on the evidence of letters from Aspinall, Smith, James Simmonds (the manager of the Princess's Theatre during Jefferson's engagement) and from Jefferson himself. These letters, in which the writers consistently denied any possibility of bribes having been given or received, were published in the *Weekly Review* on 7 February 1863, together with Blair's apology.

If the charge had been proven, Smith's career as a critic would have suffered, not only because of the suggestion that his good opinion could be bought, but also because of the likely effect on his veracity as an interpreter of moral and ethical values. Through his habit of mixing socially with the actors whose work he criticised, he became liable to flattery that may, on occasion, have led to more favourable reviews than otherwise. He was also in a position to provide valuable advance publicity and often did so. However, his determination to become a reputable critic would appear to have prevented him from taking the risk inherent in the acceptance of a large monetary bribe. When reminiscing about the theatre in later years, he took care to present himself as having been incorruptible, using an anecdote about the return of a roll of banknotes presented at the *Melbourne Punch* office by singer Anna Bishop for the purpose.[14] In the case of Joseph Jefferson, the actor's continued success provided reinforcement for the accuracy of Smith's early opinions.

Many years later, Smith remarked that he had never read 'any adverse criticism directed against him by his enemies'. His reason for this was that 'being of a sensitive disposition, he thought it better not to allow his equanimity to be disturbed'.[15] There may have been some truth in this statement. The habit of self-protection that he had adopted as a child remained an important facet of his personality. But, as is obvious from his response to Neild in *Melbourne Punch*, he was certainly aware of the continued campaign against him. Writing the letter, 'Punch to Punchinello', he adopted a tone of sorrow, rather than anger:

> ...I do feel unaffectedly sorry for, instead of angry with, him. I can imagine nothing more entitled to a tender consideration and a clement judgment than a jaundiced mind and a heart which evil passions have converted into a nest of snakes. I picture to myself the

irritable vanity, the wounded self-love, the morbid jealousy, the malicious envy, the perverse determination to refer pure actions to impure motives, the dishonourable suspicions, the morose malevolence, and the important and baffled truculence of the unfortunate individual who is a libeller by profession; and I can imagine nothing more terrible than his self-inflicted tortures.[16]

This was a clever reply, designed to distract attention from Neild's accusations by presenting Smith as an innocent and unfairly injured party, while also demonstrating gentlemanly restraint in the face of deliberate and perverted malice. But, as a means of preventing further attacks, it was a failure.

Neild attempted to discredit Smith in another way by accusing him of plagiarism. This was a charge less easily refuted than that of bribery. *Melbourne Punch*, like most nineteenth century periodicals, was compiled of a mixture of original and reprinted material. Much as colonial editors might wish to have an entirely original product, there was usually insufficient local material available to fill the pages of their journals. *Melbourne Punch* relied heavily on imported skits and jokes, or, as Neild described them, 'pilfered caricatures and stolen sarcasms',[17] as fillers. This reprinted material was sometimes acknowledged; more often, it was used casually without details of origin. Smith's newspaper work was also the subject of suspicion. In the *Weekly Review* article 'Manufactured Literature', Neild remarked that three-quarters of the drama and fine arts criticism in the *Argus* was taken from the work of other critics, while articles ostensibly written for that paper, as well as other local publications, were obviously reprints.[18] It could not be denied that Smith made considerable use of supporting opinion in order to add further interest to his topics. Whether or not he was actually a plagiarist in work of this kind is less certain; it is rare to find instances of lack of attribution. At the same time, Neild's charge had the effect, certainly unwanted, of underlining Smith's deficiencies as a creative writer.

Neild then accused Smith of accepting a 'consideration' for publicly promoting the Irish political elements in the colony. This charge arose out of the lecture 'On the Irish Character', which Smith delivered at St George's Hall on 17 December 1862.[19] The national and religious biases of the immigrants were naturally perpetuated in the colony and there was considerable prejudice towards the Irish Catholics amongst the predominantly British Protestant population. To the O'Shanassy ministry, then in power, prejudice such as this seemed especially inappropriate to its purpose of attempting to achieve stable government. Smith's lecture, in which he listed and described attractive attributes of the Irish character such as music, valour, wit and humour, was intended to counter anti-Irish feeling in the community. Charles (later Sir Charles) Gavan Duffy, a notable Irish immigrant who was Minister for Lands in the O'Shanassy government, was in the chair. Neild's attack on the occasion of Smith's appearance on the same platform was designed to incriminate Smith as a political turncoat for personal advantage. As Neild observed, Duffy and Smith seemed to be the best of friends:

> There was a very pretty rivalry as to which of them should say the politist things each to the other. Benevolent brotherhood seemed to beam from their several eyes, and the tender-hearted listeners were melted into sympathetic admiration as they witnessed this reconciliation.[20]

Using extracts from items published in *Melbourne Punch* during 1858 and 1859 in evidence, Neild demonstrated Smith's previous antagonism towards the Irish and to Duffy in particular. He concluded by describing the lecture as 'a burlesque in disguise', hinting that he knew more about the truth of the subject than he had revealed, which appears to have been a reference to Smith's impending appointment as Parliamentary Librarian.

The lecture was repeated on 16 January 1863, prompting a further *Weekly Review* article, in which Neild elaborated on his theme. He suggested that those who wished to appreciate the full significance of the contrast between Smith's present view of the Irish character and those expressed in *Melbourne Punch* should look also at the columns of the *Age* during Smith's employment on that newspaper. The lecture itself, Neild dismissed as being 'exactly what we should have expected from its compiler'. He continued:

> One half of it is in inverted commas, and the other half ought to be. It is borrowed partly, with acknowledgment, from various authors, and stolen, partly, without acknowledgment from various other authors. There is not, properly speaking, an original sentence in it.[21]

The old charge was thus aligned with the new. Smith, apparently deciding that discretion would prove the wisest course, made no public reply. Certainly, it would have been impolitic of him to provoke public comment over the circumstances of his entry into the public service. The repeated charge of plagiarism was one on which he was consistently to remain silent.

Neild was shortly to move to the *Herald*. There, for a while, he continued his attempts to disparage Smith. He maintained his antagonism over the following years, until, writing for *Humbug* in 1869, he made the last and most concentrated attack of the long campaign. This came in the form of the article 'Of Humbugs Generally', in particular, 'The Literary Humbug', in which Smith was placed in context as a prime example:

> It would be curious to inquire how the L. H. made his entry into literature. Was he a draper who had aspirations beyond tapes and cotton spools? or a shoemaker, like Samuel Drew, who wrote treatises on his lapstone; or a starveling schoolmaster, who thought

there was some other destiny for him than setting copies, and feruling stupid boys? or a clerk on eighty pounds a year, who yearned to write leading articles, and be a great moral power? or an ambitious printer, like Douglas Jerrold, but with none of Jerrold's genius? or did be begin life as a writer, and was he—say the editor of a small country newspaper—one of those newspapers that have a "poet's corner," and devote four columns to the chronicling of tea parties? Did he write pretty moral stories after the manner, but with none of the zest, of Miss Edgeworth? or was he great in the aesthetics of art, and compiled a book—say, about painters—which gave him the opportunity, when speaking of himself, to put after his name, "Author of 'Artists and Men, as Poets, and as Painters.'" Perhaps, in addition, he may have done some local thing about "Roman Remains," and so got for himself the credit of knowing something about archaeology. At any rate, supposing the last surmise to be the truth, when he left the old country for this new country, he brought with him, in all probability, a reputation. Nobody could say exactly why he possessed the reputation, for, though books had been written of which he was presumedly the author, nobody ever met anybody else who had read the books.[22]

Neild continued in a similarly satirical vein, demolishing Smith's carefully built up reputation by describing him as 'a delightful charlatan' who took credit for work that was not his own, and 'a brilliant journalist' who nevertheless had been responsible for several failed literary ventures. Worst of all, Neild dismissed his quarry as a swindler, one who had 'lived on pretence for the greater part of his life'.

Smith was then editor of the rival *Touchstone* and, as such, a legitimate subject for satire. But this article was obviously motivated by personal animosity and, in allowing its publication, Marcus Clarke was departing from his editorial objective of presenting *Humbug* as 'an impartial Satirist...closed alike to private malice or private interest'.[23] Smith made no public reply, perhaps thinking it undignified to respond in self-defence, especially when the result may have been a reaffirmation of some of the points that Neild was trying to make. The most serious feature of the article was its reliance on near truths. Smith did have faults of pretension; his work owed much to the skill of synthesis and it was a fact that his editorial ventures in the colony had often been short lived. It was also obvious that he sought, indeed seemed at times to crave, recognition as a public figure. However, since he held similar views to those of Neild on the promotion of culture as a necessary factor in colonial development, the feud between the two of them appears to have succeeded only in dissipating the energies that might have been combined in the pursuit of mutual objectives.

Quarrels of the kind were not uncommon among ambitious immigrants. Some were more trifling affairs; others like that between Neild and Smith lasted for years, with reconciliation seemingly unattainable. But, in their case, it was Neild himself who initiated the movement towards better understanding. Towards the end of December 1869, he wrote to Smith, apparently proposing an end to public disagreement. Both that letter and Smith's reply have been lost. Neild's second letter, preserved by Smith, was a further message of conciliation:

> Your letter gave me infinite pleasure, but at the same time suggested many regrets that for eleven years I have gone on misunderstanding you for lack of a little explanation. Be sure from this time I will believe nobody who shall try to make me believe other than that you think kindly of me. I anticipate many pleasures in the time to come from conferring with you on the various subjects respecting which I know we have similar tastes. Your reading and experience are far beyond mine, and I shall become your debtor for information concerning multitudes of things. I will endeavour to make up for the large loss I have suffered in these years of angry darkness, and I shall be glad to ask your advice whenever I lack the counsel of a friend. I fear you will find I have grown very irritable and uncompanionable but I will be as little so as possible. I thank you with all my heart for accepting my letter in the spirit in which I wrote it. Your reply has brought me sunshine & I trust there will never be darkness again.[24]

The long quarrel was thus ended; private visits to each other's homes were resumed and the disharmony that had marred their association appears to have been permanently overcome. The reasons for Neild's change of heart are unknown. Even though his letter to Smith is remarkable for the warmth of its tone, it is possible that, in addition to a genuine wish for reconciliation, he had become aware that Smith was about to be appointed editor of the *Australasian*, and wanted to preserve his own position as drama critic. He was, in any case, to assure Smith that he would be agreeable to continue working for the *Australasian* under the new editorship.[25]

Smith was to become involved in another literary controversy in 1881. The topic of Shakespeare vs. Bacon was initially one of general interest, but, as the argument continued, the focus altered until it developed into a personal attack on Smith. This controversy was stimulated by William Thomson's *On Renascence Drama*, published in Melbourne in 1880. Thomson, a physician with a particular interest in literature, believed that Shakespeare's plays were, in fact, written by Francis Bacon, a theory that appears to have originated in the United States of America and been the subject of discussion there and in Great Britain. Thomson's main argument is summarised in the following extract:

> In affirming that the various plays forming that grand body of dramatic literature were from time to time composed by Francis Bacon, for no commercial uses, nor ephemeral entertainment, but alone as opportune illustrations of a universal scheme of social and political philosophy, complete though never claimed, the preliminary query might be put by the incredulous thus: "Could Bacon alter his style, and adapt his phrase to suit the character of

any work to which he chose to direct his gigantic powers," which query the writer answers in the affirmative.[26]

In an elaboration of this theme, Thomson assessed the circumstances in which the plays might have been written, grouped them politically and discussed particular examples in what another Baconian enthusiast has described as 'an accumulation of fact and argument—rather than a presentation of the case already made'.[27]

On Renascence Drama provoked the article 'Was Bacon Shakespeare?' by Richard Colonna Close, which was published in the *Victorian Review*. Close considered that Thomson had 'shown no reason why Shakespeare should still not be considered the author of the plays', describing his proofs 'or rather self-assumed proofs' as 'meagre, far-fetched, strained and full of conceits'. He discussed and countered the various points raised by Thomson, agreeing, for instance, that Bacon had the poetic facility to write the plays, while arguing that this facility alone was no proof of authorship. He also conceded similarities of thought and expression in the works of each writer, yet found the differences 'more striking' than the similarities. In all, he remained completely unconvinced that Thomson had succeeded in proving that Bacon was Shakespeare. On the contrary, for Close, Thomson's success rested in strengthening his conviction 'that Shakespeare could not have been Bacon'.[28]

Smith's only acknowledged contribution to the controversy appeared in the *Argus* on 20 August 1881. There, in an article titled 'Shakspeare, not Bacon', he wrote about the 'Baconian craze' in general terms, without reference to Thomson's work. Smith had his own solution to the problem, citing sixteenth century sources as evidence for his assertion that 'the dramas were written by the same hand as the poems and sonnets'. His main proof of Shakespeare's authorship of the plays is based on a comparison of lines from the plays and sonnets in which the language indicates a common vocabulary. He lists words used in the same sense and gives examples of similar forms of vocabulary and expression. In conclusion, he dismisses the Baconians as 'modern crotchet-mongers' and 'wiseacres', adding, as his final sentence: 'I venture to think a more extravagant and irrational hypothesis was never propounded'.

Thomson replied to his critics with the pamphlets *William Shakespeare in Romance and Reality* and *Bacon, not Shakespeare*, both of which were published in Melbourne in 1881. The first of these pamphlets deals with the *Argus* review of the issue of the *Victorian Review* in which Close's article had appeared, as well as with the article itself. The *Argus* critic appears to have been James Smith: Thomson describes this 'Victorian reviewer' as a 'ripe Shakespearean scholar of the orthodox school and refined critic in art and letters, [who] writes pleasingly for popular reading'.[29] Apart from the introductory comment that Thomson's 'eccentric theory' had been subjected to 'some trenchant criticism, showing that the hypothesis has not a leg to stand upon, and that the gentleman's wish is father to his thought', the review had consisted largely of extracts from Close's article.[30] Thomson angrily assessed the content of this article as being 'the stolen ideas and pilfered phrase of a predatory critic',[31] an accusation of plagiarism on the part of Close that also carried the inference that Smith, as editor of the *Victorian Review*, should share the blame.

Thomson's *Bacon, not Shakespeare* was a rejoinder to Smith's *Argus* article 'Shakspeare, not Bacon'. Here Thomson is critical of Smith's reliance on external evidence in determining the authorship of the sonnets, although he does not deny that they came from the same source. He also discounts Smith's use of internal evidence in comparing Shakespeare with Shakespeare when according to his own belief, Shakespeare should be compared with Bacon. In support, he provides examples of similarities between Shakespeare and Bacon, countering Smith's list of common words and quotations. Thomson's reply is weakened by the fact that he was writing in personal affront as well as in defence of the Baconian theory. He takes Smith's derogatory allusions to the Baconians as referring to himself and says, 'It is I alone, indeed, who now stir up hostile contention'.[32] Some of this hostility was directly attributable to Smith's seeming unfamiliarity with Thomson's books and pamphlets. In response, Thomson, whose pursuit of literature was incidental to his profession as a medical practitioner and whose work, as self-described, was 'not meant to display knowledge, but only to divert',[33] referred to Smith, the working journalist, in the following terms: 'Nobly censorious, he is with every term of ordinary logic and with every canon of regulated criticism grandly supercilious, in arguing a very Malvolio at recreation'.[34]

Smith made no public response to Thomson's pamphlet and there the matter may have rested if it had not been for the publication of two anonymous articles in the *Age*, in which he was accused of plagiarism. The first article, 'Shakspeare, not Bacon', was published on 22 February 1882, the date of Smith's departure for England and Europe. After giving a short account of Smith's *Argus* article of the same title, the writer introduced the question of plagiarism. As evidence, he cited the American Charles Stearns, whose *Shakespeare Treasury of Wisdom and Knowledge* had been published in New York in 1869. In the chapter 'Did William Shakespeare Write Shakespeare's Plays?', Stearns gives a large number of parallel examples from the plays and the poetry. The *Age* writer says Stearns gives 94 instances of similarities and Smith 60, while, in fact, Smith gives 82. The actual number is, of course, less important than the charge that Smith's examples were the same as those of Stearns. The *Age* writer gives seven of these parallel examples. He also finds a similarity of argument, illustrated by extracts from both sources.

An *Argus* leader in reply to the *Age* article was published the following day. The writer, who had been unable to contact Smith at sea by telegraph or to obtain a copy of Stearns's book in Melbourne, reserved judgment as to the truth of the charge of plagiarism. He was, however, indignant at the timing of the accusation:

> We appeal to all lovers of fair play—to every right-thinking and fair-dealing man in the community—whether such a proceeding as this may not fairly be characterised as dastardly. Mr. Smith is a public man. He is a trustee of the Public Library; he was a commissioner of the late International Exhibition; he is one of the Victorian representatives to the Bordeaux Exhibition; and he is one of the oldest and most eminent of Australian journalists. On public grounds, therefore, as well as a matter of simple justice between man and man, Mr. Smith ought to have been afforded every opportunity to meet and answer the charge which has been brought against him. That he has not been afforded this opportunity is not only a reflection on the manliness and good feeling of his accusers, but it throws a shade of suspicion on the accusation itself.[35]

Smith's status as a respectable colonial figure is confirmed by the tone of this article as well as the evidence it provides. However, even though the timing of the charges may have been as unfair as his colleague concluded, the fact remained that, in themselves, they were a serious reflection on Smith's integrity.

The *Age* writer renewed his attack with 'Stearns, not Smith', published on 24 February. He explained that he had obtained a copy of Stearns's book only the day before the publication of his first article, making the timing coincidental. He adds further evidence, by means of extracts, that Smith, in 'Shakspeare, not Bacon', intended to convey the impression that the comparison of Shakespeare with Shakespeare, rather than Shakespeare with Bacon, as had been the custom with Baconian enthusiasts, was an original idea. An additional extract from Stearns proved that the two men were writing along parallel lines. The *Age* writer evidently expected some response from Smith. As he wrote in conclusion:

> It is unfortunate that he should not be on the spot to defend himself from the charge; but if none of his admirers can offer any defence for him we have no doubt the public will be good-natured enough to suspend judgment till he states his case in reply.

But, once again, Smith appears to have decided that silence was the wisest course for him to take. Since he intended to be away from the colony for twelve months, the issue could be expected to lose impact.

Considering the similarity of their approach to the topic, it is probable that Smith was familiar with Stearns's work, although there is no record of its inclusion in his private library,[36] nor was it held by the Melbourne Public Library or the Parliamentary Library. A careful comparison of Smith's article and Stearns's chapter provides sufficient evidence to suggest that the use of parallel examples was coincidental rather than deliberate: out of the total of 94 examples given by Stearns and 82 by Smith, 7 are the same and 4 are similar; the rest are different. A careless mistake in transcription by Smith adds further weight in defence. In the example 'Man have marble, women waxen minds. In women's waxen hearts to set', Smith attributed the second line to *The Merry Wives of Windsor* iv,4. But he was wrong: that reference reads 'With rounds of waxen tapers on their heads'; his example comes from *Twelfth Night* ii,2. The coincidental use of 'waxen' indicates that he, as well as Stearns, was using a concordance, thus allowing both similarities and differences in their choice of examples. Smith had access to the relevant reference material in his private library, including Alexander Schmidt's *Shakespeare Lexicon* and Mrs Cowden-Clarke's *The Complete Concordance to Shakespere*.

The identity of the *Age* writer is uncertain. J. J. Shillinglaw kept a cutting of the second article, writing at the end, 'By Marcus Clarke'.[37] He must have been mistaken: Clarke died on 2 August 1881, before the publication of Smith's 'Shakspeare, not Bacon', let alone the *Age* article. William Thomson is not a contender, appearing as a third party in the pamphlet *The Political Allegories in the Renascence Drama of Francis Bacon*, published in 1882. Here Thomson, referring to the similarities between the work of Smith and Stearns, describes Smith (though not by name) as 'a slavish copier' and the *Age* writer as 'that adapter's vengeful accuser'.[38] It seems most likely that the *Age* articles were written by David Blair, a determined proponent of the Baconian theory who had also been responsible for the publication of charges of plagiarism against Smith while editor of the *Weekly Review*. However, the identity of the writer of the *Age* articles is less important than the fact that the main subject of the controversy was an issue that had been discussed at length in past years. There were still a few enthusiasts, such as Thomson and Blair, in the colony, but, unlike the Hamlet controversy, where the participants were motivated by current productions, the matter had little local or topical relevance.

Smith made an attempt to revive another outdated literary controversy with his last book, *Junius Unveiled*, published in 1909. This was one of a number of works by various writers claiming to solve an eighteenth century mystery. Smith believed that he had discovered the identity of 'Junius', a self-appointed political censor, who, with personal invective allied to shrewd and lucid argument, had attacked the King and the leaders of government in a series of letters that appeared in the *Public Advertiser* between 1769 and 1772. The writer was careful to conceal his identity, which caused much speculation. William Pitt, Sir Philip Francis and Lord Temple are prominent among those whose names have been suggested, but, as with Smith's choice of Edward Gibbon, author of *The Decline and Fall of the Roman Empire*, the evidence seems inconclusive.[39] Smith refers in his introduction to the 'somewhat remarkable circumstances under which the clue to the authorship of the *Letters of Junius* came into [his] possession'.[40] These circumstances remained unexplained until after his death, when Annie Bright, then editor of the spiritualist journal *Harbinger of Light*, revealed that the clue to the identity of 'Junius' came from spiritual sources.[41]

Convinced that 'Junius' and Edward Gibbon were one and the same, Smith assembled supporting evidence based on personal attributes and literary style, finding that ' the proofs were already waiting to be seized upon and to be arranged and classified by whomsoever should be fortunate enough to obtain the necessary clue'.[42] He compares the life and career of 'Junius' with that of Gibbon and discusses the similarities that include military training, a knowledge and use of the French language, a friendship with John Wilkes, and common sources of information. He also gives several comparative examples of language and style. The manuscript was submitted to Sir John Madden, Chief Justice of Victoria and Sir Samuel Way, Chief Justice of South Australia, for comment. Their opinions were then included in an Appendix. Both justices admitted the value of the evidence as compiled. However, Way queried Smith's failure to compare the handwriting of 'Junius' and Gibbon, an omission that the author defended with the explanation that he believed it to be unnecessary on the ground that Gibbon would have employed an amanuensis as a safeguard against discovery.[43]

While the inspiration for the work was spiritual, the evidence in support of Smith's discovery was collected and displayed in a logical manner. He had been interested in the mystery for many years and the material on which he based his conclusions was readily available in his own library, including *Junius and His Works*, edited by J. Wade, together with Gibbon's *Decline and Fall* and his *Autobiography*, edited by J. Murray. *The Authorship of the Letters of Junius Elucidated* by John Britton is another work with which he was probably familiar. Though not, so far as can be ascertained, in his private library, it was reviewed in the *Salisbury and Winchester Journal* while Smith was editor.[44] Britton, a well known Wiltshire antiquary, makes a case for politician Isaac Barré as the writer of the letters on similar grounds to those used by Smith, including comparisons of character and career, knowledge of military affairs, familiarity with the French language and similarities of style and tone, as found in the writings. He also supports the concept of an amanuensis.

Smith was mistaken in believing that he was the first to uncover what John Wilkes described as 'the most important secret of our times'.[45] Despite his use of a similar title, Smith does not appear to have seen *Junius Unmasked*, an anonymous pamphlet published in London in 1819, in which the author also sets out to prove that Gibbon was the writer of the 'Junius' letters. Here, a list of attributes is set down, including race, education, financial circumstances, religious persuasion and political preference, among others observed in what was known of the figure of 'Junius'. Edward Gibbon is then methodically tested against each attribute and proved, to the writer's satisfaction, to be the same. The author makes uses of textual comparison and, like Smith and Britton, suggests the employment of an amanuensis. He omits, however, the important factor of a knowledge and the use of French, to which Smith devotes a whole chapter. The pamphlet, which consists of 44 pages, plus lists and tables, is less than half the length of Smith's book and, in all, a much lighter work.

Obviously, *Junius Unmasked* had been almost forgotten. In a favourable review of *Junius Unveiled*, the *Age* critic declared that Smith 'had given a new direction to the whole controversy'.[46] But it was a controversy that had lost impact, and, despite Smith's efforts to prove the ultimate identification of 'Junius', his work stimulated only a mild interest. There were other reasons besides a lack of topicality for the book's failure to arouse discussion. To some extent, *Junius Unveiled* was suspect because of its inspirational source, regardless of the logicality of its argument. However, even if this aspect of the work had been discounted, there were very few potential literary controversialists in Melbourne. Smith had outlived almost all of the immigrants with whom he might have discussed the question, and, by this time, literary controversies of the kind that he had once enjoyed were no longer in fashion.

9
SPIRITUALISM

Smith's colonial career may be divided into two parts: the first, dating from the time of his arrival until the early 1870s; and the second, which began at the end of that decade and continued into his old age. During the intervening years, he was increasingly distracted from many of his usual functions by an interest in spiritualism that developed into passionate involvement. He was drawn into spiritualist belief through his meetings with an elderly woman who had acquired some reputation as a gifted medium. Towards the end of 1870, he began visiting her at her home in Carlton, sceptical of her reputation but curious to see her mode of operation. Then, disturbed by the evidence she appeared to present, he returned to test his impressions until, convinced that the phenomena he had observed required serious consideration, he began spending regular afternoons with this medium in pursuit of spiritual communication. This was to become a consuming fascination that affected his capacity for rational thinking and caused the neglect of his career. At the height of his first enthusiasm, he wrote and lectured about little else. When his new-found beliefs settled into assured personal conviction, he was better able to separate his spiritualist activities from his other work. Meanwhile, his reputation suffered; he lost credibility both because of his conversion to spiritualist belief and the dismissal from the position of editor of the *Australasian* that was its consequence.

Many years later, Henry Gyles Turner described the circumstances of Smith's conversion and its immediate effects:

> His successful and promising career was brought to an untimely end by his falling under the influence of a spiritualist fanatic, a Mrs. Jackson, who by hypnotic control, and a clever pandering to his egotism brought him to the belief that he was an apostle, directly commissioned from above, to establish the Kingdom of God on earth, by means of the planchette, and other media, in touch with the next world.[1]

Turner's assessment of the excessive influence of Mrs. Jackson appears to have been correct, but his remarks concerning Smith's career are less accurate. Although Smith was obviously suffering from a lack of balance at this time, he was to do some of his best work as a journalist in future years. But his acceptance of spiritualist manifestation would direct his actions during much of the 1870s and his commitment as a proselytiser govern many aspects of his life.

Given his great respect for the written word, it is not altogether surprising that Smith should seek personal contact with the spirits of those authors whose work he found most appealing. It seems likely that, if this had been his whole purpose in adopting the practice of spiritual communication, his enthusiastic approach to the subject may have been viewed with tolerant acceptance by those of his fellows who appreciated his motives, while being unable to believe in the validity of such a practice themselves. However, as he became ever more immersed in what seemed to him to be the almost limitless possibilities of extended knowledge of the spirit world, he began to see himself as a divine instrument, someone who had been specially chosen as the mouthpiece for hitherto unrealised truths that it was now his duty to reveal to his less-favoured colleagues. Such an attitude was unlikely to endear him to many of the people who read his articles or listened to his lectures on the subject. His whole personality appears to have changed with his conversion. As Turner remarked at the time: 'those who remember Mr. Smith's genial lectures on social topics, would scarce recognise him in the bitter denunciation of his conventicle appearances'.[2] After his lectures, though previously so ready to prolong friendly discussion of the issues raised by his topics, Smith would slip away without a further word to his audiences. Always introspective, despite the gregarious aspects of his nature, he found no comfort in the society of those who refused to believe what he felt forced to say.

Smith had for many years been interested in the concept of the evolution and operation of the human mind. As a writer stimulated by the ideas that others had passed on to him, he was fascinated by the possibility of continuous intellectual activity. Reluctant to accept that death might be anything more than an interruption of that activity, he pursued his enquiries into the matter as the spiritualist movement developed in Melbourne in the late 1860s and early 1870s. Meetings of spiritualists and other interested people, both in the form of small groups and the foundation of larger societies, reflected the growth of interest in spiritualism in Europe, England and the United States of America. The basic beliefs of the movement, naturally attractive to Smith, were the continuity of mind and personality, as well as the possibility of spiritual communication, not only with loved ones, but also with the great minds of past generations. Communication was established in some circles through table tapping and the use of coded answers to specific questions. In others, a person in a receptive and often trance-like state became the medium through which the messages from the spirit world were transmitted. While the movement was initially considered to be perfectly respectable, it soon provoked sceptical cricitism from uninvolved observers. In reaction, converts attempted to apply scientific methods to the testing of psychic phenomena as the means of rationalisation of belief. Dissension over the existence of the movement and the nature of spiritualist belief caused divisions in literary, cultural and religious circles in Melbourne. As one of the most vocal exponents of the importance of spiritual communication and the implication for contemporary society of messages from the spirit world, Smith became the centre of public controversy over the validity of his new found and warmly cherished beliefs.

Not all of the converts were as immoderate. In fact, most of those who became involved in the movement approached spiritualism in a relatively rational manner. Smith's fellow journalist Charles Bright, whose conversion resulted from investigations made for the *Argus* in 1869, was able to combine spiritualist belief with profitable activity as a lecturer in Australia and the United States. W. H. Terry was another of the spiritualists to display more balance than Smith. Terry helped establish the Victorian Association of Progressive Spiritualists (later the Victorian Association of Spiritualists) in 1870, and, in that year also, he founded the spiritualist journal *Harbinger of Light*. Alfred Deakin was a prominent member of the Association before entering politics, acting as President and Secretary at different times during the 1870s, as well as conducting the Progressive Lyceum, a Sunday school for the children of members. Other activities in which Deakin was involved included arranging lectures by visiting specialists, investigating phenomena and attending seances.[3] Smith may have joined the Association initially. He was an occasional lecturer, but further active involvement seems unlikely because of the extremity of his views on spiritualist practice.

At first, while still exploring the possibility of spiritual communication, he was able to maintain a certain amount of scepticism, even though the probability of conversion must have increased in proportion to the extent of his involvement. It was at this stage of preoccupation that he joined the group of interested people that met weekly at the home of Dr James Motherwell to discuss spiritualist phenomena. Motherwell, a Collins Street physician, had gathered around him a circle of men who hoped, through discussion and the sharing of psychic experience, to come to a greater understanding of the movement. Dr Walter Lindesay Richardson, father of the novelist Henry Handel Richardson and first President of the Victorian Association of Spiritualists, was another member of this group, which consisted largely of professional men who were concerned with the apparent disparity between religious belief and scientific discovery. If Smith had restrained his activities to this sort of reasonable investigation, he might have been able to continue his career without censure. As it was, when he became more and more extremist in his views, he aroused antagonism among his fellows.

Continued experience of spiritualist involvement led Smith on to conversion and complete acceptance of spiritualism in its natural manifestations (as distinct from diabolism, sorcery and other sensational phenomena). His public affirmation of belief, made in a letter to the *Argus* published on 30 December 1871, stimulated a literary controversy in which the participants argued the case in a tone of gentlemanly-like enquiry. The following extract is taken from Smith's account of his conversion, as included in his opening letter:

> My attention was directed to [intelligent manifestations of spiritualism, or naturalism] some months since by the fact that many men for whose mental attainments I entertain the highest respect, whose veracity is unimpeachable, and whom I know to be unlikely to be led away by delusions of any kind, were firm believers in spiritualism. I observed that it was exercising a beneficial influence on their health, their happiness, and their daily conduct; and I resolved to investigate the phenomena for myself. Up to that time I had read pretty well everything that had been written against spiritualism, and only one book in its favour—Peebles' *Seers of the Ages*,[4] which repelled me by the tumidity of its style. I entered upon the enquiry with great suspicion. I suspected those through whom the intelligent phenomena were said to be produced, and I watched the operations of my own mind with vigilant scrutiny. Like most men to whom their brain is their tool-chest and their bread-winner, I have been accustomed to study its workings, and to regulate my physical habits so as to keep it in the highest state of health and efficiency. Therefore I was prepared—indeed, I expected to find—an explanation of the phenomena of spiritualism in some one or more of the occult operations of the mind—in unconscious cerebration, mental transfer, latent thought, or forgotten impressions suddenly awakened or vitalised, the unsuspected opening up of long-sealed chambers of the memory, a morbid excitement of the imaginative facilities, and so forth. I am bound to confess that every one of these explanations failed to account for the phenomena. I fought against the spiritual theory, but the facts were too strong for me and I was compelled to succumb. The evidence as it accumulated, was so powerful, so consistent, so harmonious—the details were so perfectly in accordance with the leading principles, and the latter approved themselves so entirely to my reason, that conviction was irresistible.

It is obvious that, despite the application of intelligence and reasoning power, Smith was strongly attracted to the prospect of continued involvement in spiritualist experimentation. But, although the movement had grown to the point where it could become established as an association of devout adherents, there were many people in Mebourne who were firmly opposed to the practice of spiritualism and amazed that Smith and his fellows should seem so credulous.

During the next three weeks, the *Argus* published a series of letters under the heading 'Spiritualism Defended'. Those written by Smith were signed with the initials 'J. S.'; the others, in which the writers argued against the various points he made in defence of his stand, were

Spiritualism

published either over initials or pseudonyms. Not all of the writers are identifiable, but Henry Gyles Turner and Marcus Clarke, using their own initials, were certainly participants in the controversy. Turner, temperate in public, but privately appalled by Smith's acceptance of spiritualist manifestations, was concerned at the threat to his friend's career implicit in a public affirmation. He set the style for the argument in the opening paragraph of his first contribution to the series:

> The letter of "J. S.," in this morning's issue of your journal, is evidently the production of a cultivated mind caught in the meshes of the idealistic "philosophy" which is just now charming so many thinkers; and although its logic will not bear criticism, and its earnestness verges on dogmatism, it is entitled to respectful consideration on account of its temperate tone, and the absence of that imputation of mean motives to the other side which has discredited most of the correspondence recently published on the subject.[5]

Turner wrote two more letters to the *Argus* in which he refuted Smith's belief in spiritual intelligence on the grounds that instances of such intelligence were to him 'trivial and inexplicable phenomena'.[6] Inevitably, comparisons between spiritualism and religion were brought into the argument. This stimulated Marcus Clarke, who was equally intolerant of both forms of belief, into suggesting that, on the basis of common sense, science might be expected to provide the answer to this kind of enquiry.[7] At the end of the controversy, in which the participants discussed opposing points of view as carefully and logically as the subject allowed, the writer of an *Argus* leader expressed the general reaction to Smith's letters, describing his 'newly-born faith' as being 'thoroughly destitute...of any claims to the recognition or belief of reasonable human beings', and claiming that the evidence produced by Smith in its support was unlikely 'to be deemed conclusive by any but the most credulous'.[8]

Undeterred by public criticism, Smith continued seeking out further spiritualist experience, carrying on, in the meantime, with his work as a member of the *Argus* staff. In April 1872, he was given leave of absence in order to conduct a lecture tour in Dunedin, New Zealand, at the invitation of the local Mutual Improvement Association.[9] He arrived in Dunedin on 26 April and began the planned series of lectures the following evening. The first was on spiritualism, after which he turned to secular topics for a time, repeating lectures given in Melbourne. These included, among others of a similar kind, the popular 'Wit and Humour', 'Recollections of Venice' and 'Shakespeare, the Dramatist and the Man'. At this stage of his enthusiasm for spiritualism, Smith was still able to diversify his interests sufficiently to lecture on secular topics in his accustomed, pleasant manner. At the same time, he was anxious to convey the spiritual messages he considered himself fortunate to have received to this new audience. He gave two more lectures on spiritualism towards the end of the tour, attracting crowds of eager listeners, as had been the case with the whole series. These lectures were of an explanatory nature: while he obviously wanted to share his sense of exhilaration at the wider world that appeared to have opened up before him, he was still aware of the danger of alienating his audience through over emphasis on the necessity for conversion. In the first part of a lecture on 6 May, for instance, he gave an exposition of God's commandments or, as he believed them equally well described, the laws of nature. In the second part, he expanded upon the benefits that must accrue to mankind through obedience to those laws. In other lectures, he discussed the nature of spiritual teaching and explained the concept of spiritual inspiration.

Smith's spiritualist lectures provoked public controversy through letters to the editor of the *Otago Daily Times*, published in Dunedin.[10] Thomas Roseby, an Australian Congregational minister stationed at Dunedin, was the first of the defenders of traditional Christian teaching. Most of the other writers were as strongly opposed to Smith's views, although some expressed cautious support. Roseby soon dropped out of the argument, disdainful of Smith's attempts at self-justification.[11] Doctor James Copland then became the major antagonist and he and Smith continued to exchange letters for the duration of the controversy.[12] One of the important points of difference was each man's concept of rationality; another was Smith's insistence upon his role as an amanuensis and Copland's conviction that anyone who talked of interlocutors was suffering from delusions. Since there could be no reconciliation of such firmly held but opposing views, the controversy reached no conclusion. As Copland described it, Smith had 'amazed the simple and amused the curious'.[13] For Smith, it was enough; he had completed a successful tour and aired the issues raised by his spiritualist lectures through public discussion. At the complimentary farewell held on 13 May, the course of lectures was praised by the Vice President of the Mutual Improvement Society as having been an 'intellectual carnival to the people of Dunedin'.[14] As a tangible expression of gratitude, Smith was then presented with a purse containing 50 sovereigns.

Back in Melbourne, growing ever more dedicated in his belief that he was one of a select few, chosen to act as an instrument for the communication of spiritual truths, Smith became increasingly immersed in spiritualist activities. Seemingly involved to the point of complete infatuation, he claimed to have received the subject matter for his spiritualist lectures through inspiration from angelic ministers or spirit companions. His main purpose, as he believed, was to warn those less finely attuned to messages from the spirit world that the end of the material world was at hand. He had become convinced that the present generation was about to be destroyed by a wave of magnetic fire because of its refusal to live in obedience to natural laws. Only those who were obedient to spiritual guidance and receptive to the love of

Spiritualism

God, as displayed through the second advent of Christ on earth, could expect to be saved. Much of what he had to say could have been heard from a more conventional pulpit. Apart from Smith's prophecy of the imminent end of the world, his condemnation of earthly wickedness and the affirmation of salvation through obedience to divine law is not dissimilar to some aspects of Calvinist or Methodist revivalist doctrine. However, although he believed in God or an 'infinite Father', he was by now strongly anti-clerical and openly contemptuous of current modes of religious practice. This questioning of previously accepted religious belief was not uncommon in an era of expanding scientific knowledge. What was unusual and, ultimately, unacceptable to Smith's contemporaries, was his determined advocacy of a new religion based on spiritualist advice, in which life as they knew it was to be brought to a sudden end.

Henry Gyles Turner attended the first of these lectures, 'The Voice of God', delivered at the Masonic Hall in Lonsdale Street on 13 October 1872, at the invitation of the Victorian Association of Progressive Spiritualists. He found the occasion depressing; it was a cold, wet morning and, in the darkened, half-empty hall, Smith delivered his lecture in a stern, denunciatory tone that confirmed the severity of his obsession. Already concerned about Smith's involvement in the movement, Turner was alarmed at this demonstration of his friend's extremism. On the one hand, as he observed, Smith was preaching the harshest of religious doctrines, including 'the salvation of the very few' and the 'annihilation of the masses'; on the other, he demanded 'as absolute a surrender of the reasoning powers, and as blind an obedience to the ghostly teachers' as ever demanded by the Church.[15] Turner's account of the lecture was published in the *Daily Telegraph*, stimulating further public controversy. If, as he concluded, Smith's views were representative of those of the main body of spiritualists, it was unlikely that there could be any future for the movement as a religious system. The members of the Victorian Association were quick to reply that Smith's views were not consistent with the mainstream. W. H. Terry expressed his 'pain and humiliation' at the inference of Turner's report, describing Smith's ideas as 'unreasonable and retrogressive'. Furthermore, Terry insisted that, although the Association had been under the impression that Smith was a spiritualist, his lectures confirmed that he had changed his views and could no longer be called one.[16] J. Tyerman, another member, defined Smith's views as being individualistic and, in fact, inclining more towards orthodoxy than spiritualism.[17] G. S. Manns, the Honorary Secretary of the Association, joined in to justify the invitation given to Smith on the grounds that his previous lectures, in the form of spirit communications, had been listened to 'with the greatest pleasure by the majority of his hearers'; and, therefore, although the committee had heard rumours of a change of views, it had seen no reason to refuse the latest paper.[18] Smith was bound to reply. In explanation, he confirmed the statements made by Terry and Tyerman, regarding his own beliefs: 'I am not, and never have been, a spiritualist'. He dismissed the use of current methods, such as mesmerism or table tapping, for conjuring up what he described as 'earth-spirits', and claimed that, in all his Sunday lectures, he was presenting 'the Father, and him only'. If his subject matter had come from himself, he conceded that it would 'deservedly expose [him] to be branded as a monomaniac, derided as a visionary and despised as an imposter'. But, since he was speaking as a human instrument of 'the Father', nothing could prevail against the vital truths of his statements.[19]

Obviously, there could be no satisfactory conclusion to any discussion in which the proponent met rational argument with inspired dogmatism. Smith went on to prove that his convictions were unshaken with the lecture 'The World Beyond the Grave', delivered to 'a considerable audience' in the Independent Lecture Hall on 28 October.[20] There he developed his theory of the evolution of mind, the 'vital spark' that he believed must transcend human mortality. He spoke also of the necessity for man to rise above the love and gratification of self in order that his mind might be receptive to spiritual impressions and, eventually, claim the ultimate objective: 'the privilege and happiness of being an instructor on earth'. When human beings learnt to live in absolute obedience to natural laws, they would realise that 'Heaven commenced on earth and grew evermore', so that the barrier now called death proved no longer insurpassable. Those who refused to live in this enlightened manner would remain restless, disembodied spirits after death; those who 'received the love of God and allowed self to be crucified' would find eternal life, in which the mind that they had nourished would be reincarnated in a new, and different, human body. Smith's choice of topic and the manner of his delivery turned his lecture into a sermon. Most of the subject matter was unremarkable: the virtue of unselfish devotion to duty and its eventual reward was central to Christian teaching, while reincarnation, in which the quality of the next life was governed by the conduct of the present one, was an equally important tenet of Eastern faith. The fear of hell, with its fire and brimstone, was also a common feature of nineteenth century pulpits. No reputable preacher, however, would forecast the imminent end of the world, as Smith did, in vehement insistence that the present branch of the human race would be 'swept off the earth by a wave of magnetic fire', after which the world would be repeopled by another branch better attuned to spiritual truths.

This lecture was reported in the *Argus* and the *Daily Telegraph*, provoking a scornful rejoinder from David Blair, as determined as opponent of spiritualism as Turner, who claimed in a letter to the editor of the *Daily Telegraph* that 'The World Beyond the Grave' was nothing 'but a mosaic of ancient notions borrowed from many sources'.[21] Smith made no reply and the controversy appeared to be over. However, it was to be revived when he lectured on the topic 'The Second Advent' at the Independent Hall on 6 January 1873. As reported by the *Daily Telegraph*, 'there was no chairman, the lecturer entering by a side door and leaving by the same door the instant the lecture was over'.[22] On this occasion, Smith took as his text 'The Son of Man shall come in clouds, and with great power'. He asserted that, when Christ came again, he would once more be veiled in a human body, to be rejected by all those except the ones who were able to recognise the Father's voice. Those who refused to 'recognise the light' were doomed. But those who accepted it would find 'eternal happiness' as they grew ever nearer to its source. Smith concluded the lecture by warning his audience that the Second Coming was 'close at hand' and urging them to ensure salvation through obedience to 'perfect law'.[23] Although he was firm in his belief that his views were incontrovertible because they had come to him through divine law, the lecture was to receive scathing comment through the *Daily Telegraph*. The American spiritualist J. B. Peebles was also lecturing in Melbourne, accompanied by his medium Dr Dunn, and the increased publicity given to the spiritualist movement caused a further reaction to Smith.

Exasperated by the publicity given to Peebles and Dunn, Blair wrote to the *Daily Telegraph* in protest, grouping Smith and the Americans together as 'dismal Jeremiahs'.[24] Letters signed with Blair's own name as well as the anagrammatic pseudonym 'Daniel Brail' are similar in style and content, indicating a common author. He was contemptuous of the 'gross perversion and shameful ignorance of the New Testament' displayed by Smith in his lecture on the Second Advent, describing any prophet of that kind as being 'either a self-deluded fanatic, a maniac, or a deliberate and most wicked imposter'.[25] Smith replied in a tone of patient resignation, heavily tinged with satire. After suggesting that 'D.B.' had forgotten 'that Christian charity with which so pious and virtuous a censor of blasphemous lunatics ought to be over-flowing', he asked what could be expected of a madman, 'other than lunatic language and insane conduct?'[26] Blair was quick to defend his own integrity, while dismissing Smith's 'playfully piteous plea of insanity' as irrelevant. What he believed to be ultimately more important was the right of free enquiry or discussion in response to Smith's prophecies, a right denied by Smith's claim of incontrovertible inspiration.[27]

Unbound by the ties of friendship that constrained Turner, Blair was outspoken in his opposition to Smith. It is probable that he gained some personal satisfaction from the critical nature of the current controversy. At the same time, despite his often sarcastic style and frequently abrasive manner, he was obviously sincere in his efforts to expose the apparent falsity of Smith's statements. Writing in criticism of the collection of money for a testimonial to Peebles, he demonstrated an equally vehement opposition towards any aspect of the promotion of spiritualist belief.[28] Having gone thus far, Blair seems to have dropped out of the controversy, although letters from 'A Literary Detective' accusing Smith of borrowing his subject matter from ancient sources tend to reflect his style as well as his predilections.[29] Smith, governed by the conviction that he was the mouthpiece of higher authority, replied as well as he was able. Other writers joined in, including Tyerman, who disputed Smith's claims to be independent of earthly mediums and argued against his concept of reincarnation.[30] To all those who opposed him and refused to accept the importance and the urgency of the messages that he was trying to pass on, Smith reiterated his conviction that he was divinely inspired. But the discussion had run its course and, with the exception of Smith, it appears that everyone involved had tired of its inconclusive nature.

No Melbourne newspaper was now prepared to publish Smith's views on spiritual communication. Fortunately for his overwhelming desire to pass on the results of his experience as an amanuensis, he found a sympathetic editor in J. Evans, who allowed him to fill the pages of the *Maryborough and Dunolly Advertiser* with spiritual outpourings. From 10 January 1873, when the *Advertiser* reprinted the *Argus* report of the lecture on the Second Advent, until 9 October 1874, when the last of the series 'Hidden Mysteries' appeared, Smith's work was published in almost every issue. Apart from correspondence, none of it is signed, but it is clearly recognisable through the subject matter as well as the series of *Maryborough and Dunolly Advertiser* reprints, some of which are directly attributable. Most of the articles are repetitive, in that they deal with variations on similar themes such as the second advent of Christ, the concept of reincarnation, the evolution of mind, the hypocrisy of religious practice and the necessity for observance of natural laws. Several of these articles were actually the texts of lectures given by Smith in the surrounding district, such as 'On Miracles', delivered in the Mechanics' Hall at Chinaman's Flat on 1 June,[31] or 'Our "Glorious Civilization"', at the Town Hall, Carisbrook, on 23 June 1873.[32] During the following year, he concentrated mainly on articles in series, including 'Excursions in Natural History',[33] where he enlarged on the revelation of natural instruction, or 'God's Parables'[34] with its sequel 'Hidden Mysteries',[35] an explanation of the meaning of the Biblical parables. All of this material was claimed to be derived from spiritual inspiration.

The literary activities connected with Smith's particular exposition of spiritualism stimulated a lot of interest in Victorian country centres. His replies to editorial comment in other newspapers, including, for example, the *Daylesford Mercury* and the *Kyneton Observer*, were reprinted in the *Maryborough and Dunolly Advertiser*, provoking further correspondence in that paper. Lecture reports and other articles were the subject of further comment and, for the period with which Smith was associated with it in this regard, the *Maryborough and Dunolly Advertiser* was, for all practical purposes, the organ for the dissemination of his ideas on spiritual communication and the transmission of spiritual instruction. But, even though some of its readers might be appreciative, the use of of a regional paper for such a purpose, at the expense of the development of features of local interest, was not sound business practice. Evans admitted this in a letter to the editor of the *Hamilton Spectator*, written in reply to adverse comment. He continued with an explanation of his reasons for the promulgation of Smith's views: 'But truth is of more importance than gain. If your correspondent had sought for the truth instead of condemning without investigation, it would have been made plain to him that the Father is now speaking to mankind through human instruments...[36]' Smith had been writing articles on secular topics for the *Maryborough and Dunolly Advertiser* for many years during which he and the editor would, no doubt, have built up a friendly relationship. Even more importantly, Evans was sufficiently convinced of the validity of Smith's spiritualist activities to wish to act as his publisher. Other letters of support appeared in the *Advertiser* from time to time, but, on the whole, the tone of the correspondence is that of outrage and exasperation. The writer of a letter signed 'Constant Reader' described the lecture on the Second Advent as 'a transparent piece of hypocrisy, cant and humbug from beginning to end'.[37] 'Unit' went further, assessing Smith's attempt at spiritual obedience as being 'wretched, maimed [and] polluted',[38] and his writing permeated with 'malevolent smut'.[39]

While remaining himself assured of the truth of his dogmatic pronouncements, Smith's credibility was in doubt in many quarters and his reputation lower than he might ever have imagined. In many respects, he had become a pathetic figure. When speaking to the Victorian Association of Spiritualists in 1896, many years after the intensity of his spiritual involvement had declined into a quieter and more acceptable conviction, he gave the members a rare personal insight into the hardship that had accompanied his consistent work for the spiritualist cause:

> It requires, indeed, no small courage to doubt long-established beliefs, and to renounce venerable fallacies and delusions which time, custom, and ancient precedent have combined to interweave with the very roots of our mental and moral being. It is not to be accomplished without many a pang, or without serious misgivings, at times, with respect to the wisdom of our course, and the safety of the path along which we are travelling. For it is a solitary road which the doubter is bound to pursue. He meets with little sympathy, and much hostility.[40]

Yet, because of his conviction of righteousness, he persevered. He was to remain a spiritualist for the rest of his life, but, although he became a frequent contributor to the *Harbinger of Light*, he would not again be as extremist in his views as he had been during the 1870s.

Little is known about the effect of Smith's spiritualist activity on his family. Eliza, supportive in other ways, may reasonably have been expected to accept her husband's conversion, even while deploring its intensity. As an intelligent and well-educated person herself, it seems likely also that she would have agreed with Smith's educational experiments; otherwise, she must surely have intervened for the sake of the sanity of their children. As Smith described it, while lecturing in Dunedin in 1872:

> ...[the] spirits are educating four of my children in every branch of liberal instruction, including music, drawing, the Latin language, Greek and Roman history, chemistry and botany, geology and arithmetic; and this, magnetically, and without the utterance to them of a single word, except in correction of new lessons after they have been written by the children.[41]

At this time, those children would have been fourteen, twelve, nine and seven, respectively. It is not clear from Smith's account whether he was acting as an intermediary in instruction, although some parental assistance would seem to have been required. It is probable that this was the method through which Charles Smith gained inspiration for the lecture 'The Will of God', which he delivered to a large audience at the Golden Age Hotel, Maryborough, on 1 June 1873, having been introduced by his father as a child who, like the Biblical Samuel, was receptive to heavenly instruction.[42]

Smith's determined advocacy of the possibility of divine inspiration, especially for those who were well attuned to the spirit world, baffled many of his listeners. Both Blair and Turner, as Smith's most vocal opponents in the controversies that surrounded his public demonstrations of the phenomenon, refused to give Smith's claim to be an amanuensis much countenance. Blair, in fact, dismissed it outright, in contempt of all those who claimed to be seers and prophets. Turner was more tolerant, even though he, too, was unable to credit that Smith's claims were genuine. However, Turner was broadminded enough to accept the probability that Smith himself believed in the integrity of what he was doing. As Turner recalled in later years:

> I often argued with him in private, and had a long controversy with him in the Daily Telegraph. Still, I feel sure that *at the outset* he was sincere in his belief that he was a specially ordained instrument to set the world on the right path.[43]

But Turner was less sure that Smith retained this conviction after the first few years of his involvement with spiritual teachings. Certainly, after 1874, when there are few, if any, public reports of his activities as a writer or lecturer on topics such as the imminent end of the world, he seems to have given up the idea of being a divine messenger of that kind. Even so, he never lost his belief in spiritual inspiration. According to Turner, 'he kept a medium almost exclusively in his employ and spent whole days in recording the vapid outpourings of the Immortals'.[44]

Turner considered the results of this activity to be worthless, but Smith's articles, based on the messages he claimed to have received, were to find a ready audience among the readers of the *Harbinger of Light*.

As Smith's adversaries found, it was impossible to reach any definite conclusion when applying rational argument to supernatural phenomena. But, even though he would have denied it, there may well have been a rational explanation for Smith's belief in spiritual communication. He was a very quick reader, able to take in whole sentences at a glance and absorb the information that he required almost spontaneously.[45] This ability was an asset that had served him well as a journalist. The material that he required immediately could be recorded in one of his notebooks, in readiness for the time when it might be needed. He had access to the latest books and journals through his work on the *Argus*; his private library was a further source of reference. In the 'Religion and Philosophy' section of the 1910 catalogue of his books for sale at auction, there are many titles that might have been the stimulus for his articles and lectures on spiritualist topics, for instance, Alger's *A Critical History of the Doctrine of a Future Life* or Gregory's *Animal Magnetism*. Another section headed 'Natural History and Medical Science' includes titles such as Clarke's *Mind in Nature*, Geiger's *Contributions to the History of the Development of the Human Race* and Tuke's *Illustrations of the Influence of the Mind on the Body in Health and Disease*, which could have been the basis for further development as articles and lectures.[46] It might be argued that these titles and other works of similar or related content merely reflect Smith's interests. On the other hand, if he was to be at all authoritative, he had to draw his material from some reliable source, if not the supernatural. Since he was often overworked, with faculties tense and strained, yet still anxious to pursue his enquiries, it seems at least possible that he may sub-consciously have absorbed a good deal of the content of what he was reading, to recall it in the guise of what then appeared to be spiritual inspiration.

The question of the intensity of Smith's response to the spiritualist movement remains. There were a number of others in Melbourne who, like him, had become active in spiritualist practice after personal investigation of psychic phenomena. But, when compared with men of more moderate views, such as Terry or Tyerman, he was unique in the manner of his conversion and extremely vocal proselytism. The almost hysterical nature of his involvement suggests that he was in the grip of some form of aberration, if not altogether overcome by mental breakdown. His constant reiteration of the essential importance of spiritualist belief seems to have been close to the frenetic activity of a person in a psychotic state, seeing himself as one of the elect and unable to compromise because of the urgency of the force that was driving him. Inevitably, Smith's concept of the validity of spiritual communication, let alone his dogmatic defence of the phenomenon, was to prove unacceptable to most of his listeners. Yet he kept on trying to find a receptive audience, prepared to continue despite personal and professional loss because of his strongly-held conviction of his own righteousness.

Smith was often unsettled during the first part of his life as an immigrant. The restlessness that caused him to make frequent attempts to change his occupation, as well as the unexpectedly erratic manner in which he conducted the *Australasian* are further indications of a certain instability. The way in which he constantly sought new avenues of activity, joining and, where possible, playing a leading part in each new movement or organisation may also be linked with his wholehearted acceptance of spiritualist belief. It is obvious from his actions in the promotion and support of colonial culture that he regarded himself as an evangelist in the field. As such, it was not a large step to become a spiritual evangelist, or, in another of the roles he assumed in the course of his work, as a publicist for the phenomena revealed through the movement. Whether or not he would have become a spiritualist if he had remained in England is open to question. All new colonists were subject to pressures that usually decreased with time. There were various forms of relief for those who were unable to settle down easily; some went back home; others stayed behind, to begin drinking heavily, to seek extra-marital affairs, or, in extreme cases, to suicide. Smith was fortunate in contracting what appears to have been a happy marriage within a comparatively short time after his arrival. He was also able to achieve early success as a journalist and critic, allowing him the comfort of professional as well as personal security. But, perhaps more than most of his fellows, he appears to have had a strong need for the assurance of his own capacity as an undisputed leader. While he achieved leadership on many occasions, his satisfaction was necessarily incomplete because of the jealousy that provoked quarrels between his colleagues and himself and embittered the struggle for position. Under those circumstances, the prospect of becoming a spiritual leader through the elitist possession of essential truths must have had a compelling attraction.

There was also the problem of homesickness. During the whole of his life in Australia, Smith held a nostalgic, romanticised view of his homeland. But this was a feeling that gradually declined in strength and, after his visit to England and Europe in 1882, it appears to have subsided into a quiet, less troubled affection. In the early 1870s, when successive attempts to return home had failed, it is likely that the goal that had proved inaccessible seemed especially desirable. While not at first looking specifically for personal manifestations during his investigations into spiritualism, Smith was delighted when he found that the spirit of his younger brother had been contacted through a medium. As he recalled many years later:

> ...not a person in the room, besides myself, knew of my having lost a brother in England, still less that he was drowned. It occured when he was seventeen and I was five-and-twenty. We were brothers indeed, and my attachment to him was so great, that the shock nearly killed me.[47]

Smith claimed to have received 'many convincing proofs of the actual presence of departed friends and relatives' during attendance at Doctor Motherwell's circle.[48] Comforted and reassured that parting seemed no longer subject to the constraints of time and distance and aware also that the great minds of the past might be equally accessible, he became drawn more deeply into involvement with spiritual experimentation. Once he began to believe that he, and he alone, was the recipient of even more important spiritual communications, he appears to have seized the opportunity of being the kind of leader that, in his dangerously exulted state, he thought should be unchallenged. The tragedy was that, despite his efforts, few believed in him and, instead of the appreciation he expected to receive, he was reviled and ostracised on account of his messianic spiritualist activities.

After the last of his series of articles for the *Maryborough and Dunolly Advertiser* was published in 1874, Smith's purpose in presenting lectures and writing articles of an extremist kind appears to have become less determined. This may have happened because his spiritual source was no longer as fruitful; it may also have seemed to him that his task as an evangelist had lost its urgency because, by then, he believed that he had passed on all that he was required to make known. It is probable that he had begun at last to tire of his admittedly thankless role as an apostle of divine truth. If so, it is also likely that his worldly ambitions were reasserting themselves, together with other material considerations, including the need to earn a better living than was possible as a writer on exclusively spiritualist topics. The regular feature articles that he began writing for the *Argus* in the late 1870s, using the initials 'J. S.', mark his return to active journalism. However, his part in litigation over a disputed estate in 1881 suggests some continuity of obsession in his approach to spiritualist belief.

Judge Molesworth began hearing the case for revocation of probate of the will of the late George Lamont, a wealthy quartz miner and investor who had left the bulk of his estate away from his family, on 12 May 1881. The hearing was interrupted and delayed by Molesworth's subsequent illness and it was not until 17 October that the judgment was given.[49] According to the evidence set down by the judge, the estate had been left largely to a Mr. McGeorge, whose de facto wife, known as Mrs. McGeorge, was the former Mrs. Jackson, the medium who had been Smith's first contact with spiritualism. Lamont became acquainted with Mrs. McGeorge through attendance at spiritualist meetings. He later became a resident at her house in Flinders Street and it was there that he met Smith. In 1875, in consultation with McGeorge and Smith, Lamont purchased land at Hawthorn in McGeorge's name and built two houses. Lamont lived with the McGeorges in one and Smith and his wife and family in the other. In 1877, in Lamont's absence, a quarrel between McGeorge and Smith over liability for payment of rent provoked Smith's removal from the property which, in the following year, was occupied by Lamont, who remained there until his death in March 1880. When Lamont's three sisters found that his estate had been left to the McGeorges, they made application for revocation of probate.

During the course of the hearing, Smith's account of spiritual communication with Lamont appeared in the *Harbinger of Light*. The supposed message began:

> True friend of other days! Four of us have often sat together; two were true and two were false; and I have come from the world of spirits to tell you that I was not myself when I made my will. I have realised that old and well-worn truth, that sooner or later sin brings its own punishment; for the faults and follies of my early years were visited on me at the close of my earthly existence. My brain was weakened by early excesses, and Mac and that woman knew it. I became subject to them as the patient is to the electro-biologist. Under her influence I ceased to be a free agent, and directly I crossed the boundary of the two worlds, my eyes were opened, and I knew how I had been duped and imposed upon; but I cannot undo it; the money will do them no good, but in that woman's hands it will prove to be a curse to her and to her confederate. Look at her and see to what a depth of vileness a woman may descend; look at her with a lying spirit on her lips! They lied to me continually. They told me you were not my friend; they poisoned my mind against you; they kept you from me, and me from you. I wanted to add a codicil to my will, making some provision for you; but they prevented me from doing so. J.S., I swear before my God it was they and not I who did that thing.[50]

Smith's decision to make public the words he claimed to have received from Lamont did him little credit, even allowing for his frequently expressed conviction of the validity of spiritual communication. When combined with the threat of personal revenge on McGeorge at the time of their quarrel, as disclosed in evidence at the hearing, it left him in the position where Judge Molesworth, summing up, could say: 'On the whole, I would regard Smith's evidence with some distrust as to most of it.'[51] It also left him open to ridicule by his contemporaries, one of whom wrote to the *Age* under the pseudonym 'The Ghost's Best Friend', repeating Lamont's message interspersed with satirical comment.[52] The only benefit to Smith from the circumstances surrounding his involvement with George Lamont was his release from what seems to have been the almost overpowering influence of Mrs. Jackson/McGeorge.

With his interest in spiritualism apparently subdued, he concentrated on his work as a journalist for the remainder of the 1880s. These were good years. Melbourne was booming and, after his overseas trip and the re-establishment of his career, he was once more in a position of some colonial importance. Then, at a time of personal stress following the bank crashes of the early 1890s and the consequent loss of most of his savings, he turned again to the consolation of being an exponent of spiritual communication. While his work for the *Argus* continued, he began lecturing and writing on spiritualist topics. The subjects—for instance, 'The Higher Teachings of Spiritualism', a discussion of spiritualist ideals, or 'Spiritualism Through the Ages', an historical account of spiritualist practice—were uncontroversial. Encouraged by his reception to begin lecturing more often, he presented papers to the Victorian Association of Spiritualists as well as to other interested groups, such as the Victorian Theosophical League and the Victorian Psychical Research Society. The lectures were reported in the publications of these societies and, before long, he was writing the articles for the *Harbinger of Light* that were to become a regular feature of the journal.

Most of Smith's lectures and articles during this period were based on spiritualist communication received throught the medium John Wren Sutton. In 1906, his major work of the kind was published in London. This was *The Secret of the Sphinx*, based on the Biblical story of Moses and the flight out of Egypt by the children of Israel. The story is attributed to Archon, an ancient Egyptian scribe, whose spirit is alleged to have passed it on to Sutton and, hence, to Smith, the main objective being 'to rectify some of the errors of history, both sacred and profane'.[53] Moses is given receptive powers, allowing him to receive spiritual lessons on topics familiar to Smith, including among others, the concepts of evolution of mind, reincarnation, divine inspiration, materialisation, and the plurality of existence.[54] The 'perfect humanity' or mystery of the Sphinx is revealed as its secret at the end. Smith's didactic purpose is obvious, but, apart from the sections of instruction, the story develops at a pace not inappropriate to a novel of adventure in which the writer is not afraid to depart from the Biblical model when occasion demands. Speaking to Annie Bright, then editor of the *Harbinger of Light*, Smith told her that the medium provided 'the skeleton of the story', while his part was 'to clothe this framework with the living interest that words and intelligent description can give'.[55] But much of the work is recognisable as Smith's own, based on his lectures and articles on spiritualist topics. Because of its limited general appeal as well as the repetition of many of the theories that he had expounded upon at length in the past, the book was largely ignored by the press. Undeterred, Smith continued recording spiritual communications for use as the basis for further articles for the *Harbinger of Light*, the last of which appeared in the week preceding his death in 1910.

10

THE RETURN VISIT

The first of the long series of feature articles that Smith wrote for the *Argus* as 'J. S.' appeared on 19 April 1879. This was a detailed, descriptive sketch of his birthplace, Loose. Other articles in a similarly reminiscent style followed, including 'An English Country Town in 1835', about Ware at the time that he had lived there,[1] and 'An English Cathedral City', about Salisbury at a later stage of his English life.[2] These articles, which Smith obviously took pleasure in writing, had a particular appeal to those immigrants who, while now well settled in Melbourne, retained a nostalgic affection for the places with which they had once been familiar. Marcus Clarke, evidently reconciled to his former antagonist, was one of those who wrote to Smith in appreciation of such evocative recollections of English country life.[3] From this beginning, Smith worked his way back into prominence as a literary journalist, writing 'J. S.' articles on a variety of topics until he left the *Argus* in 1896.

It is possible that he was already making plans to visit England and Europe while writing the first of these articles. In themselves, they may equally well have been the stimulus for renewed interest in organising a trip that, among other objectives, would serve the long wished for purpose of taking him home as an important and successful colonial figure. Because the distance between the old and the new countries was so great, an absence from the colony of twelve months or more was required in order to undertake the trip. Apart from those who were sent abroad on official business or those who could cover the costs of extensive travel through private resources, few of the immigrants who hoped for a return visit were able to realise their intentions. Smith was fortunate in being able to combine his skills as a journalist with a year's tour of England and Europe, during which, as arranged, he would send back descriptive articles for publication in the *Argus*. He was also able to secure appointment as a Commissioner for Victoria at the Universal Wine Exhibition at Bordeaux, allowing him to travel in the official and professional capacities that he had hoped for, but failed to achieve, during the 1860s.

The return visit

James and Eliza Smith left Melbourne on the *Liguria* on 22 February 1882, travelling on the outward voyage with Henry Gyles Turner (who had also been appointed a Commissioner) and his wife Helen. They returned on the *Siam*, which arrived in Melbourne on 7 February 1883. During this year overseas, Smith visited the major cities and other places of interest in England and several European countries. Apart from his official function at Bordeaux, he appears to have been free to travel at will, storing up source material for articles in the 'Pictures of Travel' series that would appear in the *Argus* while he was away and continue for another year after his return to the colony. At the conclusion of this series, he chose 29 out of the total of 68 articles for reprinting, with little revision or alteration, as a collection entitled *From Melbourne to Melrose*.

Smith's approach to the trip as a whole is illustrated by his response to the toast 'Bon Voyage', made at a farewell given him by members of the Standard Building Society and the Standard Mutual Building Society, of which he was President and Vice President respectively. As reported in the *Argus*:

> He (Mr Smith) had worked very hard for the last 27 years, and was now going to seek that best of all kinds of rest which was to be found in change of scene, change of air, and change of occupation. He hoped most sincerely that whilst he was away he could be of some service to the colony. Wherever he saw an industry which he thought could be introduced here, or anything in municipal affairs, the treatment of the insane, of the poor, or of criminals, in the management of hospitals, the drainage of cities, in agriculture or in manufactures, which would be of service to the colony, that he would examine and report upon with the view of benefiting his fellow colonists. (Applause). He could not repay the debt he owed to the colony but by so doing.[4]

It is in the light of this publicly expressed attitude that a major function of the 'Pictures of Travel' series may be seen. They were, from the outset, designed as communications from a colonist who saw himself as a favoured representative. Aware of the advantages of privilege, he was anxious to relate his experience of travel to the place in which he had now made his home, both for his own sake and the benefit of those who were prevented by circumstances from undertaking an overseas trip.

Smith was following an established literary tradition with articles of the kind. Reminiscences of travel were a popular form of instruction and entertainment during the nineteenth century, when, although more people were travelling long distances between one country and another than ever before, there were still a great many whose knowledge of foreign places could be gained only by reading about the experiences of others. As immigrants, the colonists had travelled half way across the world themselves, but the voyage they had taken in that instance was less a sightseeing tour than an adventure of a different kind. However, having had that particular experience, they were all the more likely to be interested in the tales of others with greater opportunities for extensive travel. The publication of articles in series in newspapers and magazines allowed for consecutive accounts that followed the various stages of the writer's journey. While overseas countries known by repute, if not experience, were of especial interest, local districts opened up by exploration might also be the subject of descriptive sketches; John Stanley James (better known as 'The Vagabond'), whose lively and informative articles were a feature of the *Argus*, and later, the *Age*, was a well known exponent of this form of journalism.[5] Smith wrote occasional articles about Victorian country districts himself, but his most concentrated work of the kind is found in the 'Pictures of Travel' series.

The articles that he sent back for the series began appearing on 30 May, three months after he had left the colony. From then on, they were published at intervals varying from weekly, fortnightly and three-weekly, depending upon the mails as well as his own regularity in despatching them. If, as may be assumed, these articles reflect the itinerary that Smith followed, he went first to Italy, where, as he was to do wherever he travelled, he explored the cities and country towns, observed the people, visited art galleries, museums and theatres, investigated local industries and recorded historic and literary associations. Some of this country was already known to him, especially the northern districts that he had toured in 1853, prior to emigration. From Italy, he appears to have travelled through Switzerland to France and thence to England, where he stayed for almost three months. Returning to the Continent, he spent some time in France before visiting Belgium, Holland and Germany. After he arrived back in Melbourne, Smith wrote about the people and places that he had found of especial interest for the continuation of the series. His articles appeared weekly until, towards the end of 1883, they became irregular. The last in the series was published on 16 February 1884.

Smith's usual method in writing these articles was similar to that which he had adopted on a smaller scale with the country tales that formed *Rural Records*. He would describe the place that was central to the article as it impressed him on arrival. He then moved outwards to the surrounding district, incorporating literary and historic associations before returning to the main scene, which he would describe in detail and bring to life by filling with people.

'Naples', the first of the series, is a good example of mode and style, as applied to a foreign city that could be expected to be unfamiliar to most of his readers. He begins with a description of his approach by sea:

> The first sight of Naples at sunrise from the sea is something worth remembering. So indeed is the passage, after sunset, through the Straits of Messina, with the mountains of Sicily bulking large on the one hand, and those of Calabria towering to a considerable height on the other.[6]

The return visit

He adds interest with a classical allusion to 'the coast-hugging navigators of the Homeric epoch' who faced the dangers of Scylla and Charybdis and, as the ship moves closer to Naples, gives the history of the city from classical times until the present, leading on to a short account of the changes resulting from its incorporation into the kingdom of Italy:

> Politically and industrially, a great change has passed over the city. A new life has been breathed into it; and although it is probably impossible that anything can alter the easy, pleasure-loving nature of the great mass of the people, or infuse into them that energy, that love of work, and that insatiable desire for wealth which actuates the northern races of Europe, and notably our own, yet there is, undoubtedly, a revival in art, in literature, in manufactures, in commerce, and in the building trades more especially.

He goes on to describe the functions of municipal government as practised in Naples and, in a link that reminds the reader that he is writing for those at home, he compares the paving of the thoroughfares and the consequent freedom from dust with 'the disgraceful state of things which prevails in Melbourne whenever the wind blows from any quarter'. The thoroughfares and the people who fill them are then described in precise detail, demonstrative of his ability to pile up impressions in order to create an effect of rich and varied fullness:

> Where the streets have footpaths, which is only the case with the wider of them, the passengers overflow into the carriage-way, and, like the vehicles, "stand not on the order of their going." It may be said of the costumes of the surging throng that "motley is your only wear." There are priests in their broad-brimmed three-cornered hats, their long black cloaks, well-brushed *sottane*, and irreproachably neat silk stockings and shoes; there are monks who are both shabby and dirty; there are *bersaglieri* with plumes of cocks' feathers, emulating the "raven down of darkness" in colour and gloss, falling down one side of their faces; there are the municipal guard or city police, with their glazed military caps, dark blue coats and light blue trousers, each armed with a sword, and all maintaining a vigilant supervision of the street traffic; there are solemn-looking "swells," in the most severely respectable of broughams, with armorial bearings on the panels, and a liveried coachman and "buttons" on the box, behind as well-appointed a pair of horses as you can see outside of Hyde-park or the Bois de Boulogne; there are *pifferari*, with their primitive bagpipes from the wilds of Abruzzi; there are withered old women with more wrinkles in their tanned faces than you can count, bringing in huge flag-baskets filled with clean linen, poised upon their heads, from laundries in the suburbs; there are boys and girls with large black eyes, having all the softness and the sheen of the richest silk velvet; there are peasants bronzed by the sunshine of Calabria; there are English, French, Russian, and German tourists; there are Sisters of Mercy; and there are street Arabs and beggars, and itinerant musicians, and *flaneurs*, and women with Spanish veils

and others bareheaded, and newsboys and letter-carriers, *e tutti quanti*.

A discussion of the intellectual atmosphere of the city follows, with reference to the access of the educated classes, since the expulsion of the Bourbons, to the best of contemporary thought as provided through the bookshops, the University and the general education system. But it is not only the people of similar background to himself that appear to have interested Smith. He was also curious about common daily life, as experienced by the Neapolitan lower classes:

> ...I have been struck by the industrious habits of the *basso populo*; and as all handicrafts and most domestic occupations are pursued in front of the houses in the poorer quarters of the city, an excellent opportunity is afforded you of seeing what is going on in this respect. The wash-tub, the spinning-wheel, the cooking-stove, the cobbler's stall, the butcher's block, the carpenter's bench, the harnessmaker's "trees," the tailor's board, the seamstress's table, &c., are all in full view, and the family washing is hung out to dry from the balcony in front of the first-floor window, or is exposed on lines stretched across those architectural ravines which reach so far and rise so high above flights of steps that may be reckoned by the hundred and are among the most characteristic features of Naples... They swarm with men, women and children; for Naples, with its 670,000 inhabitants, is a human anthill; and as everybody is loquacious and voluble, and as young and old talk vehemently, declaim dramatically, and gesticulate with the utmost animation; and as the street cries are innumerable, and are uttered with a rising inflection of the voice at the commencement, and a prolonged cadence at the end... the city is a perfect Babel.

With the addition of human interest of this kind, Smith added light and colour to his word picture of the urban scene. He continued in like manner throughout the trip, writing purposefully descriptive articles designed to make his readers almost as familiar with the places he was visiting as he was becoming himself.

Once back in his home country, he travelled around England and also in parts of Scotland, visiting many new places as well as those where he had once lived. There are sections descriptive of nostalgic landscapes in the articles that he sent back at this time, including his account of a train journey towards the city of York:

> A ride from London to York by an express train, which accomplishes the journey more swiftly than did the renowned highwayman's black mare that has breathed her last so often to slow music on a bed of circus sawdust, carries you through some of the prettiest and some of the foulest scenery in England. Middlesex, Herts, Bedfordshire, Northamptonshire, Leicestershire, Nottinghamshire, Derbyshire, and a considerable portion of Yorkshire are successively traversed, and although the sky is grey, and the clouds lie low, and the sun resolutely hides his face, the countryside looks very beautiful; for the

The return visit

superabundance of moisture causes it to retain the verdure and freshness of spring. The standing crops of corn have scarcely begun to mellow, and the hay is still lying in swathes and windrows in some places, is heaped up in mows in others, and is being carted and stacked, in exceptionally favoured localities.[7]

But, in vivid contrast, he goes on to deplore the industrial blight that, through the necessity of progress, has settled upon neighbouring districts:

... the train approaches Nottingham and plunges into an atmosphere which accompanies you almost all the way to Leeds, reaching its acme of density, its maximum of sooty filth, and its climax of abominations in Sheffield, over which there hangs, even at this period of the year, a pall of smoke, heavy, motionless, oppressive, and impenetrable. Look in what direction you will, the radius of your vision does not exceed 200 yards horizontally, and perhaps not more than half so much vertically. Turn to what point of the compass you may, you see little else but black chimneys vomiting huge clouds composed of the products of combustion, with here and there a jet of pallid steam, and here and there the baleful glare of an open furnace. The atmosphere is saturated with soot. You taste it, smell it, touch it. It is omnipresent and all-pervading.

This is the manner in which much of the British section of the trip is treated. Since the places that Smith visited then were likely to be better known to most of the colonists than the European cities that he wrote about in such detail, it must have seemed of more potential interest to publicise the changes and developments that had taken place during the years since they had emigrated. But information and instruction were not confined to social and commercial matters. As had been the case in Europe, articles on cultural topics were also included.

Throughout most of the articles in the series, Smith's tone is deliberately impersonal. There is no mention of Eliza, although she was known to have been travelling with him. That they visited her birthplace, Tewkesbury, is evident from the article 'In Shakespeare's Country',[8] but Smith gives no indication that the 'delightful old town' had any other than historical associations for its colonial visitors. He obviously felt no need to write at much length about the places in which he had lived himself, because they had been dealt with in earlier 'J. S.' articles. However, without naming the village, he included a section on Loose in 'A Canterbury Pilgrimage':

Nothing seems to change in these sequestered places. You come back to them after 30 or 40 years' absence, and find them unaltered. The village appears to have contracted somewhat in dimensions; the houses look smaller and the high road narrower and the church spire lowlier than they did; but to other respects everything is pretty nearly as it used to be. The low windows of the roadside inn are filled with geraniums and calceolarias, which glow as brightly in the autumn sunshine as ever they did; the signboard which swings from its substantial frame bears the same illegible blazon it always bore, and the water-trough, overshadowed by the ancient elms, is only a trifle more ragged at the edges than it was of yore.[9]

He went on to describe the tap room, the shops, the manor house and the village green. But, while the village seemed to be much the same in outward appearance, there were inevitable changes. The interior of the church had been 'restored' until it was almost unrecognisable and the office of Parish Clerk, once held by his grandfather, had been abolished. The boys with whom he had played as a child upon the green were now middle aged or older and, even though he noticed 'some of the old names' above the shops, he no longer had any connection with Loose; there was now little apart from his idealised memory of childhood to hold him to his birthplace.

Smith's reaction to London after his long absence was uninhibited by sentiment. He was amazed by the growth of the capital and the way in which it had spread out over rural districts, sweeping away old landmarks in the course of progress. He found much to admire in the standard of domestic architecture, the well stocked shops and 'the establishment and equipment of new clubs, theatres, palatial hotels, expensive restaurants [and] refreshment-rooms'.[10] But, in what appears to have been an especially inclement English summer, he missed the 'warmth of tone and colour' to which he had become accustomed in Australia. The London climate that July was 'simply abominable',[11] and there, as well as in some of the provincial centres, he was reminded of the melancholy that might be induced by frequent exposure to cold, wet days:

> No gleam of sunshine breaks through the low-lying vault of grey vapor or dun-coloured rain-clouds which overhang and bear down upon you with their dreary uniformity of tint and tone; and the drip of the mist from the trees is so like a shower of tears as to suggest that nature is expressing her unhappiness in this lachrymose fashion. England has need of home comforts and fireside enjoyments to counteract the feelings of depression and despondency occasioned by the sad and sombre aspects of external nature during the total and prolonged disappearance of the sun.[12]

The adverse effects of the climate had been an important influence on Smith's decision to emigrate. Now, back in his homeland, the dreary weather affected his pleasure in returning. As he described it, the climate was 'the one great drawback' to feelings of wishing to remain.

There were other reasons for Smith to dismiss any but the most tentative consideration of the prospect of renewing life in England. His family ties in Australia had replaced those 'at home' and his colonial friends and acquaintances were better known to him than those that he had left behind. As had been the case with any of his plans to leave the colony, opportunities for financial reward were comparatively limited.

He was now 62 years old and, as a colonial journalist who was little known in England, it is unlikely that he could have found permanent, well-paid employment. Most significantly, he was no longer the Englishman he had been at the time of emigration. Neither was he altogether an Australian, although colonial life had modified some of his Britishness. This was something that he obviously realised himself. While describing a visit to Paris and comparing that city with London, he remarked that 'an Anglo-Australian can institute these comparisons and note these contrasts without partiality or prejudice...'[13] But, in claiming impartiality on this ground, he was also admitting that he had passed the point of return to his former life. After the trip was over, Melbourne appears to have become his home in a way that previously might have seemed impossible.

From a professional point of view, the 'Pictures of Travel' series fulfilled the important purpose of re-establishing Smith's reputation as a feature writer. The appearance of the articles during his absence helped to keep him in the public mind, while the continuation of the series for a further year extended the value of his trip as a profitable source of subject matter. When making a selection for republication, he chose articles descriptive of the places he had visited while touring in Italy, Switzerland, France and Great Britain, leaving sufficient material for a later collection, if required. The *Argus* review of *From Melbourne to Melrose* was favourable:

> Everyone who has roamed knows how the pleasure is increased if before you dash into a new city you can spend an evening with some traveller of "light and leading" who will converse to you about the place, mention the objects that have impressed him, and tell you the historic reminiscences or the art legends that invest the scene or the edifice with interest. Mr. James Smith is such a friend.[14]

However, regardless of its interest as a travel book, the publication of the collection in 1888, five years after the series had ended, indicates that Smith was likely to have had the additional objective of achieving prominence as a colonial author during the centennial year of European settlement in Australia. The use of 'Melbourne' in the title is appropriate in that context, although 'Melrose' appears to have been chosen more for the sake of euphony than significance. Apart from its association with Sir Walter Scott, whose poems are quoted in the Scottish section of the book, the town is not a focal point.

After their return to Melbourne, James and Eliza Smith settled down again at 'Amwell', the large brick residence on the corner of Burwood Road and Yarra Street, Hawthorn, which he had purchased in 1878. This property was part of the St James estate, originally owed by Sir James Palmer and purchased by George Coppin after Palmer's death for subdivision and resale. Smith continued working for the *Argus*, reporting and commenting on cultural events, writing book reviews and contributing feature articles. He also wrote descriptive and informative articles for some of the nationalistic publications that appeared during the 1880s. One of these was the *Picturesque Atlas of Australasia*, edited by Andrew Garran, to which Smith contributed most of the content of the sections covering Victoria and Tasmania.[15] Another was the *Australasian Federal Directory of Commerce, Trades and Professions*, edited by J. W. F. Rogers, for which he wrote 'The Social Development of Australasia'.[16] This was a comprehensive account of the colonisation of Australia and New Zealand in which the discussion of various aspects of development was supported, where appropriate, by the inclusion of statistical information. Though obviously a commissioned article composed largely of derivative material, there was scope for the expression of personal satisfaction at the remarkable extent of colonial progress. The following extract is taken from Smith's conclusion:

> Thirty years ago men and women migrated to Australia in search of health or fortune with something of the feeling that they were going into exile, and that they must relinquish many of the comforts, most of the social enjoyments, and nearly all the luxuries that had been accessible "at home." That sentiment has pretty well died out. There is nothing in any of the principal cities of Australasia to remind the new-comer that he is in a new country, except the absence of the antiquities, the brightness of the atmosphere, the general air of vivacity and alertness which characterizes the people he meets with in the streets, and the non-appearance of the squalor and mendicancy which obtrude themselves upon your notice in the centres of population in Europe, and even in many of the larger cities in the United States.[17]

The atmosphere that Smith conveys is one of ongoing prosperity that, more than anywhere else in the Australian colonies, was then applicable to Melbourne. The city to which he had returned to make a permanent home had developed in a way and at a speed that altogether surpassed immigrant expectations.

During the 1880s, Smith and many of his fellows shared the conviction that they were citizens of the most important city in the Southern Hemisphere. The visiting English journalist George Augustus Sala called it 'Marvellous Melbourne', a description approved by most of those who had lived through the transition from a dusty goldfields town into a substantial capital city. Writing for the *Argus* in 1885, Sala elaborated upon the reasons for his enthusiasm:

> The metropolis and seat of government of the colony of Victoria has at present, within a ten-mile radius, including the city and suburbs, a population of more than 282,000 souls. The rateable property in the city is valued at ten millions sterling, with a net annual value of nearly a million. The principal thoroughfares are a mile in length, 99ft. in width, and intersecting each other at right angles. Omnibuses,

hansoms, and hackney waggonettes swarm in the streets; and very soon an extensive system of cable and horse tramway cars will be thrown open. The Anglican and Roman communions have splendid cathedrals, and there is a multitude of handsome and commodious places of worship for other denominations. The Town-hall is gigantic and imposing; the General Post-Office vast, comely and admirably arranged. There is a splendid university. Government-house is not, perhaps, architecturally a thing of beauty which should live for ever; still it affords a spacious and dignified residence for His Excellency Sir Henry Loch and his lady. There are half a dozen theatres, more or less. There is a very grand permanent Exhibition building, and a fine aquarium. When the new Houses of Parliament are finished they will form a sumptuous pile indeed. There is one thoroughly excellent and admirable hotel in Melbourne—Menzies'—and a few other far from uncomfortable caravanserais. There are asylums, markets, hospitals, coffee palaces, public and private schools, clubs, parks, gardens, racecourses, and recreation-grounds in profusion in and about the city; and I need scarcely say that there are any number of big banks and insurance offices which in their architecture are more than palatial. The whole city, in short, teems with wealth, even as it does with humanity.[18]

As was the case with most observers, it was the rapidity of the development as much as its extent that had impressed Sala. Though then little more than 50 year old, Melbourne had expanded into a metropolis that seemed to rival many longer-established cities.

The 1880s were boom years. Between 1881 and 1891, the population of Melbourne increased from 268 000 to 473 000.[19] Housing estates sprang up along with the extension of public transport and communication services, both of which grew by 100 percent during that period.[20] Land development went ahead so rapidly that, in some of the inner suburbs, pockets of new slums were added to those already in existence, while sanitation and other necessary services fell behind. But the mood of the city was one of optimistic faith in continuous growth and there were few who doubted that the deficiencies that accompanied intensive progress would be remedied in good time. Smith shared in the general atmosphere of prosperity. In January 1888, he claimed to have earned £40 000 from literary work since his arrival in Australia.[21] This figure appears to be accurate. In order to have earned that amount over 34 years, he would have had to have an average annual income of close to £1200, which, although not in the top level of professional incomes, was rather more than the average for doctors, solicitors or salaried managers of business enterprises.[22] The relevant figures that are available include Smith's *Argus* salary of £500 in 1856, his government salary as Parliamentary Librarian of £800 in 1869 (which was probably counted), and the list of payments for journalism totalling around £440 in 1863 diary. While it is likely that his earnings were lower during the less productive years of his early involvement with spiritualism, it could be expected that his salary as a journalist, together with payments for freelance writing and lecturing, would have increased in later years, bringing his total earnings close to the figure claimed.

Widespread financial prosperity was the stimulus for the Centennial Exhibition of 1888, conceived in a manner appropriate to a period of expansion. It was not the first international exhibition to be held in Melbourne. In 1880, the Exhibition Building erected for the purpose in Carlton housed exhibits of art and industry from 26 foreign countries, as well as Great Britain and the British colonies. The Centennial Exhibition was intended to be a repetition of the earlier one, but, as Turner has described it, 'on a scale of greatly increased splendour'.[23] Invitations to become exhibitors were sent to heads of government around the world, provoking a response that temporarily reversed the desirability of overseas travel for the colonists. Instead of Victorians having to go away to see the world, the world seemed to be coming to Victoria. The exhibition opened on 2 August and continued until the end of the following January. During that time, Turner estimated the number of visitors to be 'very nearly 200 000'.[24] Melburnians and their guests filled the exhibition halls to see important paintings and other examples of the finest of creative and decorative arts. They could also marvel at innovative displays of electric lighting and the intricate operation of modern machinery. In addition, they were entertained at frequent musical performances given by massed choirs and orchestras.

James Smith was one of the Commissioners. He was also the author of the 'Report on the Exhibition of Large', which formed part of the *Reports of the United States Commissioners to the Centennial Exhibition at Melbourne, 1888*. There he informed his readers that the specially erected buildings covered an area of 35½ acres, though originally intended to be not more than 24. The main building, erected in 1880, was surrounded by a continuous gallery for the display of the fine arts, while extensive annexes were divided into sections for the use of exhibitors from Australia, New Zealand, Great Britain, the United States of America and many European and Asian countries. The report continued with detailed descriptions of the various sections of the exhibition. Victoria was a prominent exhibitor:

> This, the most compact of all the colonies on the mainland, with an area closely approximating to that of the United Kingdom, and a million of inhabitants, occupies nearly 8 acres of space in the Exhibition building with its multifarious exhibits. Gold, wool, wheat, and wine are the main sources of its prosperity; and no pains have been spared to impress these facts upon the minds of visitors.[25]

But, despite the demonstration of Victorian prosperity to the rest of the world, Smith could not deny that, financially, the Melbourne Centennial Exhibition had been a failure. Since he was writing for an American audience, the amounts he takes from the balance sheets issued by the Executive Commissioners after the first five months are in United States

The return visit

dollars. However, they show a substantial loss. Turner's breakdown of the final figures are, more appropriately, in sterling. He cites the cost of the erection of the annexes, together with alterations and improvements to the main building, as £170 000. The musical entertainments cost over £30 000, while wages and other running costs brought the total expenses up to £400 000. But the amounts that were deducted for admissions, sales of surplus materials and the value of the improvements, reduced this total to £238 000[26]. This was a very large amount, equivalent to approximately ten shillings per head of the population of Melbourne. Even so, public confidence remained high. Most Victorians at this time were unlikely to have been critical in accepting the explanation that Smith provided: 'the indirect advantages of all such industrial and artistic displays are considerable, but do not admit of exact calculation'.[27] The revenue returns of Victoria had risen by almost 16 percent over those of the previous year. Under those circumstances, as Smith and many of his contemporaries believed, 'the people [could] afford to sustain the loss entailed by the luxury of indulging in a Centennial Exhibition'.[28] Their riches had been displayed and there seemed little reason to suspect that the second century of Australian colonisation would be any the less prosperous than the first.

11
A NEW GENERATION

Although Smith eventually recovered much of the status that he had held before his conversion to spiritualist belief, he was not again to be as authoritative a figure. This was partly due to the inflexibility that arose from his belief in his own ability to make absolute judgments. His standing in cultural circles was also affected by the fact that his generation of immigrants was being overtaken by a younger group of colonists, some of whom were later immigrants, and others native born. Traditional British and European values and customs still commanded wide acceptance in the colony, but members of the younger generation were less inclined to treat them with exaggerated respect. In Smith's time as a new immigrant, colonial progress had been equated with the transplantation of ideas and the re-establishment of familiar institutions. For the immigrants of the 1850s, this had been a necessary part of the process of adaptation to colonial life. But, by the 1880s, the cultural foundations that had been laid by those immigrants were ready to be built upon through the development of fresh ideas more suited to the particular demands of a thriving colonial city.

Apart from the Hamlet controversy of 1867, Smith's position as a knowledgeable critic had not been seriously challenged. Even then, it was his interpretation of the text that was open to question rather than his critical judgment. His views on the fine arts were generally held to be equally authoritative. According to a contemporary assessment, 'in knowledge and experience of art he could hold his own in any city of Europe'.[1] His approach, however, remained firmly centred on the Ruskinite criteria that formed the basis of his cultural appreciation. The conservatism of his long-held attitudes was to bring him into conflict with a group of experimental painters, commonly known as the Australian impressionists. Tom Roberts, Frederick McCubbin, Charles Conder and Arthur Streeton, members of the Heidelberg school, were deliberate exponents of the art of reproducing what they had seen themselves and not what their critics expected them to see. Smith reacted strongly, apparently unable to appreciate that impressionism could be a valid form of art, when it broke established rules of form and composition and set its own standards of perception.

A new generation

He made the following comment on the development of French painting in 'The Art Treasures of Paris', published in the *Argus* in 1883 as part of the 'Pictures of Travel' series:

> It is difficult to understand the vogue of Corot, Courbet, Millet, Diaz de la Pena, and Theodore Rousseau. In the house of Sir Frederick Leighton, at Kensington, he was good enough to show me some pictures by the first-named artist which he evidently prized; but they seemed to me, like the three examples in the Luxembourg, and like most of the works of the other artists I have named, to be mere sketches, hasty records of fugitive effects, and to be wanting in everything but fidelity to the first impression produced upon the painter's mind by the scene before him.[2]

The artists referred to here were not a coherent group. Each one had an individualistic style and the main link between them, as Smith provides it, was that their paintings were being exhibited as representative of the best of contemporary French art. However, it is obvious from Smith's brief assessment that he had some appreciation of the objectives of what was later to be termed impressionist painting, though seemingly unprepared to accept the results of that mode. This attitude foreshadows his reaction towards the work of the Heidelberg painters, who, while influenced to some extent by the French impressionist movement, were a distinctive group whose vision of the local scene was their own.

In 1885, Roberts and McCubbin had set up camp at Box Hill, east of Melbourne, where, away from the city but with materials close to hand, they could paint directly from nature instead of making sketches for later finished compositions that they believed would lose the impact of first impression. Streeton joined Roberts and McCubbin in 1887 and, in 1888, with Charles Conder as another leading member of the group, they formed an artists' colony at 'Eaglemont', near Heidelberg.

One of the problems associated with the acceptance of their work was that paintings done in an immediate attempt to capture a transitory moment were likely to appear unfinished to the conservative eye. When they held an exhibition in Melbourne in 1889, consisting of oil paintings on the lids of cedar cigar-boxes measuring approximately 9 × 5 inches ('9 × 5 impressions'), Smith's review for the *Argus* was almost wholly condemnatory. It began:

> Such an exhibition of impressionist memoranda as will be open today at Buxton's Art Gallery, by Messrs. Roberts, Conder, Streeton, and others fails to justify itself. It has no adequate *raison d'être*. It is as if a dramatist should give a performance on the stage of such scraps of dialogue, hints of character, ideas for incidents, and suggestions of situations as had occured to him while pondering over the construction of a play, or as if a musician should invite people to listen to crude and disconnected scraps of composition, containing the vaguely indicated themes for a cantata, a symphony, or an opera; or as if a sculptor should ask us to inspect certain masses of marble

from which he had just blocked out the amorphous outlines of various pieces of statuary. None of these is to be regarded as a work of art. Neither is a painter's "impression." It is simply a record in colour of some fugitive effect which he sees, or professes to see, in nature. But, like primeval chaos, "it is without form and void." To the executant it seems spontaneous and forcible. To the spectator it appears grotesque and meaningless.[3]

The emphasis here is on the preliminary or unfinished state of the paintings as it appeared to the viewer whose expectations were governed by accepted modes of art. That Smith's views on impressionism were preconceived is evident through comparison with his remarks about modern French art during his visit to Paris, especially his use of the words 'fugitive effects' in both extracts. There is no suggestion of cautious appraisal of a new style that might prove valid with experience. Instead, there seems to be a complete lack of understanding between 'spectator' and 'executant', given which Smith could do little more in the way of interpretation than disparage the exhibits:

...four-fifths are a pain to the eye. Some of them look like faded pictures seen through several mediums of thick gauze; others suggest that a paint-pot has been accidentally upset over a panel nine inches by five; others resemble the first essays of a small boy, who has just been apprenticed to a housepainter; whilst not a few are as distressing as the incoherent images which float through the mind of a dyspeptic dreamer.

Smith's sense of outrage at what he obviously considered to be a frivolous exhibition was modified to some extent by the better exhibits. Impressions by Roberts, Conder and Streeton were among the few that merited faint praise: 'Some of the impressions, in which sufficient work has been put to entitle them to be spoken of as sketches, show that the artists are capable of much better things'. The review was concluded with an appropriate quotation from the mid-Victorian English artist W. P. Frith: 'Impressionism is a craze of such ephemeral character as to be unworthy of serious attention'.

Smith's attitude towards the Australian impressionists is reminiscent of that displayed by Ruskin in response to Whistler's innovative style. When Whistler's 'Nocturne in Black and Gold (The Falling Rocket)'[4] was exhibited in the Grosvenor Gallery in London in 1877, Ruskin made the following derogatory comment:

For Mr. Whistler's own sake, no less than for the protection of the purchaser, Sir Coutts Lindsay [the director] ought not to have admitted works into the gallery in which the ill-educated conceit of the artist so nearly approached the appearance of wilful imposture. I have seen, and heard, much of Cockney impudence before now; but never expected to hear a coxcomb ask two hundred guineas for flinging a pot of paint in the public's face.[5]

A new generation

The indignant Whistler sued Ruskin for libel and was awarded damages to the extent of one farthing. Whistler's success was, therefore, nominal, although neither Ruskin's comments nor the publicity surrounding the case harmed his career. Ruskin's loss was far greater. He had helped establish a tradition that was now under attack and his critical reputation suffered because of his consequent reluctance to accept experimental techniques and abstract forms as a valid demonstration of art. Smith, in Melbourne, was affected in much the same way because of his criticism of the impressionist painters.

While the 9 × 5 exhibition was intended mainly to provide opportunities for critical evaluation, the artists had another important purpose in making viewers aware of the possibilities of their current style. In order to arouse public comment, a copy of Smith's review was displayed at the door of the gallery and visitors were invited to decide at first hand whether or not they agreed with it. Further interest was stimulated by the comments of Edward Vidler, then fine arts critic for *Table Talk*. Although unconvinced of the effectiveness of the impressions, Vidler's response to the exhibition was more favourable than that of Smith. He appreciated both the aims of the impressionists and the validity of the exhibition as a focus for the discussion of innovative art. However, he described the sketches as being 'really so slight that they cannot stand the full blast of windy criticism', and cautioned his readers that 'the majority of visitors make the mistake of seriously treating the sketches as pictures'.[6] Evidently aware that their objectives required further explanation, Roberts, Conder and Streeton combined to make a public statement of the principles on which they had been working:

> They are these: that we will not be led by any forms of composition of light and shade; that any effect of nature which moves us strongly by its beauty, whether strong or vague in its drawing, defined or indefinite in its light, rare or ordinary in colour, is worthy of our best efforts and of the love of those who love our art. Through and over all this we say we will do our best to put only the truth down, and only as much as we feel sure of seeing.[7]

The artists went on to discuss the question of seeing for themselves and, in so doing, assisting in the development of their own ideas instead of relying upon the work of others and the repetition of conventional modes.

Smith's reply, which appeared in the *Argus* the following day, was designed to justify his attitude and confirm his judgment, both as personal assurance and reference to other authorities. He was particularly concerned to reply to the artists' statement that 'in the formation of taste in this new country where art is so young and tentative, every public expression of opinion and every show of works must have a more or less strong influence in the making of that taste.' His answer to this was: 'It was precisely on that very account that we condemned the recent exhibition, because whatever influence it was likely to exercise could scarcely be otherwise than misleading and pernicious'.

The conflict here was a question of ultimate responsibility. Because of his active interest in the fine arts and the reputation he had gained as one of the few immigrants with sufficient knowledge of the subject to act in a critical capacity, Smith obviously regarded himself as a well-qualified arbiter of public taste. As such, he could not allow a group of young and relatively untried artists to usurp his function as interpreter and instructor. He objected also to the artists' contention that 'as it takes an artist to paint a picture, so also it takes one to appreciate it', by using Italian princes and prelates, Venetian, Dutch and English merchants and American collectors as examples of patrons and connoisseurs.

The matter of taste and its exercise, important to Smith in general terms, was an adjunct to his rejection of the 9 × 5 impressions because of their lack of finish. He wrote on this aspect of his criticism as follows:

> Our correspondents further inform us that their "impressions' were not, as we hoped, mere sketches or memoranda in colour, but "very serious and well-considered efforts to represent effects and moods and thoughts of nature," and, this being so, those serious efforts go to prove either that there is some visual defect, common to the exhibitors, which prevents them from seeing nature as she really is; or that the impressions conveyed by natural objects are distorted and deformed in their passage through the minds of the artists, and are presented in a perverted form upon panel or canvas. Our main objection to their work is that it is wholly foreign to nature, and is destitute of all sense of the beautiful.

The impressions, because of their nature as an immediate response to the landscape rather than a careful one, were to be judged as unfinished works. Further, as Smith believed, the vision that inspired the artists was incompatible with that of earlier artists, as shared by him and described in the course of his criticism.

Smith's reaction to the exhibition was consistent with his previously expressed views on the purpose of the fine arts and their particular function as an important factor in the development of colonial culture. It may also be seen as part of the wider conflict between lay criticism and artistic practice that now existed and which, in 1886, had influenced some of the professional members of the Victorian Academy of Art to leave the Academy in order to form the Australian Artists' Association. Although these rival groups had been reunited as the Victorian Artists' Society in 1888, there was still a certain resentment among professional artists at the long-established amateur control of the fine arts in Victoria. From this aspect, the posting of Smith's review at the gallery door appears to have been a deliberate challenge to his authority. The artists' letter to the *Argus*, though largely an explanation of working principles, also had the effect of giving emphasis to the possible validity of their

A new generation

point of view. So far as Smith was concerned, the aims of the impressionist painters defied everything that he believed essential to the proper practice of the fine arts. To the artists, who had far less reverence for the fixed ideas that were the basis of Smith's critical appreciation, he was a reactionary critic whose views had become outmoded. Their impatience with his attitude as an expert and authoritative figure in the Australian art world was, perhaps, best expressed by Conder, who, in a letter to Roberts, anticipated the time when 'the irrepressible Mr. J. S. be gathered to his fathers'.[8]

Smith showed himself to be equally reactionary in his approach to the Melbourne production of Ibsen's *A Doll's House*, when despite his appreciation of Janet Achurch's interpretation of the role of Nora, his attitude towards the play itself was adversely critical. *A Doll's House* had its first performance in Copenhagen in 1879. Janet Achurch had played Nora Helmer in the first London production in June 1889, when her husband Charles Charrington took the part of Doctor Rank. In Melbourne, later in the same year, Achurch resumed her role as Nora and Charrington played Torvald Helmer. The play opened at the new Princess's Theatre on 14 September and continued until 27 September. During the remainder of the three-week season, Achurch and Charrington appeared in two other productions, *The New Magdalen* by Wilkie Collins and *Pygmalion and Galatea* by W. S. Gilbert. Their appearance in Melbourne so soon after a successful London season is an indication of the reduction of colonial cultural isolation in the late nineteenth century. However, on occasion, mid-Victorian attitudes remained: the recent production of *A Doll's House* had proved acceptable to London audiences, but, in Melbourne, the controversy stimulated by the play at its first performance was to be revived.

There were two main points of difficulty. The first was that the play was one where, in a departure from the continuous drama to which theatre audiences had become accustomed, the action was interrupted by the discussion of social issues. The second and more important point was the manner in which the drama ends with Nora's renunciation of her duties as a wife and mother, in search of self. Each of the main characters displays qualities that, if the play had a happy (and conventional) ending, might prove them worthy of admiration, but Torvald is not the perfect husband that he seems and Nora is not the perfect wife. Ibsen's couple, unlike many nineteenth century stereotypes, are not idealised stage figures, but human beings who must learn from their mistakes that self-sacrifice, though noble, does not necessarily lead to happiness.

Public reaction against the ending of the play caused Ibsen to rewrite it himself in order to prevent outside interference with the script. The alternative ending, in which Nora is ultimately unable to leave her children, was written for the German actress Frau Niemann-Raabe, who believed the original to be unnatural to motherhood. In Melbourne,

Smith discussed the advisability of altering the play with J. C. Williamson. His letter to Williamson has not survived, but, as is obvious from Williamson's reply, both men favoured an alternative ending:

> Thanks for your note. I am quite of your opinion that it would be wise to alter the ending of "Doll's House" to suit our audiences. it struck me that after Nora's final exit as at present arranged the children should come on and ask for their mother, Helmer tell them that she has gone, the children cry out for her and their cry bring her back again, but I am in doubt as to whether anything should be spoken after she rushes back to embrace them, though she might say "My darlings, I cannot leave *you*!"
> What do you think?[9]

The immediate result of this correspondence is unknown. However, as evident from the reviews of the first Melbourne performance, the play was produced without alteration. Smith's reasons for wishing the ending to be changed are in line with his approach to the drama as a potentially elevating force and, more directly, with his belief that Nora's actions were unsympathetic to the extent of lacking credibility. Williamson's approach seems more likely to have been dependent upon practicalities: if the first-night audience disapproved of the current ending, the play was less likely to have a successful run. The paternalism that is apparent in both of these attitudes is closely linked with the notion of the critic as arbiter that appears to have been held by Williamson as well as Smith.

The *Argus* review of the opening performance, which seems obviously written by Smith, opens with a synopsis of the plot and continues with an exposition of the reviewer's objections:

> The fundamental fault of the play is that it is excessively didactic, and insufficiently dramatic for an English audience. In a French, German, and probably in a Scandinavian theatre, people will listen with considerable attention to long dialogues on ethical, social, and religious questions—"Daniel Rochat" was a case in point—so long as they are written in good literary form; but English playgoers are impatient under similar circumstances. They demand continuous action, and the more rapidly a drama advances towards its *dénouement* the better they are pleased with it. Hence "The Doll's House" sins against one of the most arbitrary canons of British taste... Another objection to "The Doll's House" and one which militated against its success, is that the character of Nora in the third act is unnatural, and repels rather than invites sympathy; while the lesson which the dramatist wishes to convey is neither a wholesome, nor an elevated or elevating one. The noblest men and women who have ever lived, the sublimest manifestations of our common humanity, have extorted the admiration of mankind by the spectacle of their self-effacement and self-sacrifice. Ibsen's ideal woman in this play deserts her home, which has been a very happy one; forsakes her husband, who, whatever his faults may be, has made an idol of her; and abandons her children, to whom she

professes to be tenderly attached, for the despicably selfish reason that she has been treated as a doll, and not as a colleague and companion, the discovery of the fact being a curiously sudden one.[10]

For those who, like Smith, approached *A Doll's House* from a conventional point of view, Ibsen's work was foreign on several levels of understanding. But, while deploring the vehicle, Smith was fully appreciative of Achurch's performance as Nora, discussing it act by act and commenting upon the varying moods and emotions that she displayed in the part: 'all impulse, vivacity and joyousness' in the first act; 'woman...on the verge of hysteria' in the second, 'a prey to feverish excitement, every nerve in a state of painful tension, and her whole system overwrought and quivering with the strain imposed upon it by conflicting emotions'; and, in the third, 'qualities of quiet but deep intensity, strong emotion controlled by an artistic sense of the value of restraint, and an earnestness entirely free from exaggeration, which entitle her to unqualified praise'.

The play ran for a fortnight, as planned, perhaps because of the use of the original ending rather than in reaction to it. A critic for the *Age*, whose identity is unknown but whose attitude was more flexible than that of Smith, opened his review of the first performance with a brief tribute to Ibsen as 'one of the most noted moral and social reformers of the age', one 'who makes the stage his medium of instructing the multitude on his own views of right and wrong'. This review continues with a synopsis of the plot and an enthusiastic appreciation of Achurch's acting. Apart from the remark, 'the attempts made to transplant Ibsen into English soil have not been quite so successful [as productions in Norway and Germany]', there is no criticism, either direct or implied, of the resolution of the drama.[11] Smith, by comparison, seems to have been out of touch with modern dramatic trends and, in his acceptance of the demands of an English audience as the standard in an English-speaking country, restrictively provincial. His attempt to have the ending changed was also an error of critical judgment. Ibsen's alternative 'happy ending' had proved unsuccessful overseas because, in effect, it was a contradiction of the logical progress of the remainder of the action, and the original version was the one most often used.

Smith displayed a similar attitude towards what he obviously considered to be another extreme of modernity in his criticism of Ethel Turner's *The Story of a Baby*, published in London in 1895. But, in this case, he followed up his public statement of critical approval with a personal letter of encouragement and advice. He appears to have done this because, in spite of his conservative approach, he saw himself as a link in a continuous literary tradition, in which the work of a promising new Australian writer might find a place. *The Story of a Baby* was the second of Turner's novels. The first, *Seven Little Australians*, a story for children published in 1894, had been warmly received, inspiring the sequel *The Family at Misrule*, published in the following year. *The Story of a Baby*, which was an adult novel, appeared in between the two children's books. Smith believed it to be superior to Turner's first work in several aspects:

> Miss Ethel Turner's *Story of a Baby* ... displays greater maturity of thought and purpose, plan, and procedure than its predecessors, *Seven Little Australians*. The dialogue is crisply written, and the plot dramatically worked out.

The subject matter was less acceptable and its treatment in one particular section less assured than the 'character painting in the nursery', assessed as Turner's 'strong point'. Smith disapproved especially of Dot's proposed abandonment of her husband and baby, averted only through the restraint of the man with whom she intended to run away. Here he writes:

> ...the resolute wrongheadedness of the young wife, whose vindictive revolt against the somewhat tyrannical exercise of her husband's authority impels her to propose an elopement to her high-minded teacher of singing, strikes us as a mistake, as well from an artistic as from an ethical point of view. The incident is exotic in origin, and there is, in it, more of the enervating perfume of a Parisian boudoir, than of the wholesome atmosphere of the weatherboard cottage on the Red road.[12]

Smith's criticism of the incident is in accord with his exposition of the ethical and moral considerations of Nora's abandonment of her husband and family in his review of *A Doll's House*. While Ibsen's play was more exotic in plot and action than Turner's otherwise 'wholesome' novel, and the respective writers were very different in attitude and style, there is a basic theme in common, and that is, the growth of maturity through self-knowledge. This is a concept that Smith would surely have approved, though not the means of illustration chosen both by playwright and novelist. What he rightly saw as an artistic mistake in Turner's work was the incompatibility of the incident with the tone of the remainder. He confirms this aspect of his criticism of the novel in his *Australasian* review:

> In a drama by Ibsen, or a novel by Maupassant, the dramatic situation might be allowed to pass unchallenged. In *The Story of a Baby*, where we get into a different moral atmosphere, Dot's relations with Mr. Sullivan Wooster strike one as being a little unnatural, if not inconsistent with her character as pourtrayed in the earlier chapters of the book.[13]

As Turner was herself to realise, resolution of the conflict between husband and wife required working out in terms of the basic premises of the story, as already told.

Smith's letter to Ethel Turner regarding *The Story of a Baby* has not

A new generation

survived. The following extract from her reply, dated 21 November 1895, is sufficient indication of encouragement and constructive criticism:

> I appreciated your letter more than I can tell you. There are not many men who, after writing long and favourable critiques, would trouble also to write privately to a beginner to give her still further encouragement. It has added another rose to the path you speak of. I am so glad you speak so happily of a literary career, so many shake their heads at it and talk of the difficulties and disappointments; to me, just starting, it seems the ideal life and I would not give it up were the thorns predicted like those of the latana-moa, rather than the roses.
>
> I liked your criticism both in the *Argus* and the *Australasian* very much. What you say about The Story of a Baby is only too true. I have seen it myself—ever since it was too late to alter it. That incident is exotic in its origin—it brings the colour to my face to think of it, I never open the covers of it. It is as if I had finished a copy book and dropped a great blot at the end and that no penknife in the world could erase. I am afraid it is the result of a course of very modern literature,—I thought I had been "domestic" to the point of boredom and it behoved me to find a dramatic incident.[14]

Obviously impressed by Smith's attention, Ethel Turner appears to have also been anxious to show her agreement with experienced opinion. She was to become a popular author of novels and short stories. Some of her later books were intended for an adult readership, but she wrote mainly for the children who eagerly awaited each of her new stories.

Smith's approach to colonial literature was generally one of critical encouragement, although, in 'The Social Development of Australasia', written in 1888, he expressed the belief that 'a distinctively Australian or Australasian literature...lies far out in the future'.[15] As evident from this essay, he appreciated the value of the poets J. Brunton Stephens, Adam Lindsay Gordon and Henry Kendall in the course of the development of an indigenous literature:

> They have given us poetry in the true sense of the word, combining, in various proportions, thought, feeling, expression, fancy and imagination, with an ardent love of nature; and clothing their ideas in language which is often singularly melodious. Let us add that some of their descriptive compositions are full of local colour, while others bear the impress of that sense of loneliness and mystery, of awe and melancholy, which is experienced by all who have had much acquaintance with the awful stillness of the Australian bush, and with the solitariness of the great far-stretching plains of the interior.[16]

This last section, which is strikingly reminiscent of Marcus Clarke's description of the Australian bush,[17] leads on to an acknowledgment of Clarke's ability as a novelist, in what appears to be a genuinely sympathetic, though brief, assessment:

> We may also claim one novelist, the late Marcus Clarke, the author of *For the Term of His Natural Life*,[18] who had imbibed something of the spirit of Balzac and felt the influence of Poe; and who gave in his writings every indication that he possessed the gift of genius. Unfortunately, he was cut off in early life. His "leaf has perish'd in the green," and
>
> > The world which credits what is done
> > Is cold to all that might have been.[19]

Writing with hindsight that included a knowledge of the novel's continued success, Smith was able to give proper credit to the work of the young writer whom he had previously opposed as a rival in literary journalism, and who had died in 1881. Smith's sentimental conclusion is a typically Victorian literary device; he was not only speaking well of the dead, but speaking in a manner that was reverently as well as appropriately poetic.

Smith attributed the slow growth of colonial literature to the necessity for the laborious construction of a new society in which, for the first generation, there were few members of what he described as a 'leisure class'. There was also another practical reason in that, apart from local periodicals, there were few established avenues for publication in a young country. These reasons are linked in the essay with a third: the nostalgic colonial preference for the works of familiar authors and the consequent lack of interest in the local product. Not all of Smith's reasons for the slow development of Australian literature are valid. Undoubtedly, the business of setting up a colony and civilising the land demanded time-consuming energy. But the process through struggle to consolidation was a potential source of distinctive literary themes. The writers who exploited those themes were not necessarily members of a 'leisure class' in the sense that they had independent means. Each of the poets he mentions had some other occupation, while Marcus Clarke was a journalist and later, a public servant, and Smith himself worked for his living. His argument that leisure was a prerequisite of literary growth is, therefore, indefensible in the colonial context. The limitation of avenues for publication was a more important factor, especially when writers were largely dependent upon periodicals of a decidedly ephemeral nature.

The views expressed in the essay appear to have been based on a speech given by Smith at a mayoral luncheon in Melbourne on 9 February 1885. The visiting English historian J. A. Froude was one of the chief guests on this occasion and both he and Smith were asked to respond to a toast to literature. The luncheon was reported in detail in the *Age*, including the text of Froude's speech, but only a brief reference to the effect that Smith had also spoken. The *Argus* report took the form of a paragraph summarising Froude's speech. Smith's speech may have

A new generation

been omitted through lack of space. It also seems likely that its omission may have been due to the deference paid to overseas visitors of some distinction, as well as the comparative importance of Froude's views generally and the development of the local product. However, it is possible to reconstruct Smith's theme through the *Age* editorial of 21 February, which began with the following expression of disagreement with Smith's concept of a leisured literary class:

> One of the speechifiers at the recent Mayoral dinner—if we remember rightly—Mr. James Smith—apologised for the paucity of literary men in Australia and the poor figure which Australian Literature cuts in the world of books on the ground that a young community is too busily engaged in the material work of subduing nature to its wants to have any leisure for worshipping at the shrine of Minerva. The explanation is an old one, and one that is usually considered satisfying in the oratory of the table cloth; but it is an explanation that will nevertheless not bear five minutes' critical examination.

The writer continued by giving several examples of authors in England and Australia whose works were the result of the leisure remaining after other kinds of employment. He also gave, as his own reason for what he agreed was the slow growth of Australian literature, the lack, as yet, of distinctive traits of colonial character. He concluded the editorial with an appreciation of American literature based on an older and, as he believed, a more mature civilisation than his own.

The identity of the *Age* writer is unknown, but it appears from the tone of his argument as well as its content that, while furthering his own views on the subject, he was also intent on challenging Smith's authority. This, in itself, is an indication that Smith's views were still considered of sufficient importance to be the subject of challenge. Other instances of contemporary recognition suggest that his place in Melbourne's cultural life was fairly secure at this time. One of these is the letter written by Richard Twopeny to F. E. Haddon (then editor of the *Argus*) on 11 February 1884. Twopeny asks: 'Would you be so kind as to ask Mr. James Smith whom I have not the pleasure of knowing, if he would do me the favour of giving me a few notes towards a chapter on Literature and Art for the second editon of *Town Life in Australia*'.[20] Whether or not Smith supplied the notes as requested, the second edition of Twopeny's book failed to materialise. A letter to Smith from Janet, Lady Clarke (undated, but apparently late 1888 or early 1889) is interesting also as evidence of continued public acceptance of his literary experience. Many years earlier, Smith had given Lady Clarke's father a list of suitable books for her to read as a means to further education. Now she asked for similar assistance on behalf of her own daughter:

> Years ago you gave to my Father a list of works for me to read as a sort of continuation of my education and I thought it so splendid

> that I in my turn am going to ask you to be so very kind as to guide me in my little daughter's education. She is now 14 and reads with Miss Bateman. She is a clever child and older than her years in many ways. I want her to as far as possible be gradually educated in the world of books. She has four years before her. I do not know if it is best for her to read the same book steadily through taking an hour each day or if it would be better to take a history one day and on the alternate day something quite different, travels, or biography—what do you think—of course she has many other things to learn, Latin, Italian, Drawing and Music besides her general English work.[21]

Smith's reply has not survived and it is not known whether the course he suggested included works by Australian writers. But it must reasonably be assumed that he took pleasure in compiling the list and, in acceding to Lady Clarke's request, demonstrating the value of the literary experience that he had gained over the previous 30 years or more as a book collector and a critic.

He was to make another speech on the development of Australian literature at a farewell dinner to bookseller Samuel Mullen on 29 October 1889, prior to Mullen's departure for an extended visit to England. Again, his speech was in response to a toast, this time, 'Success in Literature'. In the relevant section of his reply, which was summarised in the *Argus*, he repeated his belief that Australian literature 'would have to be born in the next century'. But his reasons seem to have become influenced by recognition of a growing generation gap. According to the *Argus* reporter's summary:

> The present generation seemed to be too much devoted to the worship of muscle and too little to the worship of brains. There was too much demand for shilling shockers, penny dreadfuls, *Ally Sloper's Half Holiday*, *Tit-Bits*, and publications of a similar nature. Still, he hoped for better times, and the growth of an Australian literature.[22]

Smith was now 69 years old. His disapproval of young, modern colonials is, perhaps, an indication of his increasing age and his awareness of the challenge to the standards which, for him, had been absolute guidelines. The fact that the development of Australian literature was considered a worthy subject for formal toasts also indicates the growing movement towards colonial nationalism that led to Federation in 1901. The wish for cultural activities that were recognisable as being distinctively Australian—whether in literature or the fine arts—was an important part of that movement.

Smith's continuing perception of himself as a linking figure between traditional forms of culture and the developing colonial product is evident in his critical reaction to Joseph Furphy's *Such is Life*, published in Sydney by the *Bulletin* in 1903. As he had done after reading *The Story of a Baby* by Ethel Turner, Smith reviewed the work and

A new generation

followed up his public comments with a private letter to the author. But, whereas Turner was already on the way to becoming established at the time of her correspondence with Smith, Furphy was a unknown writer whose reputation was to be built upon a single monumental work. Because of its extreme length, Furphy's original manuscript was split into two parts by A. G. Stephens of the *Bulletin;* one was published as *Such is Life* and the other as *Rigby's Romance*.[23] A further chapter was revised for publication as *The Buln-Buln and the Brolga*.[24] *Such is Life*, 'being certain extracts from the diary of Tom Collins' was an unusual work that defied categorisation as a novel. Furphy, writing as 'Tom Collins', explained his idiosyncratic approach in the first chapter:

> Whilst a peculiar defect—which I scarcely like to call an oversight in mental construction—shuts me out from the flowery pathway of the romancer, a co-ordinate requital endows me, I trust, with the more sterling, if less ornamental qualities of the chronicler. This fairly equitable compensation embraces, I have been told, three distinct attributes: an intuition which reads men like signboards; a limpid veracity; and a memory which habitually stereotypes all impressions except those relating to personal injuries. Submitting then, to the constitutional interdict already glanced at, and availing myself of the implied license to utilise that homely talent of which I am the bailee, I purpose taking certain entries from my diary, and amplifying these to the minutest detail of occurrence or conversation. This will afford to the observant readers a fair picture of Life, as that engaging problem has presented itself, to me.[25]

It might be expected that Smith, a determinedly conservative critic, might reject a work of this kind as being outside the mainstream of general literature. However, he was to applaud it in his review for the *Age*, which is recognisable as his work both in style and tone as well as its affinity with his letter. He began by comparing *Such is Life* to works by the 'picaresque' school of Spanish novelists because of the variety and vitality of the characters. Furphy's skill in characterisation was assessed as follows: 'You are made to feel that the author of the book has lived among them, has studied their ways, looked into their hearts and minds, and acquired their vocabulary'. Furphy's literary style met with equal approval: 'He is evidently a man who has read much, reflected much, and has so saturated his mind with the writings of Shakespeare as to make the phraseology of the poet a part of his daily speech'. The review continued with extracts from the text, illustrating Furphy's powers of natural description and the expression of his sense of humour. In some parts of the book, Smith found himself

> conscious of being in company with a thinker, as well as of a close observer of human character, and a man whose sympathies are broad and comprehensive, and whose views of men and things are thoroughly unconventional and touched with the conviction that the worst of his fellow beings are not all evil, nor the best of them exempt from imperfection.[26]

He was obviously greatly impressed with the work, which, while 'not a story in the strict sense', was 'overflowing with character'. The review in the *Leader* appears to have been written by Smith also; it is similar in style and tone and the same points are selected for comment. In this review, he concluded with the following recommendation:

> The philosophical reflections of a man who has studied deeply, both in books and human nature, are also full of matter to be read, marked, learned and inwardly digested. Taken altogether, *Such is Life* is a delightful volume, to which a hearty welcome may be given.[27]

The reviews of Furphy's book were generally favourable and Smith was not alone in his applause. Although unconventional, the moral and ethical basis of the novel was sound and the author, despite his unusual style, was remarkably literate. He also had a lively, if wry, sense of humour, making his work thoroughly entertaining as well as thought provoking. It is not altogether surprising, therefore, that Smith appreciated its value, although it is also possible that he might have missed the full irony of Furphy's philosophical reflections.

The extent of Smith's appreciation is evident in the letter that extended the *Age* and the *Leader* reviews. As he wrote to Furphy:

> I cannot resist the temptation to tell you privately what I have endeavoured to express publicly; namely, the pleasure I have received from reading your "Such is Life".
>
> The vein you have struck may not be entirely new, but your method of developing it is; while the freshness and originality of the work are greatly enhanced, to my mind, by the literary culture which it displays; which is always an added charm in the eyes of a bookish man.
>
> As probably the oldest working journalist and writer of books in Australia—my first essay in that direction bears date 1845—I remember with gratitude how I was heartened in my career by kind words of encouragement from Douglas Jerrold, John Forster, William Hazlitt, and Mary Russell Mitford; so perhaps you will not find me intrusive in offering you these few words of congratulation and cordial cheer.[28]

It is obvious from this letter that Smith's approval of Furphy's literary background had influenced his acceptance of the book as an important work. This is an attitude that seems to have been closely linked with his perception of himself as a literary figure who had built his reputation on a similar background. He appears to have seen himself also as a patriarch of literature, linking his career with those of established writers and acting in relation to Furphy as Jerrold, Hazlitt and others had to himself.

Furphy received Smith's letter through A. G. Stephens. But, when writing to his friend William Cathels, he asked:

> Whisper—who is James Smith? I have seen honorable mention of his name, for instance in Alex Sutherland's large history of Victoria,[29] and frequently in columns of the profane rag above referred to [the *Argus*]. Yet I feel a most cordial interest in his personality and welfare, for as much as he has gone out of his way to send me...a very kind letter of approval and encouragement touching *Such is Life*.[30]

To Furphy, Smith seems to have been known as little more than a working journalist. However, taking Smith's self-aggrandisement at its face value, he described him in another letter, this time to his mother, as 'the highest literary figure in Australia', again citing Alexander Sutherland as his authority.[31]

Despite the apparent flippancy of Furphy's approach to the matter of Smith's status, he seems to have been warmly appreciative of Smith's comments. His letter in reply to Smith can be taken as a sincere response to critical approval. It may also have been a generous attempt to respond in like manner so that Smith, now an old man, need not be disillusioned of his position as the holder of continual cultural power. As Furphy wrote:

> I am at a loss to express my estimation of your approval in any terms which would not appear fulsome. It is enough to say that I never anticipated the notice—favourable or otherwise—of one who must be regarded as being, without exception, the most competent literary authority in Australia. And along with the honour which your kindly interest confers upon me, I feel a sense of responsibility not realised hitherto—a tacit obligation to justify in future the good opinion which has really taken me by surprise.[32]

The novel did not immediately gain widespread acceptance as an important work of Australian fiction. Because of its originality, as well as its complexity, it confounded many early readers. But those who persevered found it to be as enjoyable reading as Smith had promised and, eventually, it was to become a classic of Australian literature.

12
DECLINING YEARS

Although still actively employed during the 1880s, Smith was moving towards the retirement that he might confidently have expected to be financially comfortable. Most of his savings were invested with building societies at attractive rates of interest. This must have appeared to many Melbourne investors the most sensible way in which to maintain their current prosperity. With all the evidence of growth and development around them, few people could have anticipated the end of the land boom and the disastrous consequences of the depression that would follow. As the boom declined and the widespread speculation that had been so profitable at its height was no longer a means to easy wealth, investors began to withdraw their money from the banks and the building societies that had proliferated over previous years. The Commercial Bank of Australia, of which Henry Gyles Turner was general manager for Victoria, was the first to close its doors, when customers made a run on its funds on 7 April 1892, in an effort to recover their capital.[1] Other banks followed until all except the Union Bank and the Bank of Australasia had suspended business. Members of all levels of society were affected. Many of those who had invested large sums became insolvent; businesses closed down, leaving employees without work; houses were repossessed and more people shared the stigma and the hardship of poverty than ever before in the city's history. There was to be a gradual recovery from financial depression, but Melbourne, for so long the premier city of Australia, lost population to Sydney. New South Wales, also suffering economic difficulties, was less badly affected than Victoria. Western Australia, where gold had recently been discovered, was another attractive destination. Some Victorians went further, returning to England and Europe in an attempt to remake their lives. Melbourne also lost status as a cultural centre when artists and writers moved away in search of better opportunities.

The building societies were especially vulnerable to failure. Many of them had used investors' funds for speculation in buying and selling land and, unlike those banks that were more conservatively based, they were unable to recover from the crashes. As noted in his diary, Smith

Declining years

was a regular depositor in an unnamed building society in 1863.[2] He became President of three societies: the Freemasons' Building and Investment Society, the Standard Building and Investment Society (later the Standard Mutual Building Society) and the Southern Terminating Building Society.[3] The records of these societies are no longer extant, but it is probable that he invested in them all. His possession of shares in the Standard Mutual Building Society is confirmed by the list of his assets for probate purposes, which includes 81 permanent shares, then worth £3/2/6 each. Other investments include 160 shares in the liquidated Victorian Permanent Building and Investment Society (which appears to have evolved out of the Victorian Permanent Building Society), as well as mining shares, most of which were of little or no value in 1910. His total assets at the time of death were only £1500,[4] the major part being his private library, valued for probate duty at £1000.[5] Like so many of his fellows, he was a victim of overoptimistic enthusiasm in expansive colonial development, with its accompanying enticement of personal wealth. He continued to live in his house at Hawthorn, although it seems unlikely that he retained full ownership.[6] He had to cancel a proposed trip to England and Europe, but, more fortunate than most of those who had lost heavily in the crashes, he was neither bankrupt nor out of work.

By this stage of his working life, Smith was almost an *Argus* institution. Although past the usual retirement age, he had a still active mind and his habits of wide reading and careful observation, combined with long practice in literary skills made him a useful contributor. However, the depression was to affect the profitability of the *Argus*, making less work available to him than he needed. Eventually, his position declined to the extent that he began to consider moving interstate in search of more consistent employment. His reply to J. J. Shillinglaw's request for a particular review in May 1895 is an indication of his disillusionment:

> With respect to Professor Petrie's work,[7] I do not possess the slightest influence in regard to procuring a review of it in the Argus. Occasionally a book is placed in my hands for review, but the selection of any book for that purpose rests entirely with the editor.
> Under the policy of retrenchment rendered necessary by the change in the price of the paper, my own connection with it has become so slight and unremunerative, that, in the event of a more eligible offer from a neighbouring colony or elsewhere, I should feel reluctantly obliged to terminate a service of forty years.[8]

As it appears, there were no suitable offers of alternative employment. Work of the kind he wanted was scarce in other places besides Melbourne and Smith had no choice but to continue writing for the *Argus* in the hope that his situation would improve. What he did not realise was that he was gradually being phased out.

His resumption of active involvement with the spiritualist movement during the 1890s was something of an embarrassment to the *Argus* proprietors, even though he took care to separate his activities from his work as a journalist. The lack of available work also suggests that, apart from the 'J. S.' articles that remained a feature, his particular style of journalism was no longer appropriate for use in a progressive newspaper. Whatever their exact reasons, the proprietors decided that it was time to terminate his employment. On 22 July 1896, he was asked to retire, 'in consequence of his leaning towards spiritualism'.[9] Since the *Argus* had allowed him to remain on the staff after his dismissal from editorship of the *Australasian* in 1872, compulsory retirement on this ground so many years later must have been a considerable shock. Not only were his deepest convictions challenged once again, but also his ability to define his interests according to his audience. Since he was now in a much reduced financial position, he knew that, at 76, he would have to go on working for as long as possible for whoever he could persuade to employ him.

Smith's dismissal from the *Argus* also dismayed those among his friends and associates who were tolerant enough to accept his involvement in spiritualism as a particular interest that need not affect his concentration on other topics as occasion required. J. C. Williamson seems to have been especially disappointed that Smith would now cease work as a drama critic. On 27 July, soon after Smith's break with the *Argus* had become known, Williamson expressed his regret in the following terms: 'Theatrical critics combining knowledge and ability are so rare that your withdrawal from the list will be an incomparable loss to theatrical art in Australia.'[10] But, despite any representations that might be made on his behalf, the dismissal was final and, for some time, Smith was without a forum for criticism of any kind. He was eventually to be employed by David Syme, but the date of his return to the *Age* is unknown. Syme's letter, inviting Smith to write two or three articles a week, is undated,[11] and there is no acknowledgment of work by Smith in the *Age* until the appearance of a new series of 'J. S.' articles in 1905. He was still looking for regular, paid employment in 1899, as indicated by his letter to Alfred Deakin of 3 March of that year, regarding the possibility of appointment as secretary to the proposed Commission of Technical Education. As he told Deakin, he desperately needed work:

> I am stranded, after 45 years of hard work, coupled with thrift, and do not like the idea of quitting Melbourne and beginning a fresh career elsewhere. Hard lines! and all the harder because I have been treated with callous injustice by the Argus manager, and all my savings went in the financial crash.[13]

There was no position available to him and it seems likely that he continued working as a freelance journalist for some years after his enforced retirement. He was still lecturing, mostly to spiritualists, but occasionally to other groups more interested in general and literary topics. Much of his increased leisure time appears to have been spent in transcribing the spiritual communications that were the basis for many of the articles that he was now writing regularly for the *Harbinger of Light*. Between 1890 and 1904, as estimated by the editor Annie Bright, his contributions to the journal would have filled 'seven or eight octavo volumes of 300 pages each'.[14]

Though writing little in the way of fine arts criticism, Smith was responsible for two pamphlets that included critical appreciation of the artist who was the subject: the first, *An Appreciation of the Late James W. Curtis*,[15] and the second, *Catalogue of Exhibition of Australian Landscapes by J. Mather*.[16] He was to find further employment as editor of the *Cyclopedia of Victoria*, published in three volumes from 1903–1905. This was a comprehensive account of historical and commercial development in the colony since first settlement, including descriptive and biographical sections. Apart from his duties as editor and general contributor, he was responsible for detailed sections on the drama and the fine arts. It is rather ironical that Smith, who had been reduced to comparative poverty by the financial disasters of the 1890s, should have been commissioned to edit an encyclopedia subtitled 'an epitome of progress'. However, its appearance in series over three consecutive years indicates the faith of subscribers as well as promoters in the inevitability of colonial progress, despite the hindrance of depression.

In December 1904, Smith celebrated 50 years' residence in Victoria. Henry Gyles Turner and R. L. Ievers were responsible for arranging a commemorative dinner, at which Smith was presented with a purse of sovereigns, accompanied by a formal address in appreciation of his services to literature. This dinner, held on 17 January 1905, was attended by friends and associates, including members of the Melbourne Shakespeare Society, the Alliance Francaise and the Dante Society. Turner and Annie Bright were notable among the speakers who, according to the report in the *Leader*, 'spoke in eulogistic terms of Mr. Smith's abilities, paying tribute also to his estimable personal qualities'.[17] As the *Leader* reporter went on to say: 'The recipient of these enconiums responded modestly, deprecating the catalogue of his virtues and pleading that what he had done in journalism or literature had been for the benefit of others—to amuse, to interest, and, when practicable, to instruct'. While Smith's disclaimer was appropriate to the occasion, he had, in fact, undertaken his literary career in Melbourne with the view to making a distinguished name for himself, as well as with the objective of promoting colonial culture. It must, therefore, have been most gratifying to him to be recognised in this particular manner.

In 1907, James and Eliza Smith celebrated their golden wedding. Always reticent about his family life, Smith said little in public about his wife and children. However, when preparing the manuscript of

'Handbook for the Homeward Bound', a projected travel book that does not appear to have been completed, he wrote the following inscription on the title-page: 'Dedicated with much gratitude and affection to my travelling companion in the fiftieth year of our married life.'[18] These words in appreciation of what, in the absence of contrary evidence, seems to have been a successful marriage, were also a reminder that Smith, if not his much younger wife, had arrived at advanced old age. He had lived through most of the nineteenth century and, in the early years of the twentieth, he began writing his reminiscences. The 'Recollections of an Octogenarian', published in a series of twelve articles in the *Leader*, covers the period of childhood in England through to his early years in Melbourne. During the course of the series, he recalled the fellow immigrants with whom he had shared many convivial evenings at the Argus hotel in Collins Street. One was Butler Cole Aspinall, another Charles Bright, others Edward Whitty and William Akhurst. But, as he wrote, quoting Charles Lamb, they were 'all gone, the old familiar faces',[19] leaving him as the sole survivor. In the section 'Talent in Exile', he referred to former colleagues such as Charles Whitehead and R. H. Horne, as well as some of the artists whose work he had admired, including Nicholas Chevalier and Louis Buvelot. In a further section, 'Some Journalists', he recalled Edward Wilson, Ebenezer Syme, George Higinbotham, David Blair and other newspaper identities. In later articles in the series, he wrote about some of the politicians he had known and also the actors who had played in Melbourne, such as G. V. Brooke and Joseph Jefferson. The series as a whole forms an interesting record of Melbourne life; it is also, as Smith himself obviously realised, a picture of the colonial scene in which, through all the vicissitudes of his career, he had been a central figure.

His last book, *Junius Unveiled*,[20] was published in 1909. From then on, he was to write little else for publication, except for the 'J. S.' articles that had now become a feature of the *Age* and his spiritualist articles for the *Harbinger of Light*. Although he had been so prolific a writer for the whole of his working life, his deteriorating health caused him to tire of the effort to maintain his accustomed pace. During the last years of his life, he suffered from cystitis, a chronic illness that gradually deprived him of physical energy. Visiting him at home not long before his death, Annie Bright noticed that 'he lay weak and despondent on his couch in the verandah, and longing for his release'.[21] But his intellect seems to have been unimpaired and he managed to continue his work for the *Age* and the *Harbinger* until the last few days. He died at his home in Hawthorn on 19 March 1910 and was buried at Boroondara Cemetery two days later. After his affairs were settled, Eliza moved to Ballarat to live with their son Charles, then editor of the *Ballarat Star*. She died there in 1927.

Long and detailed notices were published in Melbourne newspapers on Smith's death. The writers had ample information on which to draw:

biographical articles for which Smith had supplied material had appeared in *Table Talk* in 1889 and the *Harbinger of Light* in 1904. The entry under Smith's name in the *Cyclopedia of Victoria* was also up to date and, since it was most probably written by himself as editor, the information it contained might be assumed to be reliable. It might also be assumed that Smith, who, among his other duties for the *Argus*, had acted on occasion as necrologist—or writer of obituaries—could have prepared the basic material for his own. In each of the biographical sources referred to, the following are common facts: the details of Smith's early career as a writer and newspaper editor in England; his emigration to Victoria and his employment on, firstly, the *Age* and then the *Argus*, as a leader writer and literary, dramatic and fine arts critic; his work as editor of, and contributor to, other Victorian newspapers and periodicals; his term as Parliamentary Librarian; and his active membership of Melbourne clubs and societies. Using these facts as a basis, the writers of the obituary notices enlarged upon his activities and paid tribute to him as a leader in colonial cultural affairs.

The writer of the notices in the *Argus* and the *Australasian* appears to have been the same person because of noticeable similarities in style and content. It probably was Henry Gyles Turner, who, of all Smith's friends and associates in Melbourne, was the one who had known him the longest and the only one of his fellow immigrants to outlive him. Turner praised his old friend as a journalist, a lecturer and a cultural activist. But, unlike the *Age* writer, who spoke in generally comparable terms, he referred also to Smith's spiritualist activities, saying, in the *Argus*: 'Mr. Smith's most absorbing subject for 40 years was spiritualism; but his writings upon it were mostly confined to elect believers; it was not a subject on which he had many opportunities to address a sceptical public'.[22] A similar paragraph appeared in the notice in the *Australasian*. It is not surprising, given Turner's antipathy to the practice of spiritualism, that he should choose to mention Smith's belief in spiritual communication. Perhaps for reasons of diplomacy, the *Age* writer concentrated on other aspects, describing Smith as 'the doyen of Australian journalists'.[23] However, spiritualism had been a most important part of Smith's life in his later years and no obituary was complete without mention of this special interest.

While obituary notices are limited as a means of estimating contemporary opinion because of their naturally complimentary tone, most writers of notices on Smith seem to have been agreed that his colonial career had been distinguished, given Turner's proviso that his spiritualist activities were less praiseworthy than the rest. For Turner, primarily a business man, despite his interest in literature, the 'dual existence' that he sensed in Smith surpassed ordinary comprehension.[24] Only those, like Annie Bright, who had a sympathetic appreciation of the importance that Smith placed on the spiritual side of his personality could begin to understand his reasons for jeopardising his career, or realise the effort he had made to restore it after the first hysteria of conversion had passed. But, while Bright was naturally sympathetic because of their common interest in spiritualism, her respect for his ability and also his industry was not confined to that sphere. She was a respected figure in literary circles herself. From 1894 until 1896, she edited the *Cosmos Magazine*, a Sydney periodical that was largely literary, even though the title reflected her interest in spiritual and other cosmic forces. After leaving the magazine because of a change in proprietorship, she continued developing her investigations into spiritualist practice and, following the death of her husband Charles Bright in 1903, came to Melbourne.[25]

Because of her own professional experience, Annie Bright was able to give full credit to Smith's activities, both as a literary journalist and a practising spiritualist. In the biographical article written for the *Harbinger* in 1904, she had referred to the 'ceaseless intellectual training' that he had undergone, allowing him to take his place among those 'writers and speakers of the first class' who were open to higher inspiration.[26] She continued this article by discussing his activities as a writer on general topics, in the belief that

> it was necessary to briefly indicate Mr. James Smith's position in the literary world to place in its proper light the unswerving fidelity to conviction and fearlessness in his advocacy of the truth of Spiritualism, with which, in spite of prejudice and misrepresentation on all sides, he has kept on his way since he became convinced of the reality of the spiritual world and its all-important influence upon our present state of existence.

After Smith's death, writing the 'Editorial Notes' that preceded her obituary, Annie Bright commented on the 'highly appreciative notice' in the *Argus*, where the writer had spoken 'most ungrudgingly of James Smith's remarkable career as a brilliant man of letters...' As made clear in this notice and, as she herself had long been aware, 'his only fault in the eyes of the world was that he was a Spiritualist, and brave enough to say so'. To her, he had been, not only a 'distinguished journalist', but also a 'beloved friend', a 'generous helper' and an 'unwearied and steadfast worker in the cause of truth and enlightenment'.[27]

When taken together, the obituaries written by Turner and Bright provide a reasonably well balanced view of the man. But, since both of them were his personal friends, their view of him is necessarily a subjective one. A notice by a *Bulletin* contributor, whose identity is unknown, but who appears to have been familiar with Smith only through professional connections, is more objective. It reads:

> James Smith, whom nobody in the inky way has ever dared to mention with disrespect these last 25 years, finished his long life on Saturday. Another month and he would have been 90. And all his years he was a very busy Smith. How far back his industry went we

moderns can judge by the fact that he claimed to have given in England the first public reading from Dickens. All but 70 years ago—69 to be exact—he was editing the Herts County Press; then he joined Douglas Jerrold in the Illuminated Press; and 56 years ago he came out to the Age. Later he passed on to the Argus but got at last back to the Symes, and was still writing for them when his last illness came. He had written acres about politics in his time, but he loved art and letters better, and he liked his own opinion on these matters. For a journalist I expect he was fairly well off; for though he took a hand in a host of unsuccessful ventures, he was a careful man and he wasted few hours.[28]

Because the writer was unhindered by reverent appreciation, the picture of Smith that is presented here is probably a closer reflection of contemporary opinion than that provided either by Turner or Bright. Whereas they, and especially Bright, appear to have seen him as a continuing achiever, the *Bulletin* writer, who was obviously a much younger person, places him firmly in an antiquarian context, treating him more as a literary curiosity than a figure of current importance.

In many respects, the *Bulletin* writer was correct in his assessment of Smith's place in the modern world. He had, as that writer duly recognised, been a man of praiseworthy achievement in the past, but, even though he had continued writing feature articles for as long as he was physically able, his work as a literary journalist belonged to an earlier period. His cultural activities were also closely linked with the colonisation process and, as such, of comparatively little relevance to the federated Australians of the next century. Like most people who outlive their contemporaries, Smith had become something of an anachronism. Many of his Victorian values were out of date and his central position in immigrant circles forgotten. This is the picture that, if they know of him at all, has come down to later generations. But, if there is to be any real understanding of the basis of cultural growth in Victoria, it is important that Smith, and, through him, the aspects of immigrant society that he represents, be re-evaluated.

If he had remained in England, he would probably have furthered his career in journalism and continued to develop the interest in active involvement in cultural affairs that had begun while a member of the Salisbury Literary and Scientific Institute. However, whether living in London or remaining in a provincial town such as Salisbury, he could not have had the same sense of purpose that inspired his efforts to become a prominent figure in colonial cultural circles. In England he had been known by his immediate circle of friends and acquaintances and, perhaps, a little beyond, as a newspaper editor and minor author. But, in Melbourne, he and his fellow immigrants of similar interest were more likely to belong to the few who, relying on their own ability and experience, attempted to set the cultural tone for the remainder of the colonists. Because Smith was part of this group he gained recognition more quickly and to a greater extent than if he had stayed at home. This was the case with many of the 1850s immigrants who had achieved some local status before leaving England and Europe. The prospect of increasing that status in a new and potentially more favourable environment was very often an influential factor in the decision to emigrate.

In 1869, when lecturing on the prospects for the future development of the colony of Victoria under the title 'The Frog and the Ox', Smith made the following statement: '...no person, however insignificant, can rightly estimate the value of his own example, or foresee the extent of his individual influence for good or for evil'.[29] He was then speaking in general terms, but it is obvious from his cultural activity at the time, that the concept of individual example seemed equally appropriate to himself. This is reflected in the way in which he sought recognition, including the instructive mode of his work as a journalist and critic, as well as his constant readiness to accept positions of authority in the many clubs and societies that he joined as an active member. His didactic approach to moral and ethical questions also confirms his belief in the propriety of using whatever authority he was able to claim for the good of the colony.

Recognition of the kind sought by ambitious immigrants might provide its own satisfaction; it could also be the cause of tensions that were peculiar to the colonial situation. The re-establishment of familiar cultural institutions in a new setting gave the founders opportunities for immediate distinction, but personal rivalries sometimes made the prize less worthwhile in attainment. Smith achieved leadership as much because of his perception of himself as an important colonial figure as for his active involvement in almost every aspect of immigrant culture. Without that perception, it is improbable that he would have shown such concern to establish himself as an acknowledged leader. But this estimate of self-importance was not restricted to himself. Immigrants with similar preoccupations such as David Blair and J. E. Neild believed themselves equally well able to direct the organisation of cultural affairs. The jealousies that accompanied the struggle for distinction were a major cause of conflict between those immigrants, spoiling relationships and preventing the easy achievement of colonial distinction. Smith, who seems to have had an even stronger wish for leadership than most, suffered perhaps more than others in consequence.

Homesickness was another major cause of tension for the immigrants during their early years in the colony. This was a feeling that was compounded by distance and the prospect of permanent separation from families and friends at home. But, while sentiment and nostalgia formed a substantial part, the reasons for the kind of homesickness that prevented those immigrants who were responsible colonists from becoming easily settled were more complex. As representatives of their countries, and, more especially, of Britain, they were anxious to transfer traditional values in order to provide themselves with the security of a recognisable framework within which to pursue colonial objectives. This was an essential part of the colonisation process and they could not have been expected to act differently. However, undue concentration on what had been familiar at home tended to have the effect of accentuating the desirability of much of what they had left behind them. As well, the longer they clung to British standards as absolutes, the less likely they were to appreciate that those standards might not have equal validity in a new environment.

Dependence upon established modes of culture also prevented the immigrants from becoming more innovative. Their institutions and their periodicals were based directly upon overseas models and the actors, artists and writers who entertained and informed them were judged largely by previously set standards that allowed little room for experimentation. This approach was acceptable during the early years of immigration. But, later in the nineteenth century, when those immigrants who had concerned themselves with the foundation of colonial culture were declining in numbers, many of the attitudes that they carried with them had become outmoded. Smith, as one of the few who were left, tried harder, in consequence, to maintain the standards that he and his fellows had worked to perpetuate. Because of his conviction that this remained his proper role, he found it difficult to accept the fact that the authority he had confidently assumed from the time of his arrival had begun to lose its power. His reaction to the next generation of cultural colonists was governed to a large extent by his inability to appreciate that, while his efforts towards consolidation had been important at the time, this was an aspect of colonial life with which he need no longer concern himself. The foundations were laid and others with standards that were now more applicable to the colony would build upon them.

The new generation of colonists was reacting, in turn, against the confines of Victorianism. Partly inspired by nationalist sentiment and partly by the wish to develop new methods of cultural expression that might prove more appropriate in relation to the new country than the old, they may more realistically be described as the founders of a distinctive colonial culture than the immigrants who nurtured imperial ideas and attitudes. But the activities of the new generation were not applicable only to the Australian colonies. They were a reflection of a much wider reaction against Victorianism that was to continue through the end of the nineteenth century and into the middle years of the twentieth. It was a reaction that would be strengthened by the outbreak of two World Wars—the first in 1914 and the second in 1939—and the loss of many of the concepts that were dependent upon peaceful existence for realisation. Both between the wars and for some years later modernity seemed to be the major criterion for cultural activity. But the cycle is now turning and the appreciation of the Victorian values upon which the immigrants based their culture is becoming recognised as a means of better understanding of the lives and activities of people, like James Smith, who held them so dearly.

NOTES

Chapter 1: Melbourne in 1855

1 *Salisbury and Winchester Journal*, 14 April 1855.
2 Ibid.
3 These figures are taken from the tables at Appendix I and Appendix II of Geoffrey Serle, *The Golden Age: a history of the colony of Victoria 1851–1861*, Melbourne, Melbourne University Press, 1963, pp. 382–83.
4 *Salisbury and Winchester Journal*, 14 April 1855.
5 A number of land acts, each intended to make good the deficiencies of the last, went through the Victorian Parliament from 1860 until the amending act of 1869 that effectually opened up the remaining unalienated land for selection.
6 *Salisbury and Winchester Journal*, 19 May 1855. This letter was reprinted in the *Age* on 4 September 1855. Smith used it as the basis for the following articles: 'Melbourne Five and Twenty Years Ago', *Argus*, 2 August 1879; 'Old Melbourne', *Victorian Review* 9, 1883–84, 404–09 [by 'W.F.T.', a pseudonym apparently based on the initials of Smith's friend, Salisbury astist Walter F. Tiffin]; 'Melbourne in the Fifties', *Centennial Magazine* 2, 1889, [344]-49; 'Recollections of an Octogenarian', 4: 'Melbourne in 1854–55', *Leader*, 20 July 1970, pp. 42–43.
7 The city area of intersecting streets within a rectangle was laid out in 1837 by the senior surveyor Robert Hoddle.
8 *Salisbury and Winchester Journal*, 19 May 1855.
9 Both sides suffered casualties during the battle at the Eureka Stockade on 3 December 1854.
10 *Salisbury and Winchester Journal*, 26 May 1855.
11 This information is contained in the entry for James Smith in *The Cyclopedia of Victoria*, edited by James Smith, Melbourne, The Cyclopedia Company, 3 vols., 1903–1905, 1,333.
12 *Salisbury and Winchester Journal*, 23 June 1855.
13 *Salisbury and Winchester Journal*, 6 October 1855.
14 See *Australians: a historical library. Australians: historical statistics*, edited by Wray Vamplew, Sydney, Fairfax, Syme and Weldon Associates, 1987, Table IEO 1–9, p. 4. Michael Christie suggests that there were probably between 11 000 to 15 000 Aborigines living in Victoria: M. F. Christie, *Aborigines in Colonial Victoria 1853–86*, Sydney, Sydney University Press, 1979, p. 7. Christie outlines the difficulties involved in attempting to make exact estimates in Appendix A, 'Victorian Aboriginal Population Figures 1834–86, p. 206.
15 *Salisbury and Winchester Journal*, 6 October 1855.
16 'Melbourne in the Fifties', *Centennial Magazine* 2, 1889, 349.

17 'Old Melbourne', *Victorian Review* 9, 1883–84, 405.
18 Ibid.
19 'An Address to the Beefsteak Club, 10 August 1918', Turner papers, MS 1625, La Trobe Collection, State Library of Victoria.
20 See 'Recollections of an Octogenarian', 5: 'Bygone Celebrities', *Leader*, 27 July 1907, p. 43.
21 *The Eureka Stockade* was published by the author in Melbourne in 1855.
22 'Melbourne in the Fifties', p. 345.
23 'The Abolition of Labour', *Victorian Review* 1, 1879–80, 361.

Chapter 2: England: 1820–1854

1 Details of the double baptism are recorded in the *Register of Baptisms in the Parish of Loose in the County of Kent*, Kent Council Archives.
2 Private Diary, 10 March 1863, Smith papers, MSS 212, Mitchell Library, State Library of New South Wales.
3 The baptism of Mary Smith on 22 September 1822 is recorded in the *Register of Baptisms*.
4 Lucy Smith was not baptised. Her burial on 3 January 1825 is recorded in the *Register of Burials in the Parish of Loose in the County of Kent*, Kent Council Archives.
5 The dedication reads: 'To the memory of a beloved brother', *Rural Records*, London, Longman, 1845. Smith refers to the death of this brother by drowning at the age of seventeen in 'Interviews with Prominent Spiritualists. By Mrs. Charles Bright. Mr. James Smith', *Harbinger of Light* 35, 1904, 8451.
6 *Ralph Penfold*, 1: 'Early Dawn', *Victorian Review*, No. 8, 8 February 1861, p. 115.
7 Ibid.
8 'On Christmas Eve' was published in the *Queenslander* Christmas Supplement, 25 December 1880, pp. 1–4.
9 This legacy is noted on the 'Statements of Assets and Liabilities', Probate Jurisdiction in the State of Victoria, in the Will of James Smith, No. 115/839, Office of the Registrar of Probates, Melbourne.
10 Personal visits to Loose: 8 July 1980 and 27 July 1985.
11 'An English Village Fifty Years Ago', *Argus*, 19 April 1879.
12 'Recollections of an Octogenarian', 3: 'An Idyllic Interlude', *Leader*, 13 July 1907, p. 43.
13 Ibid.
14 As mentioned in 'Charles Lamb', *Age*, 26 February 1910.
15 'Mr. James Smith. An Australian Man of Letters', *Table Talk*, 30 August 1889, pp. 4–5.
16 Dickens attended the school from 1821–22. See Edgar Johnson, *Charles Dickens: his tragedy and triumph*, London, Allen Lane, 1977 (first published 1952), p. 23.
17 'Reminiscences of Rochester', *Argus*, 14 August 1880.
18 See J. N. T. Boston and E. I. Puddy, *Dereham: the biography of a country town*, Dereham, Coleby, 1952, p. 199.
19 *The Curse of Protection, a paper read before the Reform Club, 1st July 1895, by Mr. James Smith*, Melbourne, Rae and Munn, [1895], p. 9.
20 This river, which starts at Ware, provided the first water supply to London, pumped through oak pipes into a pool at Islington.

Notes

21 Personal visits to Ware: 19 July 1980 and 28–29 September 1985.
22 *Ralph Penfold*, 5: 'Schoolboy Experiences', *Victorian Review*, No. 12, 8 March 1861, p. 181. This description of Ware was revised and extended for 'An English Country Town in 1835', *Argus*, 6 March 1880.
23 See 'Minutes of the Ware Charity Meetings 1808–1845', Hertfordshire County Record Office.
24 This relative appears to have been based on Mrs Maria de Horne Hooper, the daughter of the poet John Scott, who lived in Amwell House.
25 *Ralph Penfold*, 6[7]: 'Further School Experiences', *Victorian Review*, No. 14, 22 March 1861, p. 210.
26 Ibid.
27 There were two Melbourne periodicals of the same title: the first *Victorian Review* ran from 1860–61 and the second from 1879–86.
28 *Ralph Penfold*, 5: 'Schoolboy Experiences', *Victorian Review*, No. 12, 8 March 1861, p. 181.
29 'An English Election in the Olden Times', *Argus*, 26 June 1880.
30 The Select Committee of the House of Commons on the Hertford Borough Election met in 1833.
31 *Ralph Penfold*, 5[6]: 'The Players', *Victorian Review*, No. 14[13], 15 March 1861, p. 199.
32 The story of Ralph Penfold's years on Jersey is told in Chapters 8–10, published in the *Victorian Review* on 20 and 27 April and 4 May 1861, respectively.
33 'On Christmas Eve', *Queenslander* Christmas Supplement, 25 December 1880, p. [1].
34 *Ralph Penfold*, 11[12]: 'A Smooth Passage', *Victorian Review*, No. 21, 11 May 1861, [269].
35 The first of the sketches appeared in June 1843 and the last in November 1844. Jerrold was editor of the *Illuminated Magazine* from 1843 to 1845. His undated letter accepting the first of the sketches and suggesting that others on similar lines could follow is included in the Smith papers, MS 2398, National Library of Australia.
36 Smith acknowledged his debt to Mary Russell Mitford by sending her a copy of *Rural Records*. Her letter of thanks is included with the Smith papers, MS 2398, National Library of Australia.
37 This information is included in records of interviews for *Table Talk* and the *Harbinger of Light*, as well as in obituary notices and other biographical sources.
38 *Hertfordshire Mercury*, 25 May 1841.
39 Smith's marriage was registered as No. 460 for the parish at the General Register Office, London.
40 James Bartlett Smith was 22 when he died in Australia in 1867. Charles Henry Smith's dates of birth and death are unknown.
41 'Recollections of an Octogenarian, 5: 'Bygone Celebrities', *Leader*, 27 July 1907, p. 43.
42 As detailed in Robert Rhodes James, *Albert Prince Consort*, London, Hamish Hamilton, 1983, p. 65.
43 See 'One Man One Vote', *Argus*, 4 November 1891.
44 'An English Cathedral City', *Argus*, 1 May 1880. Salisbury here is called 'Southminster'.
45 For further details regarding the *Salisbury and Winchester Journal*, see James Grant, *The Newspaper Press, its Origins, Progress and Present Position*, vol. 3,

The Metropolitan Weekly and Provincial Press, London, Routledge, 1871–[1872], pp. 242–44.
46 Annie Smith's death is recorded on Certificate No, 409 for the district of Salisbury.
47 See *City of Salisbury*, edited by H. de Shortt, London, Phoenix House, 1957, p. 105.
48 Ibid, p. 106.
49 This marriage was registered as No. 360 in the District of Collingwood.
50 See note 79.
51 James Bartlett Smith's death was registered as No. 650 in the District of Princhester, Queensland.
52 This letter appeared on 16 July 1849.
53 See *History of Wiltshire*, edited by R. B. Pugh. Vol. 6 of the *Victoria History of England*, London, Oxford University Press, 1953, p. 143.
54 This meeting was reported in the *Salisbury and Winchester Journal* on 8 December 1849. As advised by the County and Diocesan Archivist for Wiltshire by letter on 18 March 1980, none of the Institute's papers has survived.
55 *Salisbury and Winchester Journal*, 19 January 1850.
56 Ibid, 2 February 1850.
57 Letters from prospective lecturers and readers are included in the Smith papers, MS 2398, National Library of Australia.
58 This claim is included in the specific biographical details supplied by Smith (as by all those listed) for *Johns's Notable Australians and Who's Who in Australasia*, Adelaide, Fred Johns, 1980, p. 284.
59 See Johnson, *Charles Dickens*, p. 402.
60 As announced in the *Salisbury and Winchester Journal* on 17 December 1853.
61 *Salisbury and Winchester Journal*, 9 October 1852.
62 Ibid, 16 April 1853.
63 'Mr. James Smith. An Australian Man of Letters', *Table Talk*, 30 August 1889, p. 4.
64 *Oracles from the British Poets* was published in London by Henry Washbourne in 1849; in London by Washbourne and in Salisbury by G. Brown in 1851; in London by Virtue in 1862.
65 *Oracles from the Poets* was published in New York and London by John Wiley in 1844 and re-issued in 1849.
66 'Preface', *Oracles from the Poets*, p. [v].
67 Ibid, p. [vii].
68 *Wilton and its Associations* was published in Salisbury by G. Brown and in London by J. B. Nichols.
69 Smith's copy of *Wilton and its Associations* is included in the Smith papers, MS 2398, National Library of Australia.
70 The articles taken from *Wilton and its Associations* are: 'The Story of an English Country Town', *Victorian Review* 10, 1884, 457–80, 542–57 (Chapters 1–4); 'Sir Philip Sidney', *Victorian Review* 11, 1884–85, 139–85 (Chapter 5); and 'Philip Massinger', *Victorian Review* 11, 1884–85, 302–20 (Chapter 6).
71 *Lights and Shadows of Artist Life and Character* was published in London by Bentley. The book was advertised in the *Salisbury and Winchester Journal*.
72 As advised by the Director, Editor and Manager of the *Salisbury Times* and *Journal* Company in a letter dated 14 April 1980.
73 'Titian's Life and Work', *Argus*, 12 November 1892.
74 This lecture was announced in the *Salisbury and Winchester Journal* on 15 October 1853.

Notes

75 This lecture was reported in the *Age* on 20 January 1855.
76 Articles on travel during 1853 included 'Recollections of Travel', *Colonial Monthly* 1, 1867–68, 66–73; 'Recollections of Italian Travel, *Argus*, 22 November 1879; 'Recollections of Padua', *Argus*, 1 January 1881; and 'A Recollection of Florence', *Argus*, 2 July 1881.
77 As referred to in 'England and Australia Compared and Contrasted. A Lecture: By James Smith', *Victorian Review*, No. 10, 22 February 1861, p. 146, and 'Mr. James Smith. An Australian Man of Letters', *Table Talk*, 30 August 1889, p. 4.
78 The Wiltshire Emigration Association was chiefly concerned with assistance to the emigration of agricultural labourers.
79 As searched in the indexes to assisted and unassisted migration, and passenger manifests in the Public Record Office of Victoria. Neither Smith's name, nor those of his children, appears in the 'Shipping Intelligence' notices published in the *Age* in December 1854 or January 1855.

Chapter 3: The immigrant

1 As advertised on p. 1 of the first issue.
2 See the entry for James Smith, *Cyclopedia of Victoria*, edited by James Smith, 3 vols., Melbourne, The Cyclopedia Company, 1903–05, 1, 333–34.
3 As stated in 'Legislative Assembly. List of persons claiming or supposed to be entitled to vote in the election of a member for the District of Melbourne', *Age* supplement, 14, 15, 19 and 20 May 1856.
4 Syme's letter is included in the Smith papers, MSS 212, Mitchell Library, State Library of New South Wales.
5 This marriage was registered as No. 360 in the District of Collingwood.
6 As described on Eliza Kelly's birth certificate: No. 88 in the District of Tewkesbury.
7 'Obituary. Mrs. E. J. Smith', *Ballarat Courier*, 25 May 1927.
8 Gustavus Vaughan Brooke died in the shipwreck of the *London* on 11 January 1866.
9 As noted in the 'Book of Notes and Cuttings', Smith papers, MS 2398, National Library of Australia.
10 'An Address to the Beefsteak Club', Turner papers, MS 1625, La Trobe Collection, State Library of Victoria.
11 Other titles were 'England and Australia Contrasted and Compared' and 'Here and There'.
12 This lecture was published as 'England and Australia Contrasted and Compared. A lecture by James Smith', *Victorian Review*, No. 10, 22 February 1861, pp. [145]–48.
13 'England and Australia Contrasted and Compared', *Ballarat Star*, 16 February 1861.
14 'Ballaarat Past and Present', *Victorian Review*, No. 11, 1 March 1861, [161]–52. 'Ballaarat', still preserved in historical contexts, was the original spelling.
15 This notice was published in the *Argus* on 31 March 1862.
16 Ibid.
17 See the diary entry for 7 January 1863, Smith papers, MSS 212, Mitchell Library, State Library of New South Wales. For further details regarding Smith's private diary and its contents, see 'The Year 1863'. Selected and annotated by Lurline Stuart. *Meanjin* 37, 1978, 411–33.

18 As recorded in the diary.
19 Ibid, 23 January 1863.
20 Ibid.
21 Ibid, 24 January 1863.
22 Ibid, 31 January 1863.
23 Ibid, 10 February 1863.
24 Ibid.
25 Ibid.
26 Ibid, 11 February 1863.
27 Ibid.
28 Ibid, 10 February 1863.
29 Two catalogues were published while Smith was Parliamentary Librarian: *Catalogue of the Library of the Parliament of Victoria. Part 1. Alphabetical Catalogue*, Melbourne, Mason and Firth, 1864. *[Classified] Catalogue of the Parliamentary Library of the Colony of Victoria*. By Authority, John Ferres, Government Printer, Melbourne, 1865.
30 *Victorian Review* 13, 1885–86, 351.
31 For full details of the contents of this library and its dispersal, see Lurline Stuart, 'James Smith's Private Library', *Bibliographical Society of Australia and New Zealand Bulletin* 6, 1982, 23–39.
32 This advertisement appeared in the *Argus* on 9 January 1863.
33 The letter from Spiers and Pond is included in the Smith papers, MSS 212, Mitchell Library, State Library of New South Wales.
34 The letter from Wilson is included in the Smith papers, MSS 212, Mitchell Library, State Library of New South Wales.
35 For full details of the contents, see *Catalogue of the Theatrical Library of a Gentleman Leaving the Profession*, together with the Library Register, MS 11325, La Trobe Collection, State Library of Victoria.
36 See Wallace Kirsop, 'A Theatrical Library in Nineteenth-Century Melbourne and Its Dispersal: Solving a Problem', *La Trobe Library Journal* 10, 1986, 1–8.
37 As described in the sale catalogue.
38 As referred to in 'Mr. Smith, the Librarian', *Parliamentary Debates, Session 1869*, 7, 75.
39 See Abbotsford Rate Books 1864–66, Public Record Office of Victoria.
40 The application is included in the Chief Secretary's correspondence, MS R12102, Public Record Office of Victoria.
41 'An Address to the Beefsteak Club'.
42 'Mr. Smith, the Librarian', *Parliamentary Debates, Session 1869*, 7, 78.
43 'The Death of Mr. James Smith. A Distinguished Writer', *Age*, 21 March 1910.

Chapter 4: Institutions

1 'Reminiscences of the Melbourne Stage', 2, *Australasian*, 2 August 1886, p. 248.
2 *Age*, 6 September 1855.
3 The actor David Garrick.
4 William Mower Akhurst, then a sub-editor and music critic for the *Argus*.
5 'The Garrick Club', *Age*, 22 October 1855.
6 'An Address to the Beefsteak Club', Turner papers, MS 1625, La Trobe Collection, State Library of Victoria.
7 'Prospectus of the Victorian Club', *Argus*, 8 May 1856.

Notes

8 *Argus*, 30 October 1856.
9 *Argus*, 4 December 1856.
10 Unless otherwise indicated, further details regarding the Victorian Society of Fine Arts are taken from reports published the *Argus* on 18 November 1856; 20 May 1857; 19 February 1863; 13 and 15 March 1864.
11 See Leonard Cox, *The National Gallery of Victoria 1968. A Seach for a Collection*, Melbourne, The National Gallery of Victoria. [1970], p. 11.
12 Ibid.
13 See *Encyclopedia of Australian Art*, edited by Alan McCulloch. 2 vols., Melbourne, Hutchinson, 1984, 2,777.
14 See the *Argus*, 18 January 1870.
15 See McCulloch, 1, 60–61.
16 See McCulloch, 1, 1245–46.
17 Unless otherwise indicated, details regarding the fêtes champêtres are taken from reports published in the *Argus* on 3, 8, 21 and 24 November 1856; 9 December 1856; 11 March 1857.
18 As indicated by the letter to the editor of the *Argus* from 'A Lawyer', 9 December 1856.
19 Information regarding the Press Cricket Club is taken from reports published in the *Argus* on 15 August 1859; 17 September and 6 October 1860; 15 September 1862.
20 *Laws of the Royal Society of Victoria*, Melbourne, Mason and Firth, [1859], p. 5.
21 *Transactions of the Royal Society of Victoria, from January to December, 1860, inclusive*, edited by John Macadam, Melbourne, Mason and Firth, [1861]: Proceedings, 23 April 1860, p. v.
22 Ibid, *Transactions, 1860: Reports of Committees*, p. lx.
23 Royal Society of Victoria Exploration Committee Minute Book 1858–1861, MS 552, La Trobe Collection, State Library of Victoria.
24 Ibid.
25 Ibid.
26 *Transactions, 1860: Reports of Committees*, p. xxxiv.
27 *The Rules and Objects of the Acclimatisation Society of Victoria*, Melbourne, William Goodhugh, 1861, p. [3].
28 This paper was published in the *Third Annual Report of the Acclimatisation Society of Victoria*, Melbourne, Wilson and Mackinnon, 1864, pp. 49–52.
29 See the *Age*, 21 July 1863.
30 See the *Argus*, 24 November 1863.
31 See the *Argus*, 25 September 1884.
32 *Rules and Regulations of the Athenaeum Club of Victoria, May 1868*, Melbourne, Mason and Firth, [1868], p. [3].
33 Ibid, p. 5.
34 Information regarding twentieth century activities was provided by the club.
35 The literary allusion is to Hamlet's remarks about the skull of the king's jester: 'Alas, poor Yorick! I knew him, Horatio: a fellow of infinite jest, of most excellent fancy...' *Hamlet* 5, 1, 201. There is also an associated allusion to Yorick, the parson in Laurence Sterne's *The Life and Opinions of Tristam Shandy*.
36 The Yorick Club was absorbed into the Melbourne Savage Club in 1966.
37 'Prospectus of the Victorian Proprietary Company (Limited)', *Touchstone*, 27 November 1869 [unnumbered advertisement page]. The advertisement was repeated on 4 December 1869.

38 See Chapter 11.
39 See 'Trustees. Melbourne Public Library. Minute Book 1900–1923', State Library of Victoria, p. 239. The meeting for 26 August 1909 is the last at which Smith's name is recorded as having been present.
40 *Rules of the Working Men's College*, Melbourne, Duffus Brothers, 1888, p. [1].
41 See the *Age*, 13 May 1882.
42 See the *Age*, 17 May 1882.
43 See the *Argus*, 27 June 1882.
44 See C. Stuart Ross, *Francis Ormond: pioneer, patriot, philanthropist*, London and Melbourne, Melville and Mullen, [1912], p. 84.
45 For further details of the foundation and development of the Working Men's College, see Ross, pp. 76–84; 98–108; 145–54.
46 This information is taken from the lists of office-bearers included in the *Report and Prospectus of the Working Men's College*, Melbourne, various printers, 1887–1909.
47 *The Working Men's College in the Making 1887–1913, by F. A. Campbell, M. C. E., the first secretary and director*, Melbourne, Working Men's College, 1925, p. 4.
48 Neild's letter was published on 5 January 1884.
49 The *Argus* leader was published on 5 January 1884.
50 The Kyrle Society was named in memory of John Kyrle, the 'Man of Ross', celebrated for his charity in Pope's *Moral Essays*.
51 See the *Argus*, 17 March 1884.
52 'Mr. James Smith's Address to the Kalizoic Society', *Argus*, 17 May 1884.
53 See the *Argus*, 8 October 1884 and 23 March 1885.
54 See the *Argus*, 23 March 1885.
55 See the *Argus*, 20 June 1877.
56 See the *Argus*, 29 August 1878; see also 'Nature's Scavengers', *Victorian Review* 3, 1880–81, 42–53.
57 See *Australian Health Society, Melbourne. A Twenty-five Years' Record of the Work and Progress of the Society*, Melbourne, Australian Health Society, [1900].
58 See the *Age*, 29 September 1900.
59 The modern spelling is found in later reports of the society's activities.
60 Melbourne audiences had seen G. V. Brooke (1855–61); Sir William Don (1861–62); Charles Kean (1863–64); Barry Sullivan (1862–66); W. M. Montgomery (1867–69), and Daniel Bandmann (1869–70) during those years.
61 'A Shakspeare Society', *Argus*, 24 May 1884.
62 'Melbourne Shakespeare Society. Its Genesis and Growth', *Shakespearean Quarterly* 3, 1924, 42.
63 See the *Argus*, 3 and 5 February 1885.
64 'An Address to the Beefsteak Club'.
65 For further details of the organisation and operation of the French Club, see Oscar Comettant, *Au Pays des Kangarous et des Mines d'Or*, Paris, Libraire Fischbacher, 1890, translated by Judith Armstrong, *In the Land of Kangaroos and Gold Mines*, Adelaide, Rigby, 1980, pp. 49–53.
66 See the *Argus*, 11 September 1886.
67 See Gustave Le Roy, *An Easy Method to Learn French Without a Master*, Melbourne, Evans Brothers, 1873.
68 Gustave Le Roy, *Australia's Welfare*, Adelaide, Hussey and Gillingham, 1892, p. 196.
69 See the *Argus*, 11 September 1886.
70 Le Roy, *Australia's Welfare*, pp. 197–98.

Notes

71 Comettant (Armstrong), p. 225.
72 Unless otherwise indicated, information regarding the Alliance Francaise is taken from reports published in the *Argus* on 11 September 1893; 14 September and 12 October 1894; 14 June 1895.
73 See Comettant (Armstrong), pp. 158–59.
74 The sisters opened a school—Oberwyl—in St Kilda in 1885. See (Comettant) Armstrong, pp. 259–62.
75 *Lectures on French Literature delivered in Melbourne by Irma Dreyfus*, London, Longmans Green, 1896.
76 Unless otherwise indicated, information regarding the Dante Society is taken from reports published in the *Argus* on 29 June 1896 and 25 May 1897.
77 See the *Age*, 1 August 1896.
78 Because of the loss of the society's early records, details of the original membership are unknown.
79 See 'The Death of Mr. James Smith', *Age*, 21 March 1910.
80 The citation is included in the Smith papers, MS 2398, National Library of Australia.
81 Ibid.

Chapter 5: Public heroes

1 See the *Argus*, 9 August 1860.
2 See the *Argus*, 21 August 1860.
3 See the *Argus*, 29 August 1860.
4 The reasons for the Club's refusal are given in a letter to Dardanelli dated 12 September and signed by the Club Secretary, Edward Bell. I am obliged to Ronald McNicoll, Melbourne Club Archivist, for providing a copy of this letter from the Club's 'Outward Letter Book'.
5 This review appeared on 10 September 1860.
6 See the *Argus*, 15 September 1860.
7 See the *Argus*, 26 September 1860.
8 See the *Argus*, 9 October 1860.
9 See the *Argus*, 15 April 1861.
10 See the *Argus*, 1 May 1861.
11 As detailed in 'Garibaldi Testimonial Balance Sheet', published with *List of Subscribers to the Sword of Honor, presented to General Garibaldi, by his Admirers in Australia*, Melbourne, *Punch* Office, 1861.
12 Ibid.
13 This letter was published in the *List of Subscribers*.
14 'Father Bleasdale v. Garibaldi', *Argus*, 28 November 1861.
15 *Argus*, 10 January 1863.
16 *Argus*, 10 February 1863.
17 *Argus*, 2 March 1863.
18 See the *Argus*, 22 December 1861.
19 *Argus*, 22 January 1863.
20 As cited in Alan Moorehead, *Cooper's Creek*, London, Hamish Hamilton, 1963, p. 190.
21 The entry for 21 January 1863.
22 *Age*, 22 January 1863.
23 *Argus*, 23 January 1863.
24 A misquotation of 'To scorn delights, and live laborious days', from Milton's *Lycidas* 1, 123.

25 'The Victorian Expedition', *Argus*, 26 January 1863.
26 'The Exploration Committee on Their Trial', *Weekly Review*, 31 January 1863.
27 For further details regarding memorials to the explorers, see Ian McLaren, 'The Victorian Exploring Expedition', *Victorian Historical Magazine* 29, 4, 1959, Appendix C, 239–41.
28 The statue was erected at the corner of Collins and Russell Streets in 1865. It was moved to Spring Street, opposite Parliament House, in 1886, because of its hindrance to traffic, and moved again in 1979, because it obstructed the building of Parliament station. It now stands in the City Square.
29 *Argus*, 20 May 1863.
30 As included in the diary with a list of amounts paid for journalism during 1863.
31 Although Joseph Jefferson's name is given here as the speaker of the address, according to the *Argus* of 22 May, it was 'spoken by Rose Edouin with rare animation and taste'.
32 See the *Argus*, 25 April 1860.
33 See the *Argus*, 29 May 1860.
34 See the *Argus*, 14 June 1860.
35 As recalled in the *Argus*, 6 July 1863. Mulready declined the honour: *Argus*, 22 August 1861.
36 *Argus*, 6 July 1863.
37 See the *Argus*, 6 July 1863.
38 See the *Argus*, 2 March 1864.
39 *Argus*, 25 April 1864.
40 See the *Argus*, 19 April 1864.
41 A circular is included in Lucy Coppin's memoirs, MS 968/5, La Trobe Collection, State Library of Victoria.
42 See the *Argus*, 18 June 1864.
43 See the *Argus*, 29 August 1864.
44 See the *Argus*, 2 September 1864.
45 'The Shakspeare Testimonial', Letter to the editor of the *Argus*, 7 July 1863.
46 See the *Argus*, 1 April 1864.
47 *Examiner and Melbourne Weekly News*, 16 April 1864.
48 Ibid.
49 *Argus*, 13 May 1864.
50 See Geoffrey Blainey, *A Centenary History of the University of Melbourne*, Melbourne, Melbourne University Press, 1957, p. 52.
51 'The Brooke Memorial', *Argus*, 2 May 1868.
52 'The Garrick Club and the Shakespeare Memorial', *Argus*, 4 May 1868.
53 W. J. Lawrence, *The Life of Gustavus Vaughan Brooke, Tragedian*, Belfast, Baird, 1892, p. 273.
54 *Melbourne Punch*, 22 March 1866, p. 97. The first line of the poem is taken from Master Walter's words in *The Hunchback* 1, 1.
55 See the *Argus*, 24 April 1866.
56 See the *Argus*, 23 April 1866.
57 See the *Argus*, 22 July and 13 December 1866.
58 'The Brooke Memorial Fund', *Argus*, 8 January 1867.
59 See the *Argus*, 11 March 1867.
60 See the *Argus*, 25 March 1868.
61 *Argus*, 12 October 1868.
62 'Unveiling the Brooke Bust', *Argus*, 14 December 1868.
63 *Argus*, 15 December 1868.

Notes

64 The fine white bust now stands at the entrance to the Reference and Information Centre of the State Library of Victoria. On 14 October 1981, a brass plaque, presented by a small group of contributors from the Friends of the La Trobe Library (later the Friends of the State Library of Victoria) to replace the faded gold inscription on the pedestal, was unveiled by Harold Love. The contributors then adjourned to the Café de Paris in La Trobe Street for an informal 'Brooke dinner'.
65 Details regarding the official presentation ceremony have been taken from 'Trustees. Minute Book, Melbourne Public Library, 1853–70', State Library of Victoria.
66 The quincentenary of Caxton's introduction of printing into England was held in 1976 as a result of the discovery, in 1928, of an Indulgence printed by Caxton and dated in manuscript 13 December 1476. For further details, see Lotte Hellinger, *Caxton in Focus: the beginning of printing in England*, London, British Library, 1982.
67 Unless otherwise indicated, information regarding the Caxton Fund has been taken from the Caxton Fund papers, MS 6272, La Trobe Collection, State Library of Victoria.
68 *Argus*, 7 August 1871.
69 *Argus*, 14 August 1871.
70 See *William Caxton: a contribution in commemoration of the festival held in Melbourne, 1871, to celebrate the fourth centenary of the first printing in the English language*, Melbourne, Government Printer, 1871.
71 See the *Argus*, 15 November 1871.
72 See the *Argus*, 19 December 1871.
73 See J. La Nauze, *Alfred Deakin: a biography*, Melbourne, Melbourne University Press, 1965, 2 vols., 2, 430–31.

Chapter 6: Periodicals

1 See Lurline Stuart, *Nineteenth Century Australian Periodicals: an annotated bibliography*, Sydney, Hale and Iremonger, 1979.
2 'Preface, *Illustrated Australian Magazine* 4, 1852.
3 'Origins of "Melbourne Punch"', *Punch* Jubilee issue, 27 August 1907, p. 7.
4 'An Editorial Valediction', *Melbourne Punch*, 5 February 1863, p. 217.
5 The use of the word 'Australasian' in the title reflects the prevailing concept of the federation of Australia and New Zealand under that name.
6 *My Note Book* 1, 1856, 4.
7 'Journal of Literature and Art', *Journal of Australasia* 4, 1856, 95.
8 See Charles Daley, 'The Early Defences of Melbourne', *Victorian Historical Magazine* 22, 1947, 16–22.
9 'Our Defences', *Argus*, 14 July 1859.
10 'Notice to Subscribers and the Public', *Victorian Review*, No. 25, 8 June 1861, p. 1.
11 'The Editor's Address', *Australian Monthly Magazine* 1, 1865, [1]–2.
12 See Brian Elliott, *Marcus Clarke*, Oxford, Oxford University Press, 1958, p. 109.
13 See Samuel R. Simmons, *A Problem and a Solution: Marcus Clarke and the writing of "Long Odds" his first novel*, Melbourne, the Simmons Press, 1946.
14 Rev. Julian Tenison-Woods.
15 The entry for 15 February.
16 'In Memoriam', *Touchstone*, 29 January 1870, p. 104. The poem is a parody

of Hood's 'Bridge of Sighs'.
17 *Victoria and Its Metropolis: past and present*, 2 vols., edited by Alexander Sutherland, Melbourne, McCarron, Bird and Company, 1888, 1, 495.
18 These letters are included in the Kendall papers, MSS C199, Mitchell Library, State Library of New South Wales.
19 This review was published on 3 July 1869.
20 See 'Historical Records of the Argus and the Australasian', MS 10727, La Trobe Collection, State Library of Victoria.
21 *Argus*, 18 April 1870.
22 Clarke's reply appeared in the *Australasian* on 23 April 1870.
23 See Charles Gavan Duffy, *My Life in Two Hemispheres*, 2 vols., London, T. Fisher Unwin, 1898, 2, 314.
24 'Historical Records of the Argus and the Australasian'.
25 Ibid.
26 Ibid.
27 'A Final Batch of Victorian Magazines', *Library Record of Australasia* 1, 1901, 130.
28 *Argus*, 6 and 8 July 1878.
29 Robertson's letter is included in the Turner papers, MS 8062, La Trobe Collection, State Library of Victoria.
30 'Colonial Periodicals', *Pacific Weekly*, 15 May 1880, p. 15.
31 The magazine was not registered in Sydney until 16 November 1889.

Chapter 7: The drama, the opera and the fine arts

1 See Chapter 6.
2 *Argus*, 20 September 1860.
3 *Argus*, 24 September 1860.
4 See the *Age*, 24 September 1860.
5 The entry for 6 July 1863.
6 *Argus*, 7 July 1863.
7 *Argus*, 7 February 1876.
8 The entry for 5 January 1863.
9 See the diary entries for those dates.
10 *Argus*, 16 September 1863.
11 *Age*, 15 September 1863.
12 Madeleine Bingham, *Henry Irving and the Victorian Theatre*, London, Allen & Unwin, 1978, p. 190.
13 William Hazlitt, 'On Actors and Acting' in *William Hazlitt: criticisms and dramatic essays of the English stage*, edited by William Hazlitt [junior], London, Routledge, 1851, p. 2.
14 'The Acted Drama', *Age*, 29 January 1910.
15 'Theatrical Reminiscences', 2: 'G. V. Brooke', *Australasian*, 23 November 1878, p. 648.
16 'Festive Meeting of the *Age* Proprietors', *Age*, 20 July 1855.
17 'Recollections of the Othello of G. V. Brooke', *Age*, 11 September 1909.
18 'First Appearance of Mr. G. V. Brooke on the Australian Boards', *Age*, 28 February 1855.
19 For instance, 'Theatrical Reminiscences', 2: 'G. V. Brooke', *Australasian*, 23 November 1878, p. 648.
20 'Coppin's Olympic. Othello', *Age*, 7 August 1855.
21 William Hazlitt, 'Othello' in *Characters of Shakespeare's Plays*, London

Notes

Oxford University Press, 1970 (first published 1916), pp. 34, 35.
22 'Theatrical Reminiscences, 2: 'G. V. Brooke'.
23 As referred to in a letter from Smith to Brooke's biographer, W. J. Lawrence, dated 15 March 1892, MSS ab. 128/2, Mitchell Library, State Library of New South Wales.
24 Ibid.
25 *Argus*, 1 April 1862.
26 'Theatrical Reminiscences', 4: *Australasian*, 21 December 1878, pp. 774-75.
27 Smith is here confusing the initials of W. S. Lyster with those of Lyster's brother Fred, also a member of the company.
28 'The Social Development of Australasia', *Australasian Federal Directory of Commerce, Trades and Professions*, edited by J. W. F. Rogers, Melbourne, J. W. F. Rogers, [1888], p. xxviii.
29 'Amusements', *Argus*, 15 November 1862.
30 *Argus*, 17 November 1862.
31 Ibid.
32 Extracts are taken from reviews published in the *Argus* on 26 November, 2 and 8 December 1862.
33 'Madame Adelaide Ristori', *Argus*, 28 August 1875.
34 As quoted by Henry Knepler in *The Gilded Stage: the life and careers of four great actresses. Rachel Felix, Adelaide Ristori, Sarah Bernhardt and Eleanora Duse*, London, Constable, 1968, p. 108.
35 Knepler, p. 108.
36 'Marie Antoinette', *Victorian Review* 1, 1879-80, 546.
37 Ibid, pp. 568-69.
38 'The Opera House. Madame Ristori as Marie Antoinette', *Argus*, 21 September 1875.
39 'The Opera House. Madame Ristori as Marie Antoinette', *Argus*, 22 September 1875.
40 This article appeared in the *Argus* on 5 December 1857.
41 John Ruskin, *The Seven Lamps of Architecture*, London, George Allen, 1886 (first published 1849), 1, 5, 28.
42 Ibid, 1, 6, 30.
43 'Taste in Art', *Age*, 18 April 1908.
44 This review appeared in the *Examiner* on 26 May 1860.
45 Von Guerard's letter is included in the Smith papers, MSS 212, Mitchell Library, State Library of New South Wales.
46 'Death of M. Louis Buvelot', *Argus*, 31 May 1888.
47 'The Social Development of Australasia', p. xvi.
48 'Road near Fernshaw', *Australasian Sketcher*, 1 November 1873, p. 134.
49 'Death of M. Louis Buvelot'.

Chapter 8: Literary controversies

1 'Mr. Walter Montgomery', *Argus*, 20 July 1867.
2 'Mr. James Anderson in "Hamlet"', *Argus*, 15 July 1867.
3 'Mr. Walter Montgomery as Hamlet', *Argus*, 22 July 1867.
4 'Mr. Montgomery's Hamlet', *Argus*, 30 July 1867.
5 'Mr. Montgomery's Hamlet', *Argus*, 31 July 1867.
6 'Mr. Montgomery's Hamlet', *Argus*, 1 August 1867.
7 See 'Mr. Montgomery's Hamlet', *Argus*, 2 August 1867.
8 See 'Mr. Montgomery's Hamlet', *Argus*, 3 August 1867.

9 See 'Mr. Montgomery's Hamlet', *Argus*, 6 August 1867.
10 See 'Hamlet's Character', *Age*, 6 August 1867.
11 See the *Argus*, 17 December 1867.
12 *"Rip Van Winkle": the autobiography of Joseph Jefferson*, London, Reinhardt and Evans, 1949, p. 184.
13 This article was published in the *Weekly Review* on 11 October 1862.
14 See 'Reminiscences of the Melbourne Stage. By an Old Playgoer', No. 7, *Australasian*, 18 September 1886, p. 570.
15 'Mr. James Smith. An Australian Man of Letters', *Table Talk*, 30 August 1889, p. 5.
16 This letter appeared in *Melbourne Punch* on 27 November 1862, p. 137.
17 'Cant', *Weekly Review*, 15 November 1862.
18 This article was published in the *Weekly Review* on 13 December 1862.
19 This lecture was reported in the *Argus* on 18 December 1862 and published (by request) as *A Lecture on the Irish Character, from an Englishman's Point of View*, Melbourne, Samuel Mullen, 1863.
20 'Mr. Duffy and His Friend', *Weekly Review*, 27 December 1862.
21 'The Recanting Journalist', *Weekly Review*, 21 February 1863.
22 This article appeared in *Humbug* on 15 September 1869, pp. 12–13.
23 'Introductory Notice', *Humbug*, 8 September 1869, p. 4.
24 This letter is included in the Smith papers, MSS 212, Mitchell Library, State Library of New South Wales.
25 As indicated in a private letter, Smith papers, MSS 212, Mitchell Library, State Library of New South Wales.
26 *On Renascence Drama, or History Made Visible*, Melbourne, Sands and McDougall, 1880, p. 19.
27 As quoted by Thomson in *William Shakespeare in Romance and Reality*, Melbourne, Sands and McDougall, 1881, p. [32].
28 'Was Bacon Shakespeare?', *Victorian Review* 3, 1880, 54.
29 *William Shakespeare in Romance and Reality*, p. 17.
30 'Victorian Review', *Argus*, 13 November 1880.
31 *William Shakespeare in Romance and Reality*, p. 92.
32 *Bacon, not Shakespeare* by W. T., Melbourne, Sands and McDougall, 1881, p. 3.
33 *William Shakespeare in Romance and Reality*, p. 93.
34 *Bacon, not Shakespeare*, p. 5.
35 *Argus*, 23 February 1882.
36 Smith's library was sold by his executors in 1910, by auction and also direct to the Melbourne Public Library. Stearns's book is not listed, either in the sale catalogue or the appropriate Accession Book.
37 This cutting is included in the Shillinglaw papers, MS 243/7, La Trobe Collection, State Library of Victoria.
38 *The Political Allegories in the Renascence Drama of Francis Bacon*, Melbourne, Sands and McDougall, 1882, p. 21.
39 The Swedish philologist Alvar Ellegard has made computer-based stylistic comparisons between a number of possible authors, based on frequently used words and phrases, resulting in the conclusion 'that Sir Philip Francis was "Junius" may henceforth be allowed to stand without a question-mark'. See Henrik Alvar Ellegard, *Who Was Junius?*, Stockholm, Almqvist and Wiksell, 1962, p. 119.

See also *The Letters of Junius*, edited by John Cannon, Oxford, The Clarendon Press, 1978, Appendix 8, 'A Note on Authorship', pp. 539–72. Cannon, who refers to Ellegard's work, agrees with him to the extent of believing that

Notes

Francis seems to be 'the most probable contender' (p. 571).
40 *Junius Unveiled*, London, J. M. Dent, 1909, p. [1].
41 See 'Cavalier James Smith', *Harbinger of Light* 41, 1910, 6.
42 *Junius Unveiled*, p. 4.
43 See 'Appendix', *Junius Unveiled*, pp. 94–96.
44 *Salisbury and Winchester Journal*, 8 July 1848.
45 As cited on the title-page of *Junius Unveiled*.
46 'New books', *Age*, 10 July 1909.

Chapter 9: Spiritualism
1 'An Address to the Beefsteak Club', Turner papers, MS 1625, La Trobe Collection, State Library of Victoria.
2 'Sunday Morning with the Spiritualists', *Daily Telegraph*, 15 October 1872. This report is unsigned, but Turner inscribed his own cutting with the initials 'H. G. T.', MS 3062, La Trobe Collection, State Library of Victoria.
3 See J. A. La Nauze, *Alfred Deakin: a biography*, 2 vols., Melbourne, Melbourne University Press, 1965.
4 Peebles was an American spiritualist whose book had been published in Boston in 1869.
5 'Spiritualism Defended', *Argus*, 3 January 1872.
6 'Spiritualism Defended', *Argus*, 8 January 1872.
7 See 'Spiritualism Defended', *Argus*, 6 January 1872.
8 The *Argus* leader was published on 17 January 1872.
9 Information regarding the tour and reports of lectures are taken from the *Otago Daily Times*.
10 Letters to the editor of the *Otago Daily Times* were published in each issue from 4–16 May.
11 Roseby's letters were published on 4, 7 and 16 May.
12 Copland's letters were published on 7, 9, 13 and 15 May.
13 'Mr. Smith's Lectures', *Otago Daily Times*, 9 May 1872.
14 'Presentation to Mr. James Smith', *Otago Daily Times*, 14 May 1872.
15 See 'Sunday Morning with the Spiritualists', *Daily Telegraph*, 15 October 1872.
16 'Split among the Spiritualists', *Daily Telegraph*, 16 October 1872.
17 Ibid.
18 'Mr. James Smith's Explanation', *Daily Telegraph*, 18 October 1872.
19 'Mr. James Smith's Explanation', *Daily Telegraph*, 17 October 1872.
20 'The World Beyond the Grave', *Argus*, 29 October 1892.
21 'Beyond the Grave', *Daily Telegraph*, 30 October 1872.
22 'Mr. James Smith on the Second Advent', *Daily Telegraph*, 7 January 1873.
23 Ibid.
24 'The Seers Smith, Dunn and Peebles', *Daily Telegraph*, 9 January 1873.
25 Ibid.
26 'The Smith Controversy', *Daily Telegraph*, 10 January 1873.
27 'The Smith Controversy', *Daily Telegraph*, 11 January 1873.
28 'The Peebles Testimonial', *Daily Telegraph*, 10 January 1873.
29 Letters from 'A Literary Detective' appeared in the *Daily Telegraph* on 4, 7, 10, 11 and 26 February.
30 Tyerman's letters to the *Daily Telegraph* appeared on 7 and 10 February 1873.
31 'On Miracles', *Maryborough and Dunolly Advertiser*, 29 August 1873; *Reprints*

from the *Maryborough and Dunolly Advertiser*, No. 11, Maryborough, 1873.
32 'Our "Glorious Civilization"', *Maryborough and Dunolly Advertiser*, 21 November 1873; *Reprints from the Maryborough and Dunolly Advertiser*, No. 22, Maryborough, 1873.
33 'Excursions in Natural History', *Maryborough and Dunolly Advertiser*, 13 March–24 August 1874.
34 'God's Parables', *Maryborough and Dunolly Advertiser*, 12 June–19 August 1874; *Reprints from the Maryborough and Dunolly Advertiser*, No. 26, Maryborough, 1874.
35 'Hidden Mysteries', *Maryborough and Dunolly Advertiser*, 21 August–9 October 1874.
36 This letter appeared in the *Hamilton Spectator* on 18 June 1873, under the heading 'The Maryborough Advertiser'. It was reprinted in the *Maryborough and Dunolly Advertiser* on 25 June 1873.
37 'Mr. James Smith's Lecture', *Maryborough and Dunolly Advertiser*, 15 January 1873.
38 'Mr. James Smith and Self-Sacrifice' *Maryborough and Dunolly Advertiser*, 23 April 1873.
39 'Mr. James Smith and Future Punishment', *Maryborough and Dunolly Advertiser*, 28 April 1873.
40 'Doubt as an Element of Spiritual Progress', *Harbinger of Light* 27, 1896, 5731.
41 'Spiritualism', a letter to the editor from James Smith, *Otago Daily Times*, 16 May 1872.
42 See 'The Will of God', *Maryborough and Dunolly Advertiser*, 2 June 1873.
43 'An Address to the Beefsteak Club'.
44 Ibid.
45 See 'Men Who Made the Argus and the Australasian', compiled by C. P. Smith, MS 10727, La Trobe Collection, State Library of Victoria.
46 See *Important Auction Sale of a Valuable Library of Books...* North Melbourne, Andrew and Taylor, printers, [1910].
47 'Interviews with Prominent Spiritualists. By Mrs. Charles Bright. Mr. James Smith', *Harbinger of Light* 35, 1904, 8451.
48 Ibid.
49 For a full account of the judgment, see 'The Lamont Will Case', *Age*, 18 October 1881.
50 'A Voice from Beyond the Grave', *Harbinger of Light* 12, 1881, 1848.
51 'The Lamont Will Case'.
52 'Mr. James Smith and the *Harbinger of Light*', *Age*, 18 October 1881.
53 James Smith and John Wren Sutton, *The Secret of the Sphinx*, London, Philip Wellby, 1906, p. 10.
54 See *The Secret of the Sphinx*, pp. 44–47; 67–68; 152–53; 211–12.
55 'Mr. James Smith. Joint Author with Mr. John Wrenn [sic] Sutton, of "The Secret of the Sphinx"', *Harbinger of Light* 37, 1906, 9010.

Chapter 10: The return visit

1 This article appeared in the *Argus* on 6 March 1880. It was reprinted in the *Hertfordshire Mercury* as 'Ware as it was Forty-Five Years Ago', on 11 June 1880.
2 This article appeared in the *Argus* on 1 May 1880.
3 In a private letter that is included in the Smith papers, MSS 212, Mitchell

Notes

Library, State Library of New South Wales.
4 'Bon Voyage', *Argus*, 18 February 1882.
5 Thomas's articles on south-eastern Victoria have been collected and republished as *Vagabond Country: Australian bush and town life in Victoria*, edited and introduced by Michael Cannon, Melbourne, Hyland House, 1981.
6 *Argus*, 20 May 1882. This article also forms Chapter I of *From Melbourne to Melrose*, Melbourne, The Centennial Publishing Company, 1888.
7 *Argus*, 30 September 1882. This article also forms Chapter XXV of *From Melbourne to Melrose*.
8 This article was published on 2 December 1882.
9 *Argus*, 23 December 1882.
10 'London', *Argus*, 16 September 1882. This article also forms Chapter XXIV of *From Melbourne to Melrose*.
11 'The London Climate and the London Theatres', *Argus*, 9 September 1882.
12 'Westward Ho!', *Argus*, 14 November 1882.
13 'Paris Revisited', *Argus*, 4 January 1883. This article also forms Chapter XXII ('Paris') of *From Melbourne to Melrose*.
14 'From Melbourne to Melrose', *Argus*, 11 February 1888.
15 *The Picturesque Atlas of Australasia* was published in parts Sydney by the Picturesque Atlas Company Limited from 1886 to 1888, and then in volume form in 1888. (Facsimile edition, *Australia: the first hundred, years*, Sydney, Ure Smith, 1974).
16 *The Australasian Federal Directory of Commerce, Trades and Professions* was published in Melbourne by J. W. F. Rogers in 1888.
17 *The Australasian Federal Directory of Commerce, Trades and Professions*, p. xxxiii.
18 Sala's article was published in the *Argus* on 15 August 1885 as part of the series 'The Land of the Golden Fleece'.
19 See Graeme Davison, *The Rise and Fall of Marvellous Melbourne*, Melbourne, Melbourne University Press, 1978, p. 7.
20 Ibid, p. 9.
21 *Table Talk*, 6 January 1888.
22 See Davison, p. 191.
23 Henry Gyles Turner, *A History of the Colony of Victoria*, 2 vols., London, Longmans Green, 1904 (facsimile edition, Melbourne, Heritage Publications, 1973), p. 264.
24 Ibid, p. 266.
25 'Report on the Exhibition at Large', in *Reports of the United States Commissioners to the Centennial International Exhibition at Melbourne, 1888*, Washington, Government Printing Office, 1889. p. 122.
26 Turner, p. 267.
27 'Report on the Exhibition at Large', p. 132.
28 Ibid.

Chapter 11: A new generation

1 As cited by Alan McCulloch, *The Golden Age of Australian Painting; impressionism and the Heidelberg school*, Melbourne, Lansdowne, 1977 (first published 1969), p. 20.
2 This article was published in the *Argus* on 6 January 1883.
3 'The Impressionist Exhibition', *Argus*, 17 August 1889.
4 Described by the artist as a 'night piece', representative of a fireworks

display at Cremorne. See J. McN. Whistler, *The Gentle Art of Making Enemies*, London, Heinemann, 1904 (first published 1890), pp. 3–4.
5 John Ruskin, *Fors Clavigera* 79.11 in *The Works of John Ruskin* (Library edition), edited by E. T. Cook and Alexander Wedderburn, 39 vols., London, George Allen, 1903–12, 29, 160.
6 'Art and Artists', *Table Talk*, 23 August 1889, p. 4.
7 'Concerning "Impressions" in Painting', *Argus*, 3 September 1889.
8 *Smike to Bulldog: letters from Sir Arthur Streeton to Tom Roberts*, edited with annotations by R. H. Croll, Sydney, Ure Smith, 1946, p. 128.
9 This letter is included in the Smith papers, MSS 212, Mitchell Library, State Library of New South Wales.
10 'Princess's Theatre. A Doll's House', *Argus*, 16 September 1889. The title used in the review varies between 'A Doll's House' and 'The Doll's House'.
11 See 'Princess's Theatre. A Doll's House', *Age*, 16 September 1889.
12 'Miss Ethel Turner's New Story', *Argus*, 19 October 1895.
13 The *Australasian* review appeared on 16 November 1895.
14 This letter is included in the Smith papers, MSS 212, Mitchell Library, State Library of New South Wales.
15 'The Social Development of Australasia' in *Australasian Federal Directory of Commerce, Trades and Professions*, edited by J. W. F. Rogers, Melbourne, J. W. F. Rogers, [1888], p. xv.
16 Ibid, pp. xi-xvi.
17 See Marcus Clarke, 'Waterpool near Coleraine, by Louis Buvelot' and 'The Buffalo Ranges, by Nicholas Chevalier', in *Photographs of the Pictures in the National Gallery, Melbourne*, edited by Marcus Clarke, Melbourne, Bailliere, 1873–75. See also Clarke's preface to Adam Lindsay Gordon, *Sea Spray and Smoke Drift*, Melbourne, Clarson, Massina, 1876.
18 The longer title was first used by the publishers, Richard Bentley, in 1882.
19 'The Social Development of Australasia', p. xvi.
20 This letter is included in the Smith papers, MSS 212, Mitchell Library, State Library of New South Wales.
21 This letter is included in the Smith papers, MSS 212, Mitchell Library, State Library of New South Wales. I am grateful to the Hon. Michael Clarke for supplying family information that confirms the estimated date.
22 'Farewell Dinner to Mr. Samuel Mullen', *Argus*, 30 October 1889. The periodicals to which Smith refers were English penny weeklies.
23 *Rigby's Romance* was serialised by the *Barrier Truth* in 1905 and published in volume form in Melbourne in 1921 by C. J. de Garis.
24 *The Buln-Buln and the Brolga* was published in Sydney in 1948 by Angus and Robertson.
25 *Such is Life*, Sydney, Bulletin Company, 1903, p. 1.
26 'Life in the Riverina', *Age*, 15 August 1903.
27 'Literary Gossip', *Leader*, 22 August 1903, p. 31.
28 This letter is included in the Kate Baker papers, MS 2022, National Library of Australia.
29 *Victoria and Its Metropolis*, 2 vols., Melbourne, McCarron, Bird and Company, 1888.
30 Miles Franklin, in association with Kate Baker, *Joseph Furphy: the legend of a man and his book*, Sydney, Angus and Robertson, 1944, p. 82.
31 Ibid, p. 84.
32 This letter is included in the Kate Baker papers, MS 2022, National Library of Australia.

Notes

Chapter 12: Declining years

1. Michael Cannon, *The Land Boomers*, Melbourne, Melbourne University Press, 1966 (corrected edition, 1967), p. 19.
2. This information is contained in the financial records for the year.
3. Brief reports of the monthly meetings of these societies appeared in the *Argus* from 1867 onwards.
4. See the 'Statement of Assets and Liabilities in the Probate Jurisdiction of James Smith's Will', Supreme Court of Victoria, No. 115.839.
5. Five thousand of Smith's books were sold at auction by Tuckett and Styles on 1 and 2 December 1910. There is no record of the amount raised by this sale, but, according to the information available in the relevant Accession Book, the Melbourne Public Library spent almost £650 on 2300 volumes, the titles of which are additional to those in the sale catalogue.
6. Smith's name appears as 'owner and occupier' in the Hawthorn Rate Books up to and beyond the date of his death, but there is no reference to real estate in the 'Statement of Assets and Liabilities'.
7. Sir Flinders Petrie, a distinguished English Egyptologist and a grandson of the navigator Matthew Flinders.
8. This letter is included in the Shillinglaw papers, MS 243/81/1, La Trobe Collection, State Library of Victoria.
9. See 'Men Who Made the Argus and the Australasian', compiled by C. P. Smith, MS 10727, La Trobe Collection, State Library of Victoria.
10. Williamson's letter is included in the Smith papers, MS 2398, National Library of Australia.
11. Syme's letter is included in the Smith papers, MSS 212, Mitchell Library, State Library of New South Wales.
12. Smith would have been employed on piece-work. His name is not listed among salaried staff in the 'Wages Book of David Syme and Company, 1886–1913', MS 10602, La Trobe Collection, State Library of Victoria.
13. This letter is included in the Deakin papers, MS 1540, National Library of Australia.
14. 'Interviews with Prominent Spiritualists. By Mrs. Charles Bright, Mr. James Smith', *Harbinger of Light* 35, 1904, 8450.
15. This pamphlet was published in Melbourne in 1901.
16. This pamphlet was published in Melbourne in 1904.
17. 'Mr. James Smith', *Leader*, 21 January 1905.
18. The title page of this manuscript is included in the Smith papers, MS 2398, National Library of Australia.
19. 'Recollections of an Octogenarian', 6: 'Vanished Hotels and Their Tracks', *Leader*, 3 August 1907, p. 43.
20. See Chapter 8.
21. 'The Passing of a Great Writer. Cavalier James Smith', *Harbinger of Light* 41, 1910, 61.
22. 'Death of Mr. James Smith', *Argus*, 21 March 1910.
23. 'Death of Mr. James Smith. A Distinguished Writer', *Age*, 21 March 1910.
24. See 'An Address to the Beefsteak Club', Turner papers, MS 1625, La Trobe Collection, State Library of Victoria.
25. Annie Bright's autobiographical novel, *A Soul's Pilgrimage*, was published in Melbourne in 1907.
26. 'Interviews with Prominent Spiritualists'.
27. 'Editorial Notes', *Harbinger of Light* 41, 1910, 49.

James Smith

28 This notice appeared in the *Bulletin* on 24 March 1910.
29 This lecture was given to the Early Closing Association at the Princess's Theatre on 26 July 1869. It was published as *The Frog and the Ox...* Melbourne, Stillwell and Knight, 1869. The extract is taken from p. 13.

SELECT BIBLIOGRAPHY

A comprehensive bibliography may be found in the author's thesis: 'James Smith: his influence on the development of literary culture in colonial Melbourne', Monash University, 1983. Copies of this thesis, to which is appended a checklist of Smith's works, are held by the Monash University Library and the State Library of Victoria.

Most members of the cultural circles to which Smith belonged are the subject of entries in the *Australian Dictionary of Biography*, edited by Douglas Pike and others, 11 vols., Melbourne, Melbourne University Press, 1966–1988.

Manuscripts

Henry Kendall Papers. Mitchell Library, State Library of New South Wales.
Henry Gyles Turner Papers. La Trobe Collection, State Library of Victoria.
Melbourne Public Library Trustees. Minute Books 1871–1909. State Library of Victoria.
'Men Who Made the Argus and the Australasian 1846–1923'. Compiled by C. P. Smith. La Trobe Collection, State Library of Victoria.
Royal Society of Victoria Exploration Committee Minute Book 1858–1861. La Trobe Collection, State Library of Victoria.
Victoria. Legislative Assembly. Minutes of the Proceedings of the Library Committee 1860–1869. Parliamentary Library of Victoria.

Newspapers and periodicals

England

County Press (Hertford)
Hertfordshire Mercury
Illuminated Magazine
Salisbury and Winchester Journal

Australia (Victoria)

Age
Argus
Austral Theosophist
Australasian
Australasian Monthly Review
Australasian Sketcher
Australian Builder

Australian Journal
Australian Monthly Magazine
Centennial Magazine
Colonial Monthly
Daily Telegraph
Evening Mail
Examiner and Weekly News
Harbinger of Light
Humbug
Illustrated Journal of Australasia
Illustrated Melbourne News
Maryborough and Dunolly Advertiser
Melbourne Leader
Melbourne Monthly Magazine
Melbourne Punch
Melbourne Review
My Note Book
Once a Month
Table Talk
Touchstone
Victorian Monthly Magazine
Victorian Review (1)
Victorian Review (2)

New Zealand

New Zealand Magazine
Otago Daily Times

Books and pamphlets: nineteenth century

[Anon.]. *Junius Unmasked. A Well Known, and Most Eminent Literary Character of the Last Century*. London, Effingham Wilson, 1819.

Australasian Federal Directory of Commerce, Trades and Professions, edited by J. W. F. Rogers. Melbourne, J. W. F. Rogers, [1888].

Catalogue of the Choice and Valuable Library of James Smith, Esq., comprising about fifteen hundred volumes of the best works in English, French, Spanish and Italian Literature, many of them elegantly bound and richly illustrated, and all in excellent condition, which will be sold by auction by Alfred Bliss at the rooms of Messrs. R. Perry & Co., Collins Street West, on Thursday and Friday, July 23 and 24, commencing each day at Twelve o'clock. Without reserve.—Terms cash. [Melbourne], Mason and Firth, Printers, [1863].

Comettant, Oscar. *Au Pays des Kangarous et des Mines d'Or*. Paris, Libraire Fischbacher, 1890. Translated by Judith Armstrong, *In the Land of Kangaroos and Gold Mines*. Adelaide, Rigby, 1980.

Grant James. *The Metropolitan Weekly and the Provincial Press*. Vol. 3 of *The Newspaper Press: Its origins, progress and present position*. London, George Routledge and Son, 1871–[1872].

The Hamlet Conspiracy. Was Hamlet Mad? Or, the Lucubrations of Messrs. Smith, Brown, Jones and Robinson. Edited by F. W. Haddon. Melbourne, H. T. Dwight, 1867.

Hazlitt, William. *Characters of Shakespeare's Plays*. London, Oxford University Press, 1916 (1970 reprint: first published London, C. H. Reynell, printer,

Select bibliography

1817).
Horne, R. H. *Australian Facts and Prospects: to which is affixed the author's Australian autobiography.* London, Smith, Elder, 1859.
Important Auction Sale of a Valuable Library of Books. 5000 Volumes, including works on Fine Arts, Poetry, Biography, Historical, Political, English and French Fiction, Shakespeare, French Literature, Music and Drama, Travels, Science, Natural History, Australasian, and Rare and Valuable Australian Pamphlets. By Order of the executors of the Late Mr. James Smith. Tuckett & Styles. North Melbourne, Andrew and Taylor, printers, [1910].
[Jefferson, Joseph]. *"Rip Van Winkle": The autobiography of Joseph Jefferson.* London, Reinhardt and Evans, 1949 (first published as *The Autobiography of Joseph Jefferson*. London, T. Fisher Unwin, 1890).
Lawrence, W. J. *The Life of Gustavus Vaughan Brooke, Tragedian.* Belfast, W. & G. Baird, 1892.
Ruskin, John. *Modern Painters.* 6 vols. London, George Allen, 1902 (first published complete, Orpington (Kent), George Allen, 1888).
Ruskin, John. *The Seven Lamps of Architecture.* Orpington (Kent), George Allen, 1886 (first published, London, Smith, Elder, 1849).
[Thomson, William]. *Bacon, not Shakespeare by W. T., in Rejoinder to the Shakespeare, not Bacon by J. S.* Melbourne, Sands and McDougall, 1881.
Thomson, William. *On Renascence Drama, or History Made Visible.* Melbourne, Sands and McDougall, 1880.
Thomson, William. *The Political Allegories of Francis Bacon.* Melbourne, Sands & McDougall, 1882.
Thomson, William. *William Shakespeare in Romance and Reality.* Melbourne, Sands and McDougall, 1881.
Turner, Henry Gyles, and Sutherland, Alexander. *The Development of Australian Literature.* Melbourne, George Robertson, 1898.
Twopeny, R. E. N. *Town Life in Australia.* London, Elliott Stock, 1883 (facsimile edition, Ringwood (Victoria), Penguin, 1973.
Victoria and Its Metropolis, Past and Present. The Colony and Its People in 1888. Edited by Alexander Sutherland. 2 vols. Melbourne, McCarron, Bird, 1888 (facsimile edition, 3 vols. Melbourne, Today's Heritage, 1977).
William Hazlitt. Criticisms and Dramatic Essays of the English Stage. Edited by W. Hazlitt [junior]. London, Routledge, 1851.
William Caxton: a Contribution in Commemoration of the Festival held in Melbourne, 1871, to Celebrate the Fourth Centenary of the First Printing in the English Language. Melbourne, Government Printer, 1871.

Books and pamphlets: later

Armstrong, Edmund La Touche. *Book of the Public Library, Museums and National Gallery of Victoria 1856–1906.* Melbourne, Trustees of the Public Library, Museums and National Gallery of Victoria, 1906.
Astbury, Leigh. *City Bushmen: The Heidelberg School and the Rural Mythology.* Melbourne, Oxford University Press, 1985.
Bingham, Madeleine. *Henry Irving and the Victorian Theatre.* London, George Allen and Unwin, 1978.
Blainey, Ann. *The Farthing Poet. A Biography of Richard Hengist Horne 1802–84. A Lesser Literary Lion.* London, Longmans, 1968.
Bonyhady, Tim. *Images in Opposition: Australian landscape painting 1801–1890.* Melbourne, Oxford University Press, 1985.

Bruce, Candice, et al. *Eugène von Guérard: a German Romantic in the Antipodes 1811–1901*. Martinborough (New Zealand), Alister Taylor Publications, 1982.
Buckley, Jerome Hamilton. *The Victorian Temper: A study in literary culture*. London, Allen and Unwin, 1952.
Cannon, Michael. *The Land Boomers*. Melbourne, Melbourne University Press, 1966 (corrected edition, 1967).
[Carrington, T., and Watterson, D. W.]. *The Yorick Club. Its Origin and Development, May 1868, to December, 1910*. Melbourne, Atlas Press, 1911.
City of Salisbury. Edited by H. de S. Shortt. London, Phoenix House, 1957.
Cox, L. *The National Gallery of Victoria 1861 to 1968. A Search for a Collection*. Melbourne, The National Gallery of Victoria, [1970].
Davison, Graeme. *The Rise and Fall of Marvellous Melbourne*. Melbourne, Melbourne University Press, 1978.
De Serville, Paul. *Port Phillip Gentlemen and Good Society in Melbourne Before the Gold Rushes*. Melbourne, Oxford University Press, 1980.
Documents on Art and Taste in Australia. The Colonial Period 1770–1914. Edited by Bernard Smith. Melbourne, Oxford University Press, 1971 (expanded edition, 1974 reprint: first published 1962).
Encyclopedia of Australian Art. Edited by Alan McCulloch. 2 vols. Melbourne, Hutchinson, 1984.
Franklin, Miles, in association with Kate Baker. *Joseph Furphy: the legend of a man and his book*. Sydney, Angus and Robertson, 1944.
Golden Summers and Beyond. [Exhibition Catalogue]. Compiled by Jane Clark and Bridget Whitelaw. [Melbourne], International Cultural Corporation of Australia Limited, 1985.
Grant, James, and Serle, Geoffrey. *The Melbourne Scene 1803–1956*. Melbourne, Melbourne University Press, 1957.
Gross, John. *The Rise and Fall of the Man of Letters. English Literary Life since 1800*. London, Weidenfeld and Nicolson, 1969.
History of Wiltshire. Edited by R. B. Pugh. Vol. 6 of the *Victoria History of the Counties of England*. London, Oxford University Press, 1953.
Hobsbawm, E. J. *The Age of Capital 1848–1875*. London, Weidenfeld and Nicolson, 1975.
Hobsbawm, E. J. *The Age of Revolution in Europe 1789–1848*. London, Weidenfeld and Nicolson, 1962 (Abacus edition, Sphere Books, 1977).
Holroyd, John. *George Robertson of Melbourne 1825–1898. Pioneer Bookseller and Publisher*. Melbourne, Robertson and Mullens, 1968.
Hunt, Edith M. *The History of Ware*. With a new introduction by David Perman. Hertford, Stephen Austin and Sons, 1986 (first published 1946).
James, Robert Rhodes. *Albert Prince Consort*. London, Hamish Hamilton, 1983.
Johnson, Edgar. *Charles Dickens: His Tragedy and Triumph*. London, Allen Lane, (first published 1952).
Knepler, Henry. *The Gilded Stage. The Lives and Careers of Four Great Actresses. Rachel Felix, Adelaide Ristori, Sarah Bernhardt and Eleonora Duse*. London, Constable, 1968.
Love, Harold. *The Golden Age of Australian Opera: W. S. Lyster and his companies 1861–1880*. Sydney, Currency Press, 1981.
McCulloch, Alan. *Artists of the Australian Gold Rush*. Melbourne, Lansdowne, 1977.
McCulloch, Alan. *The Golden Age of Australian Painting. Impressionism and the Heidelberg School*. Australian Art Library series. Melbourne, Lansdowne, 1969.
McNicoll, Ronald. *The Early Years of the Melbourne Club*. Melbourne, Hawthorn

Select bibliography

Press, 1976.
Moore, William. *The Story of Australian Art from the Earliest Known Art of the Continent to the Art of Today.* 2 vols. Sydney, Angus and Robertson, 1934 (facsimile edition, 1980).
Moorehead, Alan. *Cooper's Creek.* London, Hamish Hamilton, 1963.
Murray-Smith, Stephen, and Dare, Anthony John. *The Tech: A centenary history of the R. M. I. T.* South Yarra (Victoria), Hyland House, 1987.
Nadel, George. *Australia's Colonial Culture. Ideas, Men and Institutions in Mid-Nineteenth Century Eastern Australia.* Cambridge (Massachusetts), Harvard University Press, 1957.
Niall, Brenda. *Seven Little Billabongs: the world of Ethel Turner and Mary Grant Bruce.* Melbourne, Melbourne University Press, 1979.
Peebles, J. M. *What is Spiritualism?* Battle Creek (Michigan), Peebles Institute, 1903.
Serle, Geoffrey. *The Golden Age. A History of the Colony of Victoria 1851–1861.* Melbourne, Melbourne University Press, 1963.
Serle, Geoffrey. *The Rush to be Rich. A History of the Colony of Victoria 1883–1889.* Melbourne, Melbourne University Press, 1971.
Smith, Bernard. *Australian Painting 1788–1970.* Melbourne, Oxford University Press, 1971 (expanded edition, 1974 reprint: first published 1962).
Stuart, Lurline. *Nineteenth Century Australian Periodicals: an annotated bibliography.* Sydney, Hale and Iremonger, 1979.
Thomson, K., and Serle, G. *A Biographical Register of the Victorian Legislature 1851–1900.* Canberra, Australian National University Press, 1972.
Trevelyan, George Macaulay. *Garibaldi and the Making of Italy.* London, Longmans, Green and Company, 1911.
Turner, Henry Gyles. *A History of the Colony of Victoria from Its Discovery to Its Absorption into the Commonwealth of Australia.* 2 vols. London, Longmans, Green and Company, 1904 (facsimile edition, Melbourne, Heritage Publication, 1973).
The Australian Stage: a documentary history. Edited by Harold Love. Kensington (New South Wales), New South Wales University Press, 1984.
Victoria's Heritage: lectures to celebrate the 150th anniversary of European settlement in Victoria. Edited by A. G. L. Shaw. Sydney, Allen and Unwin, 1987.
Wilde, William H., et al. *The Oxford Companion to Australian Literature.* Melbourne, Oxford University Press, 1985.
White, Richard. *Inventing Australia: images and identity 1688–1980.* The Australian Experience series. Sydney, George Allen and Unwin, 1981.
Williams, Raymond. *Culture and Society 1780–1950.* London, Chatto and Windus, 1958 (1967 edition).
Wilmot, R. W. E. *The Melbourne Athenaeum 1839–1939. History and Records of the Institution.* Melbourne, Stilwell and Stephens, [1939].

Articles

Kirsop, Wallace. 'A Theatrical Library in Nineteenth-Century Melbourne and Its Dispersal: solving a problem'. *La Trobe Library Journal* 10, 1988, 1–8.
Miller, E. Morris. 'Some Public Library Memories'. *La Trobe Library Journal* 9, 1985, 49–83.
[Smith, James]. 'The Year 1863'. Selected and Annotated by Lurline Stuart. *Meanjin* 4, 1978, 411–33.
Stuart, Lurline. 'Fund-raising in Colonial Melbourne: the Shakespeare statue,

the Brooke bust and the Garibaldi sword'. *La Trobe Library Journal* 8, 1982, 1–12.

Stuart, Lurline. 'James Smith's Private Library'. *Bibliographical Society of Australia and New Zealand Bulletin* 6, 1982, 23–39.

Unpublished theses

Hayes, Gerard. 'James Smith: A colonial critic (1854–1910)'. B.A. thesis, University of Melbourne, 1979.

Jordens, Ann-Mari. 'Cultural Life in Melbourne 1870–80'. M.A. thesis, University of Melbourne, 1967.

Roe, Jill. 'A Decade of Assessment: being a study of the intellectual life of the city of Melbourne between 1876 and 1886'. M.A. thesis, Australian National University, 1965.

Smith, F. B. 'Religion and Freethought in Melbourne 1870 to 1890'. M.A. thesis, University of Melbourne, 1960.

INDEX

Compiled by Jean Hagger

James Smith is understood to be the subject of the whole work. The small number of entries under his name are meant to serve as a list of notable facets of his personality and cultural achievement.

à Beckett, T.T., 76
à Beckett, Sir William, 85
Aborigines, 5–6
Acclimatisation Society of Victoria, 45, 53–4
Achurch, Janet, 169, 171
Age (newspaper, Melbourne), 2, 28–30, 184
Akhurst, W.M., 7, 45, 51, 184
Alexandra, Princess of Denmark, 73–4
Alliance Francaise, 30, 45, 62, 183
Amwell (Hertfordshire), 14
Anderson, James, 119–23
Archer, William, 37–8, 45, 48, 53, 92
Argus (newspaper, Melbourne), 28–9, 181–2, 184
Argus hotel, 7, 30, 46, 184
art, *see* painting
Aspinall, Butler Cole, 7, 42–3, 45, 55, 85, 86, 124, 184
Athenaeum Club, 45, 54–5
Aurora Floyd, (dramatisation, James Smith), 102–3
Australasian (newspaper, Melbourne), 86, 88, 93–8
Australasian Federal Directory of Commerce, Trades and Professions (J.W.F. Rogers), 160
Australasian Monthly Review (journal, Melbourne), 86, 92
Australian Artists' Association, 50, 168
Australian Gold-Diggers' Monthly Magazine (journal, Melbourne), 84–5
Australian Health Society, 59
Australian Journal (journal, Melbourne), 86, 90, 97
Australian literature, 174–6
Australian Magazine (journal, Sydney), 83
Australian Monthly Magazine (journal, Melbourne), 86, 90–1, 92

Bacon, Sir Francis, 128–34
Baker, William, 49
Ballarat, 30, 34
Ballarat Star (newspaper), 29, 30, 31
Bandmann, Daniel, 93
Barkly, Sir Henry, 51, 52, 70
Barry, Sir Redmond, 74, 80, 144
Becker, Ludwig, 48, 49
Birnie, Richard, 31, 45, 54, 55, 94, 121–2
Bishop, Anna, 124
Blair, David, 28, 29, 31, 42, 45, 60, 86, 89, 90, 99, 122, 124, 132, 142–4, 146, 184, 188
Bleasdale, John, 45, 52, 67–8, 92
Bliss, Alfred, 40
Boldrewood, Rolf, 90
Bonwick, James, 84
Bright, Annie, 133, 151, 183–6 *passim*
Bright, Charles, 7, 45, 80, 81, 86, 87, 88, 93, 122, 137, 184, 186
Bright, Thomas, 28, 88
British influence (on colonial culture), x, xii, 8, 32–3, 164
Brittan, John, 15
Brodribb, William, 35
A Broil at the Café, (James Smith), 101
Bromby, J.E., 76
Brooke, Gustavus Vaughan, 7, 44–6

217

passim, 77, 101, 105–7, 184
Brooke Memorial Fund, 45, 77–80, 82
Browne, Thomas, *see* Boldrewood, Rolf
Bruce, J.V.A., 52
building societies, 180–1
Bulletin (journal, Sydney), 100, 176–7, 186–7
Burke, Robert O'Hara, 51–2, 68–73
Buvelot, Louis, 117–18, 184

Cadell, Francis, 52, 53
Calvert, Samuel, 88
Cambridge, Ada, 90
Campbell, F.A., 57–8
Carboni, Raffaello, 8
Carlyle, Thomas, 74
Carrington, Thomas, 85, 86, 91
Cave of Adullam, 55
Caxton Fund, 45, 80–2
Centennial Exhibition (Melbourne 1888), 162–3
Centennial Magazine (journal, Melbourne/Sydney), 86, 99–100
Chabrillan, Céleste de, 90
Charrington, Charles, 169
Chartists, 19
Chatham (Kent), 13
Chevalier, Nicholas, 8, 45, 49, 66, 85, 86, 87, 88, 184
cholera, 20
Clark, Charles, 80
Clarke, Lady Janet, 62, 175–6
Clarke, Marcus, 45, 55, 81, 85–99 *passim*, 127, 132, 139, 152, 173–4
Clarke, Sir William, 36, 45, 55, 62
Clarson, Massina and Company, 91
Clarson, Shallard and Company, 90
class structure, 36
Close, Richard Colonna, 129–30
clubs, 44–63
Collingwood Rifles, 89
colonial culture, 6, 164–9
colonial life, 1–9
Colonial Monthly (journal, Melbourne), 86, 91–2, 93, 95
Comettant, Oscar, 61
Commission of the Fine Arts, 50
Commonwealth Literary Fund, 82
Conder, Charles, 164–7, 169
Copland, James, 140
Coppin, George, 45, 50, 78, 80, 81, 105–6, 159
Corte, Cavalier Count (Italian Consul General), 62
Cosmos Magazine (journal, Sydney), 100, 186
country newspapers, 144–5
County Press (newspaper, Hertford), 19, 21
cricket, 51
Crimean War, 4, 89
Curtis, James W., 183
Cyclopedia of Victoria (ed. James Smith), 183, 185

Dante Society, 45, 62, 183
Dardanelli, B., 65–8 *passim*
Darling, Sir Charles, 76
Daylesford Mercury (newspaper), 29, 144
Deakin, Alfred, 82, 137, 182
Delacasse, Mlle (French acrobat), 50–1
Detmold, William, 88
Dickens, Charles, 13, 22, 34, 54
Dogherty, Mrs (Burke's nurse), 69, 70
A Doll's House (Henrik Ibsen), 169–71, 172
Double Harness (George Walstab), 91
drama, 101–9, 111–13, 119–24
Dreyfus, Irma, 62
Duffy, Sir Charles Gavan, 42, 80, 125–6
The Duke's Motto (adaptation, James Smith), 102, 103
Dumas, A.G., 43

Eades, Richard, 52, 68
East Dereham (Norwich), 13
Edouin, Rose, 73, 102
Edward, Prince of Wales, 73–4
Edwards, John, 102
elections, 16, 35–7
Ellery, Robert, 45, 56
Elliott, Sizar, 52
elocution, 54
Embling, Thomas, 52, 53
England: 1820–1854, 10–27; 1882, 156–7
Escott, Lucy, 71, 110–11
Eureka Stockade, 4, 29
Evans, J., 144–5
Examiner and Melbourne Weekly

Index

News (newspaper), 86, 88
Exploration Committee, *see* Royal Society of Victoria, Exploration Committee

Fauchery, Antoine, 8
Fawcett, George, 102
Fawkner, John Pascoe, 49
Ferres, John, 80
festivals, 12
Fêtes Champêtres, 45, 50–1
For the Term of His Natural Life, see His Natural Life
Forde, J.M., 77
Francis Cooke and Company, 28
Franklyn, H. Mortimer, 99
Frazer, William, 39
free trade, 13, 36, 42
French Club, 60
French Literary Club, 45, 60–1
From Melbourne to Melrose (James Smith), 153, 159
Froude, J.A., 174–5
funerals, 69
Furphy, Joseph, 176–9

Garibaldi (James Smith), 65, 101
Garibaldi Testimonial Fund, 45, 64–8, 82
Garran, Andrew, 160
Garrick Club, 45, 46–8, 74, 76, 77–9
Geelong Daily News (newspaper), 29
George, Hugh, 97
Gibbon, Edward, 132–4
Gibbons, William Sydney, 87
Gilbert, G.A., 84
Giles, William, 13
Gill, S.T., 88
Gillbee, William, 45, 52
gold-diggers, 3–4
gold-rushes, 2, 26
Gordon, Adam Lindsay, 94–5, 173
Grosse, Frederick, 88
Guerard, Eugene von, 45, 49, 115–17
Gullett, Henry, 98

Haddon, Frederick, 45, 55, 59, 81, 94, 122, 175
Ham, Jabez, 84
Ham, Theophilus, 84
Ham, Thomas, 84
Hamilton Spectator (newspaper), 145
Hamlet controversy, 119–23

Harbinger of Light (journal, Melbourne), 133, 137, 151, 183–5 *passim*
Harpur, Charles, 90
Harrison, James, 82
Hazlitt, William, 104–5, 107
Heads of the People (journal, London), 18
Hearn, W.E., 48, 86, 92, 94
Heidelberg School, 164–9
Henry, Louis, 58, 59
Herbert family, 24–5
Hertford (Herfordshire), 19
Higinbotham, George, 35, 36, 48, 81, 184
His Natural Life (Marcus Clarke), 90, 97, 174
Hodgkinson, Clement, 52
Hodson, Georgia, 71
Horne, R.H., 7, 45, 46, 47, 85, 86, 88, 90, 122, 184
Hotham, Sir Charles, 29
Howitt, Alfred, 69, 70
Les Huguenots (Meyerbeer), 109–11
Hulburd, Percy, 31
Humbug (journal, Melbourne), 86, 92–3, 95

Ibsen, Henrik, 169–71
Ievers, R.L., 183
Iffla, Solomon, 52, 56
Illustrated Australian Magazine (journal, Melbourne), 84
Illustrated Journal of Australasia (journal, Melbourne), 86, 87–8, 90
Illustrated Melbourne News (journal), 86, 88
immigrants, 2, 187–90, British, x, 6–9, 31–5; European, 9
imports, 4
impressionism, 164–9
In Memoriam G.V.B. (James Smith), 77–8
Irish settlers, 125–6
Irving, Martin, 74
Italian Dramatic Company, 111

Jackson, Mrs (medium), 135, 149
James, John Stanley ('The Vagabond'), 154
Jefferson, Joseph, 107–9, 123–4, 184
Jerrold, Douglas, 18
'John Bull', 32–3

Johnston, J.S., 29
Jones, Avonia, 77, 107
Journal of Australasia, see Illustrated Journal of Australasia
journalism, xi
Junius Unveiled (James Smith), 132–4, 184

Kalizoic Society, 45, 58–9
'Kangaroo Bull', 32–3
Kean, Charles, 76
Kelly, William Lancelot, 30
Kendall, Henry, 93, 94–5, 173
Kerferd, George, 42
Kerr, William, 29
King, John, 69
Knight, John, 45, 49, 55
Kyneton Observer (newspaper), 144
Kyte, Ambrose, 70

Lalanne, M. (French acrobat), 50–1
Lambert, J.C., 47
Lamont, George, 149–50
Landells, George, 72
Landsborough, William, 70
Langton, Edward, 43, 45
La Trobe, Charles, 29
Lawrence, W.J., 107
Leader (newspaper, Melbourne), 28, 86, 93
lectures, public, *see* public lectures
Le Roy, Gustave, 60
Lights and Shadows of Artist Life and Character (James Smith), 24–5
London, 158
Long Odds (Marcus Clarke), 91, 96–7
Looking Back (George Walstab), 92
Loose (Kent), 10–12, 152, 157–8
Lyon, Mlle (French language teacher), 62
Lyster, W.S., 69, 109–10
Lyster Opera Company, 109–10

Macadam, John, 45, 52, 70, 72
McCombie, Thomas, 87
McCoy, Sir Frederick, 52, 53
McCubbin, Frederick, 164–5
McCulloch, Sir James, 41–2
McGeorge, (landlord of James Smith), 149–50
Mackenna, William, 52
Mackinnon, Lauchlan, 29
MacMahon, Sir Charles, 43

Madden, Sir John, 133
mail, *see* postal services
Manns, G.S., 141
manufacturing industry, 2
Maori Wars, 89
Marie Antoinette (Giacometti), 111–13
Martelli, Alexander, 65–7 *passim*
Martin, A. Patchett, 98
Maryborough Advertiser (newspaper), 29
Maryborough and Dunolly Advertiser (newspaper), 144
Mason, Cyrus, 50
Mather, John, 183
Mechanics' Institute (Ballarat), 34
Mechanics' Institute (Melbourne), 5, 26
mechanics' institutes, 5, 22
Melbourne: 1855, 1–9; 1885, 160–1
Melbourne Club, 45, 46, 48, 49, 55, 65
Melbourne Elocution Society, 45, 54
Melbourne Leader, see Leader
Melbourne Monthly Magazine (journal), 85, 86
Melbourne Public Library, *see* Public Library, Museums and National Gallery of Victoria
Melbourne Punch (journal), 29, 85–7, 125
Melbourne Review, (journal) 86, 98–9
Melbourne Shakespeare Society, 45, 59–60, 77, 99, 183
Melbourne Typographical Association, 81
memorials, 64–82
Michie, Sir Archibald, 31, 45, 50, 53, 76, 122
military service, voluntary, *see* voluntary military service
Mitford, Mary Russell, 18
Molesworth, Sir Robert, 149–50
Montgomery, Walter, 119–23
Moorhouse, James, 98
Morris, Edward E., 59–60, 99
Motherwell, James, 45, 137, 149
Mouchette, Mme (drawing teacher), 62
Mount Alexander Mail (newspaper), 29
Mueller, Baron Sir Ferdinand von, 52, 53
Mullen, Samuel, 176

Index

Mulready, William, 74
My Note Book (journal, Melbourne), 86, 88

Naples, 154–6
National Gallery of Victoria, 49–50, 113, 116, 117; *see also* Public Library, Museums and National Gallery of Victoria
National Gallery School of Art, 116
Neild, J.E., 31, 45, 46, 47, 55, 58, 85–94 *passim*, 105, 120–8, 188
Neumayer, Georg, 52
Newbery, James Cosmo, 56
Newsletter of Australasia (journal, Melbourne), 87–8
Newton, Frank, 49
Norman, William, 70

opera, 109–11
Oracles from the British Poets (James Smith), 23–4
Ormond, Francis, 57
O'Shanassy, Sir John, 37–8

painting, 113–18, 164–9, 183
Palmer, Sir James, 159
Parliamentary Library (Victoria), 37–43, 126, 131
pastoral industry, 2
Peebles, J.B., 138, 143
Pembroke family, *see* Herbert family
periodicals, 83–100
Philosophical Institute, 51
Philosophical Society of Victoria, 5, 51
Picturesque Atlas of Australasia (ed. Andrew Garran), 160
Pond, Christopher, (co-proprietor of the Café de Paris), 37, 40, 101
Pope, Mark, 39
Port Phillip Club, 46
Port Phillip Magazine (journal, Melbourne), 84
postal services, 4–5
'Press Amateurs', 78–80
Presss Cricket Club, 45, 51
public lectures, xii, 26, 62, 80
Public Library, Museums and National Gallery of Victoria, 5, 45, 57, 131; *see also* National Gallery of Victoria

Ralph Penfold (James Smith), 11–17 *passim*, 15, 16, 90

Quinn, Miss, (actress), 102

Ray, Edgar, 85–6, 90
Reiff, Anthony, 71
religion, 5
Requiem Ode (James Smith), 71
Richardson, Walter Lindesay, 137
Ridgway, Charles, 37–8
Rip Van Winkle (dramatisation, Joseph Jefferson *et al*), 108–9
Ristori, Adelaide, 111–13
Roberts, Tom, 164–6, 169
Robertson, George, 98
Rogers, George, 13
Rogers, J.W.F., 160
Rolfe, George, 56
Roseby, Thomas, 140
Royal Society of Victoria, 45; Exploration Committee, 51–3, 68–73
Royal Zoological Society, 54
Rural Records (James Smith), 18–19, 154
Rusden, G.W., 76, 77
Ruskin, John, xi, 25–6, 74, 104, 113–14, 164, 166–7

Sala, George Augustus, 160–1
Salisbury (Wiltshire), 20–7, 105, 152, 187
Salisbury and Winchester Journal (newspaper, Salisbury), 1–6 *passim*, 20–6 *passim*
Salisbury Literary and Scientific Institute, 21–3, 187
Scrivenor, F.W., 60
Shakespeare, William, 59–60
Shakespeare–Bacon controversy, 128–34
Shakespeare Memorial Fund, 45, 74–7, 79, 82
Shillinglaw, John, 45, 91, 132, 181
Simmonds, James, 124
Sinnett, Frederick, 8, 31, 86, 87, 92
Slater, George, 87, 88
Smith, Annie Feldwick (née Notcutt), 19, 20
Smith, Charles Henry, 19, 21, 146, 184
Smith, Charles Lamb, 30, 31

221

Smith, Edith Mary, 31
Smith, Eliza Julia (née Kelly), 30, 61, 62, 107, 146, 157, 183–4
Smith, Emily Beatrice, 31
Smith George Paton, 43, 80
Smith, James: accused of plagiarism, 125, 130–2; as art critic, 113–18, 119–24, 164–9; childhood and youth, 10–19; as drama critic, 103–9, 111–13, 119–24; fluency in foreign languages, 17, 25, 60–2; income, 41, 161–2, 180; as opera critic, 109–11; personal attributes, 15–16, 26, 43, 148; as playwright, 101–3; political beliefs, 19, 35–7; private library, 39–41, 133; public lectures, 26, 31–2, 34, 37, 59, 76, 125, 139–43, 182–3; religious beliefs, 56; spiritualism, 57, 97–8, 133, 135–51, 181–2, 183, 185; as travel journalist, 152–9
Smith, James (father), 10, 11
Smith, James Bartlett, 19, 21
Smith, Kate Brooke, 31
Smith, Lucy, 11
Smith, Maria Theresa, 31
Smith, Mary (mother), 10–11
Smith, Mary (sister), 11
Smith, Tennyson Lancelot, 30–1
Smith, W. Jardine, 69, 87, 93
societies; 44–63
Spiers (co-proprietor of Café de Paris), 37, 40, 101
spiritualism, 57, 89, 133, 135–51
Squires, Henry, 71, 110–11
Standard Building Society, 153
Standard Mutual Building Society, 153
Stawell, Sir William 45, 48–9, 52, 70, 74
Stearns, Charles, 130–2
Stephens, A.G., 177, 178
Stephens, J. Brunton, 173
Stiffe, James, 86
The Story of a Baby (Ethel Turner), 171–3
Streeton, Arthur, 164–7
Strutt, William, 49
Such is Life (Joseph Furphy), 176–9
Sullivan, Barry, 75
Summers, Charles, 49, 50, 73, 75, 76, 79–80

Sutherland, Alexander, 98, 179
Sutton, John Wren, 151
Syme, David, 28, 29, 30, 81, 182
Syme, Ebenezer, 28, 29, 184

Table Talk (journal, Melbourne), 185
Tarleton, J.M., 50
Tenison-Woods, Julian, 92
Terry, W.H., 137, 141
testimonials, 64–82
theatre, 12, 17, 101–18
Thomson, William, 128–30, 132
Tiffin, W.F., 23–6
Topp,. A.M., 98
Touchstone, (journal, Melbourne), 86, 92–3, 94
travel articles, 152–9
Trollope, Anthony, 80
Tulk, Augustus, 50
Turner, Ethel, 171–3
Turner, Helen, 153, 162–3
Turner, Henry Gyles, 8, 31, 42, 45, 47–8, 55, 57, 60, 86, 87, 98, 135, 139, 141, 146–7, 153, 180, 183, 185
Twopeny, Richard, 175
Tyerman, J., 141, 144

University of Melbourne, 5, 15

Verdon, Sir George, 41
Victorian Academy of Art, 50, 168
Victorian Artists' Society, 50, 168
Victorian Arts Union, 50
Victorian Association of Progressive Spiritualists, 137, 141
Victorian Association of Spiritualists, 137, 151
Victorian Club, 45, 48–9, 54
Victorian culture, xi–xiii, 189–90
Victorian Fine Arts Society, 49
Victorian Institute for the Advancement of Science, 5, 51
Victorian Literary and Benevolent Fund, 82
Victorian Monthly Magazine, (journal Melbourne), 86, 88–9
Victorian Proprietary College, 45, 56–7
Victorian Psychical Research Society, 151
Victorian Review (1860) (journal, Melbourne), 15, 86, 89–90
Victorian Review (1879) (journal,

Index

Melbourne), 60, 86, 98–9
Victorian Society of Fine Arts, 45, 49–50
Victorian Theosphical League, 151
Vidler, Edward, 167
voluntary military service, 89
Von Guerard, Eugene, *see* Guerard, Eugene von
Von Mueller, Baron Sir Ferdinand, *see* Mueller, Baron Sir Ferdinand von

Walch, Garnet, 45, 55, 60, 93
Walstab, George, 86, 90, 91, 92
Warburton, Peter Egerton, 51, 52
Ware (Hertfordshire), 13–17 *passim*, 152
Ware Free Grammar School (Hertfordshire), 14–15
Watson, John, 52
Watterson, David, 96, 98
Watts, H.E., 92
Way, Sir Samuel, 133
Weekly Review and Christian Times (journal, Melbourne), 90
Weekly Review and Messenger (journal, Melbourne), 86, 90
Weekly Times (newspaper, Melbourne), 93

Wharton, Henry, 71, 111
Whistler, James, 166–7
Whitehead, Charles, 7, 86, 88, 89, 90, 94, 184
Whitty, Edward, 7, 86, 184
Whitworth, Emmeline, 82
Whitworth, Robert, 82, 90
Wilkie, David, 52
Williams, W.H., 86, 87, 90–1
Williamson, J.C., 60, 170, 182
Wills, William, 51–2, 68–73
Wilmot, W.B., 84
Wilson, Edward, 29, 30, 40, 45, 48, 50, 53, 184
Wilson, J.P., 60
Wilson, William, 49, 50
Wilton and its Associations (James Smith), 24–5
Woods, Julian Tenison, *see* Tenison-Woods, Julian
Working Men's College, 45, 57–8
Wright, William, 70, 72

Yorick Club, 45, 55, 80–1, 91
Younge, Frederick, 101
Younge, Richard, 102

Zoological and Acclimatisation Society, 54

For Product Safety Concerns and Information please contact our EU
representative GPSR@taylorandfrancis.com
Taylor & Francis Verlag GmbH, Kaufingerstraße 24, 80331 München, Germany

www.ingramcontent.com/pod-product-compliance
Lightning Source LLC
Chambersburg PA
CBHW061440300426
44114CB00014B/1770